# PRAISE for *YOU ARE A BRAND*, Second Edition!
## By Catherine Kaputa

"Self-branding is not optional in today's insecure world of commerce. *You Are a Brand!* is an excellent and welcome addition to the all-too-small library on the subject."

> — Tom Peters, Author of *The Brand You 50* and bestseller *In Search of Excellence*

"There's an old proverb that says 'You eat life or life eats you.' Catherine Kaputa and her brilliant ideas on self-branding show you how to be the diner and not the entrée."

> — Jay Conrad Levinson, Author of the national bestseller *Guerilla Marketing*

"Each individual is an important contributor to the success of his or her corporation. This insightful book shows you how to fully realize your potential and give yourself and your company maximum benefit."

> — William H. Roedy, former Chairman & Chief Executive,
> MTV Networks International, and Author, *What Makes Business Rock*

"When jobs across the spectrum of goods and services production are buffeted by global competition, personal branding becomes an absolute essential for professional career development. In *You Are a Brand!*, Catherine Kaputa gives us a no-nonsense kit for survival in the global labor market."

> — Gregory L. Miller, Chief Economist, SunTrust Banks, Inc.

I've always thought *You Are a Brand!* is a terrific, useful book…but then Catherine added two new chapters on the art of the elevator pitch and using social media. Now that terrific book has become even more sensational!

> — Anita Bruzzese, USA Today Columnist and Author of
> *45 Things You Do That Drive Your Boss Crazy*

"Catherine Kaputa has written an excellent complement to our book *High Visibility*. We talk about how the celebrity industry creates celebrities, and Kaputa talks about how people can bootstrap themselves into visibility."

> — Philip Kotler, Professor of Marketing, Kellogg School of
> t, Northwestern University

SECOND EDITION

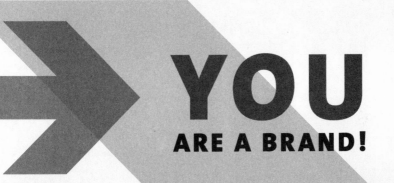

# YOU
## ARE A BRAND!

SECOND EDITION

# YOU
## ARE A BRAND!

In Person and Online, How Smart People
Brand Themselves for Business Success

## CATHERINE KAPUTA

NICHOLAS BREALEY
PUBLISHING

BOSTON • LONDON

This edition first published by Nicholas Brealey Publishing, in 2012.

20 Park Plaza, Suite 1115A
Boston, MA 02116 USA
Tel: + 617-523-3801
Fax: + 617-523-3708

3-5 Spafield Street, Clerkenwell
London, EC1R4QB, UK
Tel: +44-(0)-207-239-0360
Fax: +44-(0)-207-239-0370

www.nicholasbrealey.com

© SelfBrand, LLC

Printed in the United States of America
15   14   13   12        1   2   3   4   5

ISBN: 978-1-85788-580-4

**Library of Congress Cataloging-in-Publication Data**
Kaputa, Catherine
  You are a brand! : In person and online, how smart people brand themselves for business success /
Catherine Kaputa. — 2nd ed.
        p. cm.
  Rev. ed. of: U R a Brand. c2006.
  Includes bibliographical references and index.
  ISBN 978-1-85788-580-4 (pbk. : alk. paper)
  1. Professions—Marketing. 2. Career development. 3. Success in business. I. Kaputa, Catherine U R a Brand! II. Title.

HD8038.A1K36 2012
650.1—dc23

2012016717

*To all of you
who want to take control of your brand
so that you can open up more possibilities*

*Thence comes it that my name receives a brand.*

William Shakespeare
Sonnet 111

# CONTENTS

 **FOREWORD**

There are only two things in life worth striving for. One is happiness; the other is success.

There are a lot of happy people who aren't very successful. And there are a lot of successful people who aren't very happy. But if you have both, what more could you want?

Money? Not really. Money can't buy happiness. And most truly successful people have more money than they will ever spend.

Happiness and success, the yin and the yang of life. Like the Chinese symbols for all the principles one finds in the universe, the yin and the yang are diametrically opposed concepts. Which is why it is very difficult to achieve both at the same time.

To be happy, you need to create a positive attitude in your own mind. A powerful sense of self, so to speak. Or, as a cynic might say, "A legend in one's own mind." Let's call this the "yin."

To be successful, you need to create positive attitudes in the minds of other people. You can't make yourself successful. Only other people can make you successful.

In the same way, you can't make a sale. Only other people can decide whether to buy from you, whether you are an individual or a company.

In other words, you need to build a "self-brand," a reason for people to buy from you, whether you are selling yourself for a job or selling products and services to others. Let's call this the "yang."

Most people focus on the yin. It's logical. If you can create a powerful positive attitude about yourself, this attitude will rub off on other people. They will perceive you to be the successful person you are trying to become. That's why you can find thousands of books on this subject—*The Power of Positive Thinking* by Norman Vincent Peale, for example.

The yin is conventional wisdom wrapped in a positive thinking package: hard work, total dedication, and constant improvement in every aspect of your life are bound to bring you not only happiness but also the success you believe you deserve.

Conventional wisdom is always wrong. Positive thinking might make you happy (the yin), and it is a terrific approach to life in general, but it won't bring you success. To become successful, you need to focus on the yang.

You need to focus on creating a positive attitude in the minds of other people. In other words, you need to create a self-brand.

Building a product brand and building a self-brand require similar strategies. The problem is that building a self-brand goes against a person's natural instincts. Take one example: most people think of themselves as "well rounded," with an interest in all aspects of life, such as art, music, theater, sports, politics, etc. A great way to live a happy life, a lousy way to build a brand.

But that's getting into the heart of Catherine Kaputa's message.

I first met Catherine when she worked with us at our New York City advertising agency, Trout & Ries. That was more than twenty years ago, but I have always remembered her and her participation in the many meetings that took place in the ad agency.

She was always the smartest person in the room.

Now, it's nice to be smart, but that doesn't necessarily make you successful, as Catherine points out in this book. Sometimes being smart is a handicap. Smart people are often too smart to take advice from others.

I hope that's not true about you. (And it probably isn't if you've picked up this book.)

What is also remarkable about Catherine is that she has taken her own advice. She has built her self-brand by following the same principles you can read about in this book.

You should do the same. But you have to forget about the yin and focus on the yang. You have to focus on those strategies that will build your self-brand in the minds of others, even though many of those strategies go against conventional wisdom.

Happiness and success, the yin and the yang of life. Assuming you have the yin under control, let Catherine Kaputa lead you through the steps you need to take to achieve the yang: a success that might go well beyond anything you could possibly imagine.

—Al Ries

Coauthor, *The Origin of Brands*

# ➤ PREFACE TO THE 2012 EDITION

*Self-love my liege is not so vile a sin as self-neglecting.*

William Shakespeare
*Henry V* (II, 4)

Some things have changed since the hardcover version of this book came out. Some things never change.

The branding ideas in this book are timeless: they work in expanding markets; they work in contracting markets.

But there are new ideas we need to think about today, resulting in this new edition of *You Are a Brand!* with nearly one-third new content. There is new research with insights for personal brand builders. There are new personal branding stories to tell that have lessons for us. There are new things I've learned about how to lead, inspire, and influence others, whether it's one or two across the table from you or hundreds in an auditorium. There are new ways to build our personal brand digitally through social media that we need to harness. Indeed, the virtual world keeps growing in power. And there continues to be economic uncertainty, so we have to master branding ourselves in person and digitally if we want to succeed in challenging times. All of these changes can add urgency to working on your personal brand and finally taking control of your future. You can't accomplish much without knowing who you are—the authentic you—and communicating your value to others.

In the personal-branding mind-set, you are your most important asset—an asset, like education, that no one can take away from you. Personal branding shows you how to increase the value of that asset, both in terms of self-actualization—becoming who you can be—and in terms of human capital—maximizing the financial value of your career. Personal branding is always based on authenticity, but it's showing yourself in the best, most relevant, and most appealing way to a specific audience. Personal branding is also about self-empowerment. You need to take control of your personal story and career destiny. Yet personal branding is not taught in school and has become the most neglected aspect of education.

Thinking like a brand means creating a brand for yourself and to do that you first need to find the right personal brand strategy. To make finding the right self-brand positioning easier, I have developed an online assessment as a complement to Chapter 4 on finding a great self-brand strategy. (You'll find the URL on page 72.) Once you have your personal brand strategy, you'll need to "package" Brand You with a strong visual and verbal identity,  and marketing it, and not squandering the opportunities that constantly come your way. It's easy to shortchange yourself if you're not thinking like a brand.

A prime example? Your elevator speech, a sixty-second personal commercial that you might use in an interview or networking situation. Many people can't talk about who they are professionally and how they bring real, tangible value to a business situation in a short, conversational dialogue. So, I've added a new chapter, chapter 9, that offers a how-to guide for creating your elevator speech, a personal business pitch, in a way that's authentic, relevant, and right for the situation. The chapter has lots of ideas on how to pitch your accomplishments, your services, and your ideas so that you "click" with others anytime, anywhere, whether you're selling yourself in person or virtually via Skype or another video forum.

Since the first edition of this book, a sea change has occurred in how we communicate and connect with others. The rise of social media like LinkedIn, Facebook, Twitter, and YouTube has transformed the way we build business and personal relationships, and how we find and learn about others.

Like it or not, you have a virtual brand. People will use the Internet and social media to learn your story, either the one you've put out there or a very different one that's been put out by others. Even the total lack of an online brand presence says something significant about your personal brand. And, trust me, it isn't good. A weak Internet image today is like having a weak reputation in the old, pre-Internet days. It will minimize, not burnish, your brand.

Social media and new media give you a powerful megaphone for building your brand and your community. These new digital tools, what I call *cyberbranding*, are made for personal branders because they give power to the people. They are inexpensive and open to all. So I've added a new chapter, chapter 11, to show you how to harness the power of social media and the new digital tools without letting them take over your life.

The good news is, anyone can join the personal branding club, and with the advent of social media and digital tools, it's more exciting than ever before. This book is designed to give you the skills and process to create and market Brand You. Even the creative ability that you'll need is not out of your reach. New research has debunked that myth that creativity is born, not made. It's a skill you can cultivate just like any other.

This book is designed to take you through the three-step branding process:

1. Brand Strategy: Finding Your Self-Brand Idea (chapters 1–4)
2. Creative Development: "Packaging" Brand You (chapters 5–9)
3. Marketing Brand You: Building Visibility and Connection with Your Target Audience (chapters 10–14)

Today, we all have to be entrepreneurs and branders, whether we work for a company or have our own business. You have to master self-branding not only to learn how to be self-directed and have personal impact, but to learn how to find your purpose. You must find out what you were made to do! In today's organizations, we are expected to master *entrepreneuring*, to add value by being innovative growth agents.

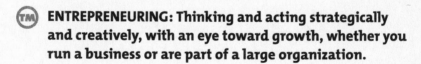

**ENTREPRENEURING: Thinking and acting strategically and creatively, with an eye toward growth, whether you run a business or are part of a large organization.**

Join me on the journey to build Brand You, a distinct personal brand that's authentic and relevant, and that empowers you in today's dynamic business world as well as brings more value to your company. This book will show you how.

 **INTRODUCTION**

*Why, then the world's mine oyster!*

William Shakespeare
*The Merry Wives of Windsor* (II, 2)

Success as an executive or as an entrepreneur (or even as a professional or employee in any type of company these days) requires careful, calculated branding, both to enter the playing field and to stay in the game.

Success also requires a dose of that great universal mystery we call "luck," that inexplicable combination of things, time, and actions and their infinite juxtapositions. But luck is not something you can count on, although there are practical things you can do to manifest more of it in your life, which this book explains.

*You Are a Brand!* is a field guide to success in business or whatever realm you are exploring.

You'll get the inside scoop—the secrets and hidden rules of success of people on the move from all walks of life—from a self-brand strategist who helped them on their journey. You'll learn how the branding principles and strategies developed for the commercial world may be used to achieve your business and personal potential.

In short, you are a brand.

Top entertainers, politicians, and athletes have long used branding principles and strategy to create stardom. Now, savvy professionals, businesspeople, and entrepreneurs are also using self-, or personal, branding, so that they can be more successful.

If you study the lives of successful entrepreneurs, well-known business executives, politicians, performers, and the like, you'll discover that hard work, or luck alone wasn't instrumental in their achievement. Rather, their success was the result of a conscious process, a strategic branding process, often undertaken with the assistance of advisers, coaches, and other mentors who propelled their achievements and celebrity.

How to achieve success is a key theme in this book: professional success in terms of getting paid what you're worth, landing the promotion you deserve, or launching a start-up that lasts. But self-branding doesn't benefit just you, and it's a mistake to think of it only in terms of self-promotion. Self-branding is a strategic process that benefits the company you work for or are building. It shows you how to bring more value to your company, your clients, and your projects by being focused and strategic, by having top-notch communication, sales, and marketing skills, and by having a valuable network of business and personal contacts.

I am also going to talk about success in a larger sense, in terms of self-actualization—being who you were meant to be. Branding is a great tool for both, because it makes you an active partner in your business and in your life destiny.

*You Are a Brand!* will teach you self-branding strategies and career moves you won't learn in business school or anywhere else.

You'll discover the career and perception problems faced by senior-level executives like Benjamin, who had to unite competing department heads around a compelling vision when he took over as president of a technology company. You'll meet sophisticated up-and-comers like Anthony, who had a fairy-tale life and a Wall Street salary until his world came crashing down on 9/11. You'll meet new entrepreneurs like Lynn, a sales professional who built a reputation for herself and her sales insights that led to a business start-up. You'll meet people like Kate, whose boss didn't think she deserved the title and salary of her peers even though she was handling the same workload.

*You Are a Brand!* is for people of all stripes who must be brand builders if they are to succeed in today's dynamic and challenging marketplace. This book is for ambitious people who want to do more with their lives. It is for people who want to consciously create success and perhaps also achieve high visibility and renown.

It is for people who want to reposition and rebrand themselves for a second act. It is for entrepreneurs, professionals, and business owners who want to fuse their personal and company brands into identities that will help them achieve maximum impact. It is for kids and teenagers, and even their parents, who want the best school brand stamped on their résumés because it will give them a head start.

It is especially for women, women like myself, who were told as children, "Don't upstage your brother" or "It's not nice to call attention to yourself." The truth is, if you don't brand yourself, someone else will, and it probably won't be the brand you had in mind.

*You Are a Brand!* will make the principles of branding available to you. In many ways, brands are like people: They have qualities, attributes, and personalities. And people are like brands. They are products that can be nurtured and cultivated to become winning brands.

You'll learn how to package your brand with a powerful visual and verbal identity without seeming promotional or obnoxious. You'll be introduced to ten strategies from the commercial world and shown how they can be applied to you. Each chapter contains examples, tips, and brainstormer exercises so that you can implement the branding process in your life. You will learn how to maximize the potential of your most important asset—you.

In short, this book will give you control over how you are perceived.

If anyone understands this, I do. I spent two decades as a branding and advertising expert.

A dominant theme or clichéd example of the classic branding story would be that of the young, ambitious executive on the way up; the clichéd location would be New York City; the clichéd company would be on Madison Avenue or Wall Street; and the clichéd person would be me. I'm Catherine Kaputa, and I lived that cliché.

I'm a baby boomer like 77 million other Americans. If I were any more typical, I'd start to become untypical; so I think most readers can relate because they either are part of the baby-boom brand or have been unduly influenced or annoyed as this dominant brand made its way through the last half of the twentieth century and into the first half of the twenty-first century.

Dad was a genuine war hero, like many others of his generation. He piloted thirty-five missions over Germany during World War II and had numerous medals that branded him as a war hero. He also had the ultimate hero branding fifty years later: interment with honors at Arlington National Cemetery. Dad was sent to Miami once for R&R. He loved it and vowed to return there to live if the Nazis didn't get him first. Dad was packaged in the strong, silent personality that was a powerful draw for men of his generation, the group Tom Brokaw branded as "the greatest generation."

Miami and the world seemed so innocent then. We rode our bikes to school and everywhere else without supervision, played marbles and hop-scotch at recess, and saw the future in terms of unrelenting rapid progress. Frank Sinatra sang the theme song, and it came from Miami Beach, too: "He's got high hopes. He's got high apple pie in the sky hopes."

Who could resist the brand of an era? I had "apple pie in the sky hopes," too, particularly in my adolescence.

Everybody's been there. Adolescence: it's personal identity time, it's absurd, it's profound, it's scary. The culture was still offering limited roles for women, and I admit I didn't have the courage or creativity to face the future without a role model. The one that intrigued me was Brenda Starr, reporter, the heroine of a comic strip. She was glamorous, powerful, and respected and got to travel all over. Journalism. That was the brand for me.

So off I went to Northwestern University and the Medill School of Jour-nalism. Then, caught up in the identity crisis of my generation. I switched gears. For the next eight years, Japanese art became my life and brand.

I was in deep: master's degree from the University of Washington, Seattle Art Museum curator job, Asian art books published, Smithsonian Fellow, Tokyo University study grant. I applied for the Ph.D. program at Harvard because Harvard was right for my brand (high hopes again). Just as I was organizing my dissertation for my Ph.D., my general uneasiness morphed into an epiphany. This is not me. This is not my brand. I want out! Dr. Kaputa was not going to happen. I took two aspirins and cried all morning.

You don't need a connection to New York City to feel its influence, but I did have a connection, and that made the city's gravity a force I could not resist. Heart and head were both pulling me. I still wasn't sure what I was going to do, but I knew where I would do it. The capital of the world.

It's been said, "You can't start off in New York; you need to play Peoria first." No you don't. I didn't.

I sold my Volkswagen Beetle, crashed at Aunt Sophie's in the Bronx, and was determined to find an exciting job in my first love—communications. The vagueness of the communications brand was the proper mind-set, since it gave me the flexibility to brand myself to an opportunity (journalism, advertising, public relations), and I needed flexibility. My previous brand was a handicap.

"Why does an Asian art scholar want to be in advertising?" was the refrain. But persistence does pay off. One ad agency interpreted my background as "creative," and I had a foot in the door.

The mark of a hot ad shop was big-name national accounts and talked-about TV campaigns. Trout & Ries didn't have sexy creative; rather, it was a hotbed of brand strategy and positioning. I was pretty mediocre in my first job as a copywriter, so I switched after two years to the account side. "Creative" had been the right brand to land the job, but my gut was pushing me to reposition my brand.

Al Ries and Jack Trout, by the way, rebranded themselves after I left. Each changed his brand position from "ad agency chief" to "marketing strategist," found the right brand position, and took off. (Boy, how brand image can change. Today, when I tell people my background, the "Wow!" is always about my having worked in my first job under the now-famous branding gurus Al Ries and Jack Trout.)

My personal career strategy was to move on to a larger, well-known agency so I could gain experience on a high-profile brand.

I was already branded as a "small agency" person after my four years at Trout & Ries. The recruiters were of one stripe: "You don't have 'big agency' experience."

When others can't help, do it yourself! In this case, I networked, talked to people, found old friends, made new friends. It worked, plus I got lucky. (Strange phenomenon: the harder you work, the more luck you have.) I landed a job at Wells Rich Greene managing the "I ♥ NY" account.

Mary Wells Lawrence had already achieved legendary status by the time I arrived at the agency. She was a woman of style and was as clever with her personal brand as she was with her extremely successful campaigns, which include Braniff's colorful planes, Alka-Seltzer's "Plop plop fizz fizz," and Benson & Hedges 100s. Mary was a Francophile, and the place was run like the French court, so it was always an interesting place to work.

The "I ♥ NY" account was a wonderful piece of business to work on. The TV commercials featuring Broadway musicals and celebrities received numerous creative awards and became a flagship creative account for the agency. Part of my job was to work with the Broadway Theater League to secure the Broadway talent and enlist other celebrity talent to appear in the commercials.

Celebrities don't exist without branding, and they're good at it, but their public brands are not always real. I won't be telling you who made outrageous demands, but I'll tell you about one of the most impressive stars who came in to pitch New York.

Mr. High Hopes himself, Ol' Blue Eyes, lived up to his brand. I was struck by his mesmerizing, alert, bright blue eyes. They really were special, as were his purposefulness and demeanor. He was shorter than I had imagined, but bigger than I had expected, too. He paid his own way on this pro bono gig when others wanted freebies for themselves and their entourages.

Frank Sinatra was a famous brand and had done some well-known rebranding in his time, from teen idol crooner to movie star to singer for the ages. Along the way, he also went through some negative branding as a Mafia associate and brawler. But we were very dear friends for about twenty minutes on the "I ♥ NY" commercial shoot, and my impression of his brand can be described in one word: class.

My next career strategy was to become a corporate advertising director. Ad agencies are notorious for wanting young people and discarding old people, and I was in my thirties. Their unspoken rationale is that they need fresh ideas and young bodies willing to work long hours, and the perception is that those things are the province of the young. So my goal became to grow old at a big company, with a big title and a big office and big money.

The recruiters were no help. They see only your past, not your future. They pegged me as an agency person, not a corporate advertising director. So I was on my own, networking. The lesson in networking is to pursue all leads no matter how obscure—even a friend of a friend of a friend of a friend, and don't stop there. Salespeople will tell you it's a numbers game, and they're right.

Through a remote contact, I got a Wall Street interview, and voilà! I landed my dream job, director of advertising at Shearson Lehman Brothers. I would end up staying for fifteen years. My title stayed more or less the same, but the firm's name changed again and again, and it was Smith Barney when I left.

You can imagine the branding challenges that came with all the identity changes and the complex nature of Wall Street businesses. Corporate branding and advertising are not just about naming products and making commercials. You need smart positioning, communications strategy, and marketing tactics. And I was pretty good at it. Maybe someday I'll write a book on the subject.

Many influences affect our brands. Many can be analyzed and explained. Many cannot. Cause and effect are certain only in pure science. Branding is a science in the way social science is a science, with the "science" part of the term based on the fantasy that human behavior can be quantified. In reality, branding's cause-and-effect relationship is never certain. Be grateful for all your experiences. It's your input that makes them help or hurt. What's important to know is that anything can happen and even bad things can have good results. I learned through fortune and misfortune to take control of my branding and to try to understand branding influences in the larger world.

Did I make mistakes? Of course, lots of them. The only people who haven't made mistakes are people who never did anything, and that's a mistake, too.

Was I successful? Well, I did what I wanted to do, and I didn't get hurt, wasn't miserable, and didn't become poverty-stricken in the process. Having desires or goals and then working to accomplish them is as close as we get to the idea of success, and it's available to everybody, even with our flaws and limitations.

Thanks, Universe; thanks, Planet; thanks, America; thanks, New York; thanks, Miami; thanks, Mom; thanks, Dad.

# PART 1

# Brand Strategy: Finding Your Self-Brand Idea

# CHAPTER 1

# Take Charge of Your Self-Brand

*And say to all the world, "This was a man."*

William Shakespeare
*Julius Caesar* (V, 5)

In 64 B.C., the Cicero brothers, Marcus and his younger brother Quintus, were political wannabes. Of course, Marcus Cicero became one of the most famous Romans of all. His personal brand not only has survived the centuries, he is known by the ultimate in branding, a one-word moniker, Cicero, and his philosophy and rhetoric have been a persistent influence in Western civilization. But in 64 B.C., the Cicero brothers were outsiders. Though from a wealthy family, they were from a small town in southern Italy and they didn't have the Roman connections or status to meet their ambitions.

So Quintus took on the role of brand manager and political adviser to his brother, a role that was preserved in a letter to his brother published by Princeton University Press in 2012 as the book *How to Win an Election*.

The goal was to get Marcus Cicero elected as consul, one of the two leaders directing Rome's powerful republic. The problem was that no one in the

Cicero family had been consul. Quintus realized that Marcus's formidable skill in oratory and rhetoric were strong assets, but that it was not enough to win the campaign. Personal branding was needed.

(TM) **Self-branding is an ancient art. Once the province of political and social leaders, it's now critical to success for people in all types of careers.**

In his writing, Quintus tells Marcus to brand himself as a "new man," turning the liability of being from a small town into an advantage: "Every day as you go down to the Forum, you should say to yourself, 'I am an outsider. I want to be consul. This is Rome.'" Quintus tells Marcus to position himself as a man of the people, while also courting the wealthy and politically connected. And Marcus's persuasive speaking ability helped him fend off his chief opponent, the corrupt aristocrat Lucius Sergius Catilina.

The branding campaign worked. Marcus Cicero was elected consul in a landslide in 64 B.C.

## Is Personal Branding for You?

Are you afraid of the idea of self-branding?

Many think self-branding may be inauthentic or manipulative or immodest or even downright phony.

Do you?

How do you imagine the consummate personal brander? For some, it's the self-promoter with the slicked back hair who talks too much about himself and his many accomplishments, selling himself like a used car.

For others it's the overly ambitious networker who is careful to use your name repeatedly in conversation as she manically hands out her business card before moving on to the next contact. Or is it the tedious Facebook friend who shares her every move with waves of self-centered status updates? That's about as far from creative personal branding as stumbling is from dancing.

Good self-branders build their brand on authenticity, on who they are and who they can be. They build mutually beneficial relationships and alliances (friends). They build positive visibility for their brand using the proven strategies that successful products and companies use.

Branding can be subtle or grating, up-to-date or out-of-date, engaging or self-centered. But one thing is clear, your choice is not whether you'll participate in personal branding, you are participating! Your choice is whether you will take control of your brand so you can be yourself and let others know who you are. The Bard, as usual, said it best, "To thine own self be true."

## Soft Is Hard and Hard Is Soft

Branding is about *soft power*. For companies today, it's not the *hard things*—tangibles like bricks and mortar, equipment and inventories—that contribute the most to a company's value. It's *soft things*—the brands and company reputation, the ideas and intellectual capital, the consumer relationships and business alliances—that have the most value.

Like it or not, branding and soft power affect us every day because they influence how we feel about something. Few of us make the decision to buy something after carefully testing and considering the merits of the different brands on the market. No one goes out and does a blind taste test of colas and then selects the one that *objectively* tastes best. Even if it's a more expensive (and consequently more considered) purchase, like a car or a laptop, we will compare hard things like product features and performance criteria, but we will decide based on soft things such as what the brand represents to us.

It's the same with people. It isn't the hard, quantifiable things, like educational credentials, experience, and job titles, that contribute the most to success. The real power lies in harnessing soft power—strategy and tactics, image and visual identity, words and verbal identity, visibility and reputation, and other branding ideas—all the things that will help attract people to you.

Business success, like brand success, depends on what other people think about you. If people think you are a dynamic business leader, you are. If people think you're a B player, you are (until you change their perceptions). It doesn't matter what is "objectively" true. Perception is reality.

Creating positive impressions in the minds of other people is the work of self-branding. It used to be about "Can you do the job?" Now, many people can do what you do. So it has to be about something more. Above all, branding is a strategic process. The goal is to provide that something more that will help you succeed in a changing, highly competitive business environment (and to be authentic and even to enjoy yourself in the process). This book is about how you can tap into soft power—your self-branding power—and harness it for career and life success.

## Find Your "Brand Idea"

You are your most important asset. In a sense, you are your only asset. And your ability to maximize the asset that is *you* is the single most important ingredient in your success.

That's why self-branding is so valuable. For people, branding is about achieving greater success, as represented by money, fame, self-esteem, or whatever measure is important to you.

But I am also talking about becoming who you were meant to be, which means that success includes becoming who you truly are. The trick to effective self-branding is to devise a strategy that works in achieving professional and life goals but also is true to you—that brings more of you into the equation.

Branding for people is about finding your brand idea—your unique selling proposition (USP) or brand promise. You want to represent something special—a belief system you stand for that sets you apart from others. This could be made up of your point of view, your decision-making ability, your vision, your style, even your mystique—the X Factor that makes you special and relevant.

Branding for people is also about "packaging" the brand that is you and using branding strategies and principles from the commercial world to enhance your identity and communicate your USP. You are the storyteller of your own life and you can create a compelling brand story that helps empower your success or not. Branding also means developing a marketing plan for reaching your goals, tactics to get from A to B (and through all the other letters of the alphabet, depending on your goals). And it means engaging your target audience (your "customers") without seeming self-promotional and obnoxious and getting your work in front of the right people. Every page of this book is designed to help you know who you are, what you have to offer, and how to communicate that to others.

(TM) **BRAND YOU: A *person*—a skill set that is interchangeable with the skill sets of other people.**

(TM) **A *personal brand*—a special promise of value that sets you apart.**

## Leverage Brand Power

Looking at yourself as a brand has enormous advantages. The truth is that being good, by itself, doesn't guarantee success. We all know talented people who are underemployed, underpaid, or even unemployed. With branding, you learn how to look at yourself as a product in a competitive framework. Branding is the process of differentiating that product—you—from the competition and taking action steps to get where you want to go.

Branding also requires that you target a market. A market is any group of people that you need to engage with in order to reach your goals. Clients or customers are a target market, as are the prospects you are pursuing. If you work at a company, you should view your colleagues and direct reports as target markets. Don't overlook your boss. In any company, your boss is probably your most important target market. After all, other than yourself, your boss has the most control over Brand You. Recruiters, industry leaders, and even competitors are also markets for your self-brand.

Branding shows you how to attract a market. Don't think in terms of what you want to say and do. Flip it. Think in terms of the reaction you want from your target market. And what you have to do to get that reaction. Branding also gives you a template for developing a marketing program directed at your key target markets. You will learn how to develop specific brand messages, tactics and a "media plan" for maximizing success with your target market as well as methods of measuring your success.

Self-branding is not just good for you personally, it is good for the company, too. Branding teaches you how to be more strategic by staying relevant to the market and the latest thinking. It teaches you how to use advertising techniques to build a powerful verbal identity to express your ideas through signature words and expressions. Branding teaches you how to package your ideas for a strong visual identity, too, so they will break through and be remembered. And it teaches you how to use other branding techniques to build consensus and lead in today's competitive global marketplace.

Any way you slice it, brands win over products hands down. A branded item is viewed as better than its generic counterpart. Brands are perceived as higher in quality. They are in demand. They sell for a premium price.

Generic products compete only on price, by offering a very low price. (And if you're reading this book, I doubt that you want to compete that way.) As shown below, the list of a brand's advantages goes on and on.

### Brand vs. Product

| | |
|---|---|
| Is bought | Has to be sold |
| Creates emotional bond | Creates no attachment |
| Has high visibility | Has low visibility |
| Is unique | Is a commodity |
| Endures | Becomes outdated |
| Has premium price | Has low price |
| Creates buzz | Is of low interest |
| Stays relevant | Is static |
| Is memorable | Is forgettable |

## Take Charge of Your Brand

My mantra to my clients is "You are a brand!" This book will take you through stories, examples, and brainstormer exercises to help you make yourself a brand.

The first thing you need to do is to commit. You must take an active rather than a passive role in defining yourself and your future.

Developing a winning self-brand requires some work. The left-brain work involves analyzing facts and trends as well as planning tactics. Right-brain work involves tapping into your intuition and creativity as you develop a personal-brand strategy, a visual identity (your packaging), and a verbal identity (your self-brand messages) in order to reach your goals.

Before you can develop a successful self-brand, you need to decide what you want. You need to ask and answer questions about who you are, where you are now, and what you want to do with your life and career.

Of course, for many of us, this is the sticky part. These are the very issues we tend to avoid until we're in a crisis. Or we live a life in which there is conflict between who we are, what we want, and where we are heading.

I often recognize this disconnect in statements like "I'm doing X now because I fell into it, but I really want to be doing Y in the future" or "I'm in it for the money, but I need something more rewarding in the future." One client told me, "I went into law because my father is a country lawyer, an icon really, like Atticus Finch in *To Kill a Mockingbird*, but I hate it. To me, law is drudgery. I long for more creative lifework."

Even though people want success, some resist self-branding because they feel that it's unseemly to think strategically and creatively about themselves and then present themselves in the best possible light. It's too calculated.

I recently met with someone who had this problem. Hal was a talented lawyer in general practice, but his business was struggling. He was referred to me by a friend who hadn't gone to the elite law school Hal had attended yet was getting top dollar for his legal counsel. Hal's friend had carved out a high-profile niche for himself as a white-collar criminal defense attorney.

When I talked to Hal about narrowing the focus of his business and developing a name for himself in that specific area, he balked. "I don't want to resort to selling myself. I have a law degree from a top school, and I won't stoop to becoming a salesperson." Which would you rather be—a top lawyer or a top-credentialed lawyer?

## Live Your Dream

Often our dreams and desires are what we have put on hold in our lives. Many people light up when I ask them to describe their dream jobs. "Oh, if I could live my dream, here's what I'd be doing." And they go on to recount something that has always intrigued them and been at the back of their minds, but which they have never pursued or acted on.

But as workplace philosophers like William Bridges and John Whyte point out, our desires are too powerful a motivator to ignore. We have all spent too much time doing what we think others want us to do, rather than what we want to do.

In working with all types of clients and situations, I have found that almost anything is attainable if you can visualize it and express it. A few people accomplish this naturally or intuitively, but most of us need a strategy and a game plan for making it happen.

## Adopt the Self-Brand Mind-Set

Each of us is unique, with a mind, strengths, and experiences that are powerful self-brand assets. Anything that you have ever done or thought about could be an asset. If you think it is an asset, it is. If you see it as a stepping-stone to your self-brand goal, it is. If you see it as a career buster, it is.

 **SELF-BRANDING: Self-branding is more than your identity and image. It's everything you do to differentiate and market yourself, such as communications agility, presence, networking, and visibility tactics.**

Few of us have been taught to think of ourselves in terms of being a *brand*, as something that can be looked at in different ways, developed into a winning brand, and marketed so that we may achieve our full potential.

Few of us have learned how to rebrand ourselves to stand for something that is in demand rather than something that is no longer in vogue. We don't know how to create positive perceptions of ourselves.

Nor have many of us been taught that we are capable of defining and molding our jobs. We can even create careers and career paths that we feel passionate about.

It's not that ability and performance aren't important. They are. But a talented, hardworking person won't do as well as a well-branded, talented, hardworking person. Effective branding will tip perceptions in your favor and bring greater success.

## Break the Dependency Habit

We can no longer count on a career at one company. That was your father's Oldsmobile. And now, Oldsmobile is gone altogether! We will not only have multiple jobs in our lifetimes, we will have multiple careers. Being relevant demands a constant addition of new skills. Many of us will spend sustained periods of our careers in some form of self-employment. If you don't empower yourself through personal branding and direct your own career, you will be left waiting in vain for someone or something, like the two characters in *Waiting for Godot*.

(TM) **Companies focus on what's good for their bottom line. Not what's good for your bottom line.**

Companies merge and split up. There are downsizings and upsizings. The boss who hired you moves on. People get into trouble and point fingers at others. Technology and global economies have made outsourcing of jobs possible in ways never imagined just a few years ago. And managerial jobs are not immune.

With these kinds of changes the norm, you can't count on your company to keep you on the payroll. Even when things are going well, conditions can change quickly. You need to control your destiny.

When you work at a company, don't count on HR or even your boss to lay out a career path for you. That's so last year. Modern companies want you to figure out your own career path. Today, it's not about climbing the corporate ladder so much as navigating a corporate lattice by making lateral moves to take jobs where you can learn new businesses, new markets, and new skills. What worked as a career strategy last year might work this year, or it might not.

You have to keep track of your career value and career identity. You are in charge. We're all entrepreneurs today, whether we work for a company or work for ourselves. That's the way it is now.

That's why this book contains a number of brainstormers like the one on the opposite page. As you do each brainstormer, write your responses in the spaces provided in cursive handwriting. Why? You'll likely find that writing in cursive engages the brain and helps you think of more ideas.

When you think as if you were a brand, your goal is to prosper, not just survive. Like any brand manager, you must change your strategy and tactics when the marketplace dynamics change. You look for new opportunities and needs for which *your* brand is the solution.

## Take Charge of Your Brand, or Someone Else Will

Self-branding is about making the most of what you've got. It's about daring to put forth a different idea. It's about responding to changes in the marketplace. It's having a career identity that is known by the right people, and a career strategy that's relevant in the current business marketplace.

Many of us keep doing the same things long after they are not working anymore. Self-branding is about playing an active role in your career and life and learning how to position and market yourself to maximum advantage.

After all, it's a myth to think that you'll be rewarded solely on the basis of your hard work. And if you don't brand yourself, someone else will. Chances are that their brand description won't be quite what you have in mind, as my client Kate found out.

## BRAINSTORMER: Who's Looking Out for You?

Envision the following scenario: One day, a major catastrophe occurs at your company headquarters, causing fear and uncertainty. The economy sours and your company's sales plummet. Then, your boss walks into your office and says, "Sorry, I have some bad news for you. We have to downsize and your job is being eliminated." The job market is dreadful, particularly in your industry and geographic area. What do you do now?

Kate had been with a large food company for ten years and was working hard running a good-size department. Unlike colleagues with similar responsibilities who had been rewarded with promotions to vice president, Kate languished at the senior director level. So why the disparity?

We all have seen it happen: similar staff and responsibilities, but different compensation and title.

Kate got an inkling of the reason when she was at a large corporate meeting. The executive vice president introduced her to a new recruit as "Kate, the person who handles promotions for Brand X."

Well, that had been true several years and several promotions ago, when she was a junior employee, yet that was where her brand was stuck in management's consciousness. Her personal brand was so weak that she was subject to whatever foolish, unproductive brand others associated with her.

Kate desperately needed to rebrand herself as a leader in the company. She took a range of actions aimed at increasing her visibility and changing the perception that her key target markets, her boss and senior executives, had of her.

 **If no one knows you and your accomplishments, they don't count.**

For starters, she volunteered for a high-profile, strategic project and joined the team that would be making the presentation to senior management. The project gave her a platform for collaborating with executives at her level and above, people with whom she did not interact in her normal job routine.

Kate had to shift her brand from that of assistant to senior management, who *organizes* the material, to that of senior management, who *owns* the material. She had to take charge of her career success not only with hard work but with more visibility internally in her company. Kate also realized that it's her job to make her great deeds known to her boss, not his job to uncover them. (Modesty is a virtue, but as I told Kate, she had been taking it too far.)

Now Kate's focus is on owning the brand she desires. With a change in mind-set and an action plan, not only does Kate see herself as a leader and not as an employee, her boss and other executives do too. Kate is on her way to being branded for success.

## It's All about Perceptions

When I was a child, my mother always told me, "Don't pay attention to what other kids say." And sometimes she would recite the old rhyme, "Sticks and stones . . ." blah, blah, blah. Most of Mom's advice was great, but, boy, was that bad advice. In business, as in life, it does matter what other people think about you and what they say about you. Your success is based on their perceptions.

In reality, your brand is what other people say about you when you aren't in the room. The words of other people are the words that matter. If people think you're management material, you will be. If they think you're mediocre, you will be in mediocre roles—until you change their perceptions. If people don't even think about you at all because you're invisible in the organization, dutifully working on your tasks, you've got a perception problem, too. You won't get anywhere until you learn the importance of networking and building visibility for yourself inside your company.

We receive feedback every day on how people perceive us. We just need to tune in to it. If you work in a corporation you're likely to get a yearly formal review, but in today's politically correct workplaces it can be difficult to get candid feedback until it's too late and your name is on a list for downsizing.

There is a lot you can learn about others' perceptions of you if you observe carefully. Are you invited to important meetings? Do colleagues return your calls and e-mails quickly?

From a branding perspective, perceptions are what count. At its core, branding is about tuning in to and creating positive perceptions about Brand You, and changing perceptions if they are negative.

## Could Self-Branding Help You?

Self-branding is for people who are smart and good at what they do but not good at branding themselves effectively. It is for people who have come to realize that they need to take control of their identities. They can't rely on luck or other people or situations. It is for people who want to do and achieve more, people who have a problem (job loss, etc.), and people who want to reinvent themselves for a second act.

All of these people have come to realize that there is no security in a job—any job. Security lies in your ability to take charge. It lies in your ability to brand yourself successfully and think in terms of market needs. Security lies in your ability to respond to change and benefit from it rather than hide from it. Security lies in your ability to develop a strategy and a game plan. Security lies in you.

### Self-Brand Mind-Set vs. Employee Mind-Set

| | |
|---|---|
| Working for yourself | Working for boss |
| Internal security | External security |
| Marketing plan | Résumé |
| Markets and customers | Boss, co-workers |
| Differentiating | Fitting in |
| Strategy | Hard work |

| | |
|---|---|
| Relationships | Transactions |
| Network | Solo |
| Long-term | Short-term |
| Planning | Reacting |
| Sound bites | Business jargon |
| Packaging | Clothes |
| Visibility | Low profile |
| Self-measurement | Performance review |

## Branding Is as Easy As 1–2–3

Branding is a strategic and creative process, one that flourishes when you approach it with a sense of play and exploration and withers when you're too analytical or try too hard. You'll be thinking and analyzing too, but approaching branding as a fun process will open up more possibilities.

In its essence, branding is a three-step process (hence, the division of the book into three parts), whether you're branding your business or developing Brand You:

1. *Brand Strategy: Finding your self-brand idea:* In many ways, this preparation phase in which you find your brand strategy is the most important part. That's why ad agencies have account planners, analytical and intuitive thinkers who spearhead finding the best brand strategy and making sure the brand connects with its target customers. Like an account planner, you are looking for your brand idea, a brand insight about the value that you bring to a business situation and to your "customers," your boss, clients, colleagues, and such. Chapters 2 through 4 will give you a quick course in account planning and developing your brand strategy. You'll learn how to do a SWOT Analysis and find ten brand-positioning strategies from the commercial world that clients have used to find a winning brand idea. At the end of chapter 4, you—like the account planner at an ad agency—will prepare a creative brief, a short document that succinctly compiles all the learning in this phase so that you're ready for creative development.

2. *Creative Development: "Packaging" Brand You:* This means creating your brand's verbal identity, visual identity, and personality. The creative phase, spearheaded by *creative directors, art directors,*

*copywriters*, and the like at ad agencies, is usually considered the fun part of branding. It should be fun for you too, because you'll be figuring out how to make your brand idea tangible to others through your communications ability, your image, your executive presence, and other creative branding tactics. Chapters 5 through 9 will help you explore the different aspects of creative development for Brand You, including how to pitch yourself in an *elevator speech*.

3. *Marketing Brand You: Building visibility and connection with your target audience:* Like a brand manager, you're now ready to take Brand You to market. Marketing is everything you do to build "customers" for Brand You. We've all got customers. If you work in a company, your customers are your boss, colleagues, and senior mangers inside your company and clients and business acquaintances outside your company. Marketing is all about building visibility and preference for Brand You, using traditional means like networking as well as all the new cyberworld tools for building visibility and connection. Chapters 10 through 14 will show you how to market Brand You, rebrand yourself after a setback, and develop a career strategy to meet your goals—they'll show you everything you can do to keep your brand in demand.

## Take Action—Now

The bottom line is, branding provides a valuable tool for leveraging the asset that is you. But it is a powerless tool unless you act. See the box on the following page for my list of the top ten self-branding actions you can take, which we will explore in the chapters that follow.

The first secret of personal branding is that the magic is in you. You can take charge and harness your passion and drive. Become emotionally and intellectually engaged in your professional and life journeys. Start to create your own luck. Seek your own solutions.

The more self-reliant you are, the more luck and solutions you will find. Start developing options for yourself rather than waiting for them. A surge in self-esteem is one unexpected benefit of finding your own solutions to your situation. And stronger self-esteem will make it easier for you to act on them. To be a successful careerist or entrepreneur today, you need to be in the personal branding business. You need to own your value, the real, tangible value that you—and only you—offer and you must be willing to take charge of the asset that is you.

 **TOP 10 SELF-BRANDING ACTIONS**

1 Celebrate yourself and your uniqueness: Do a self-brand audit.
2 Keep tabs on the big picture: Do a SWOT (strengths, weaknesses, opportunities, threats) analysis.
3 Don't avoid the competition: Go to school on your competition.
4 Find the sweet spot: Focus on the right strategy for achieving your goals.
5 Harness the power of self-presentation: Learn the principles of visual identity.
6 Tap into the power of words: Learn the principles of verbal identity.
7 Think in terms of markets: Engage in and respond to the market.
8 Expand your network and your visibility: Become known for something by somebody somewhere.
9 Execute a self-brand action plan: Develop specific tactics and implement each as scheduled.
10 Stay relevant: Measure how you are doing.

 **IN A NUTSHELL:** The first secret of self-brands: That person in the mirror is the only one you can rely on. But that's not sad. It's powerful.

# CHAPTER 2

# Think Different to Become a Brand Apart

*This above all: to thine own self be true.*

William Shakespeare
*Hamlet* (I, 3)

The cardinal rule of branding is "Be different." Copying is imitation. When you copy, you're not authentic. You are a generic version of a name brand.

You'll be viewed as a B player. And you'll always be playing the catch-up game.

You should build your professional identity around your authenticity: who you are and what you can be, not who you want to be like or who others want you to be. You need to find out what's different about yourself and your abilities. Then capitalize on it.

Best of all, when you build off your strengths and desires, you'll be enthusiastic. You'll be able to indulge your passions. You'll also find that when you accept who you are, others will, too.

## Make Your Brand a Standout

Having a different idea for your brand is powerful. It will position you apart from the crowd. There are many people competing with you, for your job, your opportunity, your money, your _____. That's why your self-brand must make you stand out from your competitors in the minds of your prospects.

Brand managers spend a lot of time delineating differences: different benefits, different look, different message, different target audience. To determine their different idea, marketers do a *brand audit*, a detailed study of the brand and its competitors. What they are creating is a distinct *brand strategy*, explaining what their brand has to offer that competing brands don't.

Many people shortchange themselves when it comes to targeting their own different ideas and the benefits to their target markets. They are too busy working hard, but that is not the same as working smart. Don't be one of them.

## Find Your Unique Selling Proposition

When you don't differentiate yourself, people won't have a reason to choose you, as my client Alexandra found out. An executive coach who had been in business for more than ten years, Alexandra had a marketing brochure and a fancy logo but no different idea. After I read her brochure, all I could remember as a takeaway message was "executive coach who works with all kinds of people and all kinds of problems."

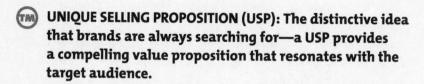 **UNIQUE SELLING PROPOSITION (USP): The distinctive idea that brands are always searching for—a USP provides a compelling value proposition that resonates with the target audience.**

A lot of entrepreneurs make this mistake. They want to cast a wide net so that they won't miss any business.

However, the opposite usually occurs. They don't get much business because people don't have anything to sink their teeth into. Alexandra offered no reason for someone to choose her and gave no sense of the *kind* of client she was best suited to help.

## Make a Different Brand Promise

We got our brand insight when I asked Alexandra, "What kind of client are you really good with?"

She said, "Believe it or not, I enjoy working with really difficult people. For some reason, I'm good at it. Companies have hired me to work with abusive or impossible managers—you know, the kind that are featured in books like *How to Work for a Jerk*."

"Why do companies even bother trying to rehabilitate these people?" you might wonder.

The reason is pure and simple: performance. Because they are talented and produce results, companies often want to keep them. But companies need to get these difficult managers to change their behavior or there will be mutiny in the enterprise.

"Are there enough people like that to build a coaching business around?" I asked Alexandra.

"Sure, tons," she assured me. "Plus I'm good with the stressed-out people who have to work with these difficult people. I've developed methods for helping people cope with impossible bosses and clients so that they are able to control the situation better."

Eureka! We had our different brand promise.

With her focus on difficult managers and the people who work for them, Alexandra had a point of difference and a USP on which to build her self-brand and company brand. She had a public relations platform for pitching reporters doing stories on how to cope with an abusive boss or a difficult client.

Alexandra's different brand strategy also became a way of being memorable and staying at the top of everyone's mind. And as we know, *out of mind* is *out of work*.

## Ask "Why?" "What If?" "How About?"

As the great Yogi (Yogi Berra, that is) said, "You can observe a lot just by watching."

While you look for ideas for a self-brand strategy, observe what attracts your attention amid all the competing messages that bombard you each day. Once you start looking, you'll find that everything communicates. Branding lessons are everywhere.

Start observing what's working and what isn't. Do it for your company, your industry, your job. For instance, what has never been questioned in your industry, business, or department? Why not? What would happen if it were? What "rules" of this industry (or company) can be broken? What's missing? How can that lead to an opportunity for you? As the marketing axiom goes, you want to be the kind of market researcher who looks at what everyone else looks at and sees something different.

Look at people who brand themselves well. What are their strong attributes? What makes them special?

Look at yourself. If you were a competitor, how would you critique yourself? How do your attributes compare with those your company prizes? (Don't just ask yourself these questions; answer them.)

Whenever you see someone lead a successful project or give an exciting presentation, ask yourself what made it so special. Whenever you see someone doing something novel and find yourself saying, "Gee, that was a great idea," think about how you might put your spin on it.

You can get self-branding ideas every day just by following stories in the media. If you're in business, read business publications like the *Wall Street Journal* or *Fortune* for success stories and cautionary tales. Or read magazines like the *New Yorker* or the *Atlantic* for thoughtful articles on opinion leaders and issues of the day.

Another way to go about exploring possibilities for yourself is to begin with the end in mind and work backward, as the next brainstormer shows.

**BRAINSTORMER: Imagining the Outcome First**

Think in terms of the outcome you want and work backward. Let's say, for example, that you want to dramatically increase your salary. Here's how you might go about it. Ask yourself the following questions. What would make an employer double your salary? What do you need to have in your self-brand profile that you don't have now?

Watch how people present themselves and their ideas on television talk shows. Even the media, with its cult of celebrities, could be a source of inspiration.

## Are You Creative?

If you watch the television show *Mad Men*, you know that Don Draper is a creative director and works in the Creative Department at the Sterling Cooper Advertising Agency, and Don has a certain disdain for noncreative types, such as the account executive Pete Campbell.

Like Don Draper, most of us have branded some people as creative types and others as noncreative types. Turns out, there is no such thing as a "creative type," and creativity, like most things, is a skill anyone can become good at.

(TM) **There is no creative gene.**
**Creativity is a skill anyone can learn.**

The key to coming up with creative ideas for Brand You and everything else is to promote free, open-minded thinking

Scientists believe that most innovative breakthroughs come out of the blue when we're doing something else, and when we're relaxed enough to take note of it. The unconscious mind takes over and makes connections, helping us to solve problems that we haven't been able to solve consciously, maybe because we're trying too hard or are too focused to see connections.

The routines that most of us have each day are the opposite of what neuroscientists believe fosters innovative thinking. Look at your morning routine: rushing out of bed into the shower and then commuting to work. You're harried. You turn on the news and it's generally gloomy. You'll miss out on creative insights with this routine.

Imaginative ideas come about when our minds are unfocused, even groggy, like when we're half awake or while taking a walk or a shower. That's when we're most likely to benefit from the unfocused, peripheral thinking that leads to innovative ideas. And having a creative idea is like a lightbulb going off. There is a burst of brain activity that shows up like a light show on brain scans.

# Ride the Creative Flow

To promote creative ideas for Brand You and all your endeavors, try chang- ing your routine. Set the alarm for fifteen minutes earlier than usual so you can have some half-awake, half-asleep time to let your mind wander and see where your thoughts lead. It's always my most creative time. Try to kill task- oriented thoughts that cloud your mind (Do I have everything in my report for my ten o'clock meeting?). See what pops up from your unconscious mind. (And keep pen and paper by your bed so that you can capture your ideas.)

Another technique that helps promote creativity is daydreaming. It's not wasting time after all; it's working on your creative power. Take a walk without your smartphone and without a specific destination in mind. Or just sit around. Let your mind wander.

Laughter and foolishness also free the mind for creative associations, studies show. In one study, people who watched short videos of stand-up comics scored 20 percent better on creative puzzles.

A stimulating, diverse environment made up of different types of people can likewise be a great catalyst for creative ideas. Even working in an open space without office or cubicle dividers is conducive to creativity studies show. It's hard to think outside the box when you're in a box.

Creative breakthroughs are more likely to come to those who live in big cities rather than small cities, as well as to people who have traveled and lived in other countries. Living abroad, like living amidst the diversity and energy of a large city, expands your thinking and opens your mind to new ways of doing things and to new ideas, and that makes you more likely to come up with creative breakthroughs, whether it's an idea for your personal brand or a breakthrough idea for a project at work.

# Start With a Hypothesis

When you first begin your self-branding journey, don't get muddled by all the "facts" as you analyze your brand and the market.

Begin by tapping into your gut or *fast thinking*. What does your intu- ition tell you about your identity and lifework? The best ideas and strategies often come through brainstorming and hypothesizing before we do any research. Deep down, we already know the answer.

The *initial hypothesis* is a technique that some management consultants use with great success. Yes, you actually can come up with the answers to your personal, business, or marketing problem before all the careful research studies and analysis get in the way and muddle your vision.

 **SELF-BRAND HYPOTHESIS: Don't neglect to consult your intuition before you do research and formal analysis. An "ignorant" idea or hunch may be more insightful and valuable than a labored study of the situation.**

The reason is simple. An initial hypothesis based on hunches and intuition may have the greatest insight into a problem. And that insight is often the solution to your self-branding, or personal, or any other problem.

Like empathy, intuition is similar to powerful radar that gives you information you can choose to act on or not. It's a powerful form of intelligence.

Intuition is not some airy-fairy hunch machine but a neurologically based behavior that developed so we could sense and quickly respond to danger. In essence, we can know more through our gut than through our brains. When we go with our gut, we discern what's really going on, not through reason or analysis of facts but through our powerful unconscious mind. Often, our gut opinion—our first reaction—is far better than what we think of after considered analysis.

Your unconscious mind can be a great resource for finding solutions that are out of your grasp during the day. Some people get their best work-related ideas while driving, others while showering, but sleep also seems to be a great place to achieve breakthroughs. When we sleep our brain tries to connect the dots and explore ideas in a trial-and-error fashion, experiments show, making it easier to bridge the gaps and solve the dilemma. (Reminder to self: keep a notepad and pen on the bedside table.)

We all have "scanning patterns." Our antennae are up to spot certain types of clues and information, but not other types. What you want to do is to increase your radar range so that you can pick up more. You'll find that the more you do this the better you will become at it, and that your gut instincts are often right.

## Creative Brainstorming

Remember, even complex problems don't necessarily need complex solutions, and a more detailed analysis doesn't necessarily lead to good results. The complex algorithms that gave AAA ratings to bad debts show the pitfalls of complex analysis.

If you are doing your initial hypothesis solo, go to a quiet place where you can let your thoughts roam. If you put together a group of friends or colleagues, choose people you think are insightful, and mix it up so that it includes people with hard and soft thinking skills. The best creative ideas come from diversity. That's why ad agencies try to put together a diverse team to work on branding assignments.

As you do creative brainstorming, you may discover some new insights or even a career path or business strategy that really pans out for you. It happens all the time.

The rule for brainstorming is "No idea is a bad idea." Censoring causes people to shut down their creative juices. Anyway, it often happens that a so-called dumb idea spurs you to think of ways to debunk it. That will help sharpen your focus.

You might even want to really get into the spirit of it and create a war-room atmosphere as ad agencies do and post the best self-brand ideas on large sheets of paper on the wall. This will help you evaluate the various ideas for Brand You. Often, the right solution will jump out from the pack.

 **BRAINSTORMER: Developing Your Hypothesis**

Here are some questions to prod your hypothetical thinking:

What's different, special, unusual, or weird about Brand You?

If you were managing this brand, where would you take it in five years?

What should you be doing to make meaning in the world?

What is the key piece of advice you would give this brand?

## Consumer Research

In preparing to develop a brand strategy, an ad agency doesn't rely on the "fast thinking" of gut instincts, brainstorming, and the initial hypothesis; they focus on "slow thinking" too, by doing *consumer research* and a brand audit.

At ad agencies, it's the job of the *account planner* to lead the consumer research and the development of the brand strategy. You need to do the same for Brand You. Your consumers or customers are your boss, your colleagues, your clients, and other senior managers. And it's important to know what their perceptions are about Brand You, about what makes you tick and the value you bring to a business situation (and, of course, what you're doing that undercuts your brand.)

This doesn't mean that your business associates get to determine your brand. Only you can define Brand You. What you are doing is gathering perceptions and insights that are critical to your brand development.

The best way to do your research is informally over coffee or lunch outside of the office where you both can relax. Don't share the topic beforehand so that the comments and suggestions are fresh and unfiltered.

You can begin the conversation by telling your interviewee that you are exploring personal branding, and while the company performance review is useful for certain performance measures, you want to get their thoughts on how your leadership style is perceived.

You want to get the other person talking about what is most meaningful about Brand You. You need to uncover the distinct, measurable value that you bring to a professional situation, and how you come across to others in the workplace. Force yourself to just listen to what the other person says, but don't disagree or try to defend yourself. Write down whatever they share. Probe and ask for examples when someone says something important. You can simply say, "Why do you think that?" or "Can you give me an example?" Then, like the best account planners and market researchers, probe to get them talking more. That way you're more likely to hear something really interesting and useful. You need to discover if others see in you the brand qualities you want to be known for. And you want to uncover your blind spots, how you come across that you aren't even aware of.

You can also pick up useful market research just by listening to your boss's or a colleague's off-hand comments after a meeting. One boss congratulated me after a presentation, but casually added, "Did you run this by any of your colleagues before the presentation?" I hadn't and that had rankled with some of my colleagues who had gone to her to complain. It was valuable intel because I certainly wanted to be branded as a team player, not a rogue.

## Family Baggage

In your pursuit of self-knowledge, you'll also want to look at family issues and messages that you are carrying around that are not useful for your brand identity. Some of the beliefs in your family creed are assets that are the bedrock of who you are and why you are successful. But other family messages can diminish your self-brand and get in the way of the career identity you desire. It's important to examine your family dynamics and core messages so that you can throw out old, limiting ideas.

My mom and dad gave me so many positive messages for which I will always be grateful. But they also hammered in traditional messages of the time like "Keep your head down and work hard, and you will be rewarded." While that may seem like good advice, if you're reading this book, you know that I believe that hard work, though important, is just the price of admission for any job. Hard work is not enough for career success. That message kept me focused on tasks for many years, and not building the relationships and visibility that are critical to career success.

I've replaced this family credo with my formula for success: Hard work + Branding = Success.

 **BRAINSTORMER: The Family Creed**

**What were your family's messages regarding work and careers?**

**What were the limits of the family creed?**

**What assets did your family give you?**

## The SWOT Analysis

Marketers often use a handy analysis called the SWOT analysis, a snapshot look at a brand's strengths, weaknesses, opportunities, and threats.

The SWOT analysis can be a useful tool for you too. It is an intensive look at your strengths and weaknesses in a real-world framework. It will help you focus on your strengths and deflect your weaknesses. It will help you zero in on opportunities and threats on your professional horizon, even uncover hidden information.

As a self-brand strategist, you must always be relevant and find new opportunities, and stay on top of how you are perceived by your target markets. We spend too much of our time following so many rules or simply plodding ahead that we don't see an opportunity or miss how we are being perceived. Doing a periodic SWOT analysis will keep you on track.

## Strengths and Weaknesses

"Strengths" and "weaknesses," the first two areas, deal with you.

Think of strengths as assets that could be links to your success. Assets are areas you can build on, and practically anything could be an asset. Start with skills, experience, and accomplishments. What parts of your job are fun to do?

Then expand the list to include personality traits. Expand it further to include anyone you have known or even met, and anything that you have explored or been interested in. The hidden assets or self-taught skills that come up through probing often hold the key.

Weaknesses are areas to avoid, because you are not on solid ground there. However, some weaknesses, such as communication skills and networking, may be areas to target for development, as they are integral to your life strategy.

## Opportunities and Threats

The "opportunities" and "threats" sections in the SWOT analysis deal with things that could affect you in the future. What is going on that could dramatically change things? What is not working well? Business is dynamic, so there is always movement and change. (Follow the business news and you'll see lots of threats to the economy, to your industry, and to business profit forecasts.) Change always creates new opportunities and new threats.

For example, if you're in school, you need to start anticipating the job market in the fields you are studying. Some areas will offer tons of growth and financial rewards, while others will be tough slogging. In the 1990s,

Wall Street and high technology were the hot spots, and many people rode that wave to fame and fortune. Today, high tech is still thriving, Wall Street less so. You need to find the best wave to ride for your future.

One way to be well prepared for just about anything the future brings is to become what Stanford calls a "T-shaped" student who has depth in one prominent area of study but also breadth across many disciplines. T-shaped students also recognize the importance of soft power skills like the ability to communicate, and collaborate with and lead diverse groups.

If you have a job, you need to keep tabs on what is taking place that could threaten your livelihood in the future, whether it's in the economy, your industry, or your company. And you want to keep your sights on the new opportunities that any change will bring about. The SWOT analysis will help you find the link between a market opportunity and your strengths and desires.

The SWOT analysis is also helpful in analyzing a potential new job or company. Many people who switch don't succeed in their new jobs. It's important to do your homework before you get romanced in the job interview process. The culture has to be a good fit for you. How healthy is the company or group you'll be joining? Some managers hire people to prop up a department or division that is already on life support. Unfortunately, they neglect to warn the job candidate that the position is a turnaround situation. Too many people find out the hard way.

Every job you take will either increase or decrease the value of your self-brand. The SWOT brainstormer on the following page will help you plot the right moves.

## SWOT Harder

The overriding goal of the SWOT analysis is to find links between your strengths and new market opportunities. You want to develop strategies that will be advantageous to you in terms of the market's future direction.

When you have completed the SWOT brainstormer, if you're like most people, you will have a long list of strengths and weaknesses. (You can always supplement your own "consumer research" with online assessment tools like Gallup's StrengthsFinder.) You'll probably have a smaller list of future opportunities as well as some threats looming on the horizon.

It's often smart to start with the list of opportunities and then review your strengths and assets. After that, you should be able to identify the ones that best position you to take advantage of those opportunities. For example, choose the two or three most critical opportunities that suit the future you see for yourself. Then, pick the strengths that play into each opportunity.

I brainstormed and did a SWOT analysis when I started my company, SelfBrand. I wanted to do something entrepreneurial after a long career working for others. I saw an opportunity to bring my strategic branding approach to companies as a brand strategist. But I also saw an opportunity to do something more novel—to take the branding process used in the commercial world and apply it to people so that they could achieve their potential in career and personal growth.

I knew that in the current world of work, many people would need self-branding skills in order to move from job to job and rebrand themselves for wholly new careers. More people will become entrepreneurs and they will need to develop a strong self-brand in tandem with a company brand.

I realized that people need to think about their careers using a strategic and creative process similar to the branding process. Plus, my clients could learn from all the mistakes that I had made along the way!

 **BRAINSTORMER: Doing the SWOT Analysis**

1.  **Strengths:** Write down anything that you are good at and love to do. Write down what your boss, clients, or colleagues give you high marks on. (It may or may not be true, but it's how you're currently perceived.)

2.  **Weaknesses:** Write down what you're terrible at and hate to do, or what your boss and friends criticize you for.

3.  **Opportunities:** This is wide open. Write down anything that could be an opportunity for you. A key is to look for unmet or unsatisfied needs in your company or business on which you could capitalize.

4.  **Threats:** Write down what keeps you awake at night about yourself or your career or business, whether real or imagined.

**Extra credit:** Circle the top two or three critical factors in each category. Look for the intersection of a new market opportunity and your strengths and assets. Brainstorm the possibilities.

## Choose an "Enemy"

You'll want to look at another page from the branding playbook: *competitive analysis.*

Go to school on your competition. A competitor is anyone who is pursuing the same goal or target market that you are pursuing.

Respect your competitors, but don't be afraid of them. Be different from them. Analyze them. (If you can analyze them, you can be better than them.)

Smart marketers think in terms of *choosing an enemy* to position their brands against. Rather than viewing competition as a negative thing, flip it. View competitors' attributes as they highlight your strengths and advantages: position your strengths against their weaknesses and reposition their strengths as less important attributes.

For example, Leonardo da Vinci positioned his younger rival Michelangelo as a mere sculptor, not a painter like himself. He even tried to brand Michelangelo as a technician, who looked like a "baker" with white marble dust on his clothes, rather than an artist.

Of course, Leonardo's branding attempt didn't stick. Michelangelo went on to paint the ceiling of the Sistine Chapel. His dynamic, muscular style of painting was influenced by his background as a sculptor and immediately became the talk of Rome. There was no doubt that Michelangelo's brand footprint was quite big enough to encompass painter and sculptor.

Picking the right enemy and using the principles of branding can dramatically transform your career identity. Until 1854, Abraham Lincoln was a local politician in Illinois whose name rarely appeared in the Chicago papers or elsewhere in the country. Then, in 1858, Lincoln challenged Stephen Douglas, the most prominent politician of the 1850s, to a series of debates over the issue of slavery.

Boy, was that a smart personal branding move. Having an important "enemy" gave Lincoln gravitas and elevated his status. Now that he had visibility, people were impressed by Lincoln and his oratory. By 1860, in just six years, Lincoln was a national figure and was elected president of the United States

Your "enemy" can even be someone you admire. The enemy represents a counterpoint to Brand You, someone you need to be clearly different from in order to succeed. One of my clients, Christopher, was promoted to a senior position replacing a very popular vice president, Ted, who had died suddenly. "How do I succeed someone who everyone loved, me included, and now is a saint in everyone's eyes?" my client asked.

Whether you're taking over from a visionary leader like Steve Jobs or a popular man of the people like Ted, don't try to fill your predecessor's shoes. They don't fit and never will, and you have to tell your team that. You must build your leadership brand on what makes you great as a leader. Don't think, "What would Ted do?" Think, "What would I do?" Realize, too, that although expressing vulnerability is usually a sign of weakness in business, it can also be a sign of strength. Tell your team that you feel inadequate following the great leader. It will help your team connect with you and your leadership.

Competition also means that your field is attractive and lucrative. After all, if it weren't, why would people want to be part of it? Your status is elevated and worth more because competition has created a lot of interest.

Marketers study their brand competitors by looking at a competitive analysis of product features, television commercials and print ads, market research studies, and the like. What can you do to study your competitors? You can always start by Googling them to see what comes up. Use the brainstormer below to position and define your competitors.

 **BRAINSTORMER: Positioning Competitors**

Describe each competitor in one positive word. Think of it as the competitor's keyword.

Describe each competitor in one negative word. This is the competitor's main weakness or strike point.

What do you have to offer that they don't? This is your value proposition.

Now, sell your value proposition against your key competitor—your "enemy."

## Find Your Different Idea

Branding is a competition. It's a competition over what you stand for versus what someone else stands for. It's a competition over ideas.

In self-branding, you're searching for your different idea, a different idea that resonates with your target market. You're searching for a different idea that will help you compete and win. The way to do well is to not run with the herd. You must look at yourself as a brand in a competitive marketplace. Find the advantage of your different idea.

Just as brands always have to be tweaked to stay relevant, so do you. After all, the goal of making yourself a relevant self-brand is to connect with other people and to be able to offer them something.

So don't neglect what's different and authentic about you. It is the most wonderful thing you have to offer the world.

---

 **IN A NUTSHELL:** The second secret of self-brands: Study yourself, your "customers," and the competition, but don't follow the herd. Find your different idea. Be sure to combine *fast thinking* (quick, intuitive brainstorming) along with *slow thinking* (thoughtful, detailed analysis).

---

# CHAPTER 3

# Search for the Sweet Spot Where You and a Market Opportunity Meet

*We know what we are*
*but know not what we may be.*

William Shakespeare
*Hamlet* (I, 5)

In self-branding, you are looking for the sweet spot: the intersection of a good idea and a market need that you can satisfy.

For most people, the problem with finding the sweet spot is not a lack of ideas and information but too many competing ideas and too much information. The hard part is figuring out which things are important and which are worthless.

Each person's situation is unique, but the self-branding process involves analyzing the facts in the marketplace and looking at ideas and options. But it also involves trusting your instincts and tapping into your intuition as you mold your future. You must use both your brains and your gut instincts as you focus your brand.

## Follow Your Instincts

Handsome and athletic, Anthony cut an impressive figure when we met. It was quite a contrast from our phone conversation a week earlier. Then, an emotional Anthony had described being laid off six months earlier by an elite Wall Street firm and his very frustrating job hunt.

Up until that day, Anthony had led what would seem to many to be a fairy-tale existence. He attended top schools and then landed a plum job as an analyst with a Wall Street investment bank.

Life was sweet for several years, until his specialty, merger and acquisitions advisory work in the telecommunications industry, went sour. And he was out on the street.

Diligent professional that he is, Anthony had spent the past six months meeting recruiters, sending out résumés, and commiserating with other newly unemployed investment bankers. Like them, he was looking for a job at an investment bank or in a corporate finance department. The problem: a dead job market and lots of job hunters with MBAs on the loose.

 **If you don't stand for something relevant to the marketplace, you have no value.**

My jaw dropped when I asked Anthony where he would like to see himself professionally in five years. His answer had almost no relationship to what he was doing now or what he was looking for.

Anthony's childhood dream was to be an entrepreneur, just as his grandfather had been years ago in India. His new twist: he wanted to develop his own business advising Western companies on increasing business with the new moneyed class in India.

"Well, if that's where you want to go, you'll never get there by looking for a job like the one you had in telecommunications," I told him. "You'll have to do different things from what you are doing now if that's where you want to end up."

Yes, change can be scary. But sometimes it's scarier not to change.

## Create Proof Points

Job number one for Anthony was to develop a self-brand strategy and action plan that would get him pointed in the right direction.

Our first problem was Anthony's glaring lack of the credentials necessary to achieve his dreams. We needed *proof points* to demonstrate that he could be successful doing business in India and that he understood the affluent Indian market. We hypothesized that his first order of business was to find employment with a Western firm that wanted to develop the new affluent market in India.

Anthony was in a classic catch-22 situation. He couldn't get such a job without experience, and he couldn't get experience without the job. We needed to create *perceptual links* between what he had been doing and what he wanted to do so that he could move forward.

To provide the perceptual links of experience and understanding of the Indian market, we hit upon a novel solution. We developed a pilot research study to measure awareness of U.S. brands among the newly wealthy in India.

Ad agencies often field a pilot research study when pitching a piece of business. They hope that the insights gained from the research will give them a strategic advantage in the new business process. It is also a tactic that you can use successfully, particularly in new geographic markets and customer segments or for radically new product areas. And it can be done affordably in smaller markets or even as a do-it-yourself project over the Internet. Don't position it as full-blown research but as a *pilot* study.

It may be more difficult to implement a pilot study for mature industries unless you come up with a new angle because there is already so much information on those markets. But the opposite is true of newer markets, like Anthony's, because not much information is available.

## Think Big

Then, Anthony started creating his own luck. Through networking, he located a businessman who wanted to explore the prospect of developing a business in India. He agreed not only to fund the study but to pay Anthony's travel expenses, too.

Next, we drafted letters to key Western companies—all the companies on Anthony's list of desirable places to work. In the letters, we said that Anthony was off to conduct a pilot research study of the newly wealthy consumer market in India and was including their brand in the study. Anthony offered to meet with them to share his findings after he completed the study.

 **The only way to predict your future is to create it.**

Were there some dead ends? Sure. But so what?

Bottom line: the strategy worked. Of the first twelve companies that received his letter, nine responded, a truly astounding rate. It was clearly the right strategy at the right time. He even booked six appointments with senior executives at target companies before he left.

In India, Anthony used the research study he was conducting as a door opener both with Western firms and with Indian nationals involved in sales and marketing, public relations, events planning, and market research.

When Anthony returned to the United States, he had a busy calendar. In follow-up meetings and interviews with senior executives, he successfully positioned himself as a rare bird—a global business executive who could bridge East and West. He was a savvy citizen of the West and also a person of Indian heritage who could speak local languages and forge strong ties.

## Uncover Hidden Assets

Anthony had another asset, one he didn't see as valuable at first.

His grandfather's name and business reputation were unique assets. Even though his grandfather was no longer alive, his business reputation in India gave Anthony a compelling and memorable story to tell and leverage wherever he went.

In India, Anthony's family heritage helped him meet lots of people in marketing, retailing, public relations, and manufacturing. In the West, Anthony made a point of mentioning that he came from a family with an established business name in India. Family heritage is important in many areas of the world and could help open doors for Western companies.

Anthony's heritage gave him an enormous advantage. But, even without it, his strategy would still have worked. After all, many Western companies had set up appointments for interviews on the basis of his initial letter outlining his proposed pilot study.

Anthony's transformation was just as powerful as anything you'd see on *Extreme Makeover*. Potential employers and business contacts now saw him in a completely different way.

Once he had a few big-name interviews under his belt, Anthony leveraged those appointments to garner meetings with other Western manufacturers. He was on his way to reaching his dream. Anthony had found the *sweet spot* where his abilities and desires intersected with a real need in the marketplace. The suggestions and questions in the brainstormer on the following page will help you recognize your dream.

## Meet Change With Change

When situations change, *you* must change if you intend to succeed.

Kayla had an extensive background in marketing and sales in the technology industry. When she first called me, the rumor mill at the company where she worked was in high gear. Reports were starting to appear in the press that another company was going to buy her company.

Like just about everyone else in her department, Kayla was worried about a merger and job cuts. She was like a deer caught in the headlights. She wasn't getting much work done on the job, and she wasn't taking much action about her situation on the outside either—that is, until the merger deal was announced two weeks later.

When Kayla and I did the SWOT analysis, we spent a lot of time looking at the changes taking place in the technology industry, especially the opportunities and threats part of the analysis. Even though the merger was being billed in the press as a merger of equals, we knew that some employees would survive and others wouldn't. We knew that all bets were off in terms of job security.

Change seemed inevitable. The consolidation train was leaving the station, and lots of companies were jumping on it. So moving to another company wouldn't necessarily increase Kayla's immunity to a merger or potential job loss.

Kayla needed a strategy for ending her paralysis and developing options for her future. Rather than sit around and worry about where the ax was going to fall next, Kayla took action.

**BRAINSTORMER: What If?**

Go to a quiet place where you can let your thoughts roam as you answer these questions. Follow your instincts.

What are you really passionate about?

What's your dream job? What would you do if you knew you couldn't fail?

What is missing from your current life that you must have going forward?

What could you do tomorrow to get started?

## Niche Your Self-Brand

The key was *focus*. Rather than position Kayla as the marketing generalist that she was, we narrowed our focus to an area that allowed her to demonstrate a touch of nonpareil excellence.

We zeroed in on social media marketing, a new area undergoing tremendous growth in which Kayla had done some exciting and successful projects. She hypothesized that social media would be even more important in the future, particularly with the young high-tech consumer that was her specialty. We thought social marketing was the sweet spot for Kayla given our take on market needs and trends.

Narrow focus goes against the grain for most people. They think that the broader their job description, the better off they will be. So most of Kayla's colleagues were positioning themselves as marketing generalists with a long list of capabilities.

Kayla had a broad background in marketing, too; but marketing generalists were becoming a surplus.

The acquiring company was weak in the emerging area of social media marketing, and this was an important factor in our decision. (Kayla had done her competitive analysis.)

 **Look for a market niche where there are few entrenched competitors.**

## Dramatize Your Résumé

Kayla's résumé was a laundry list of skills and job experience. There was no focus or message. Her résumé was full of business jargon and bland descriptions and looked downright forbidding in terms of layout. It was not a self-branding document.

The first thing I wanted Kayla to do was to shift from the idea of her résumé as job history to her résumé as an ad for brand Kayla. She needed to develop a résumé that was strategically focused and interesting, like a good ad. To do that, we put a headline positioning Kayla at the top of the résumé. Under her name, we put the following line: Social Media Marketing—The Fickle Twenty-Something Tech Consumer—Innovative Customer-Engagement Programs. We developed her self-brand message in a profile paragraph set right underneath and used the body of the résumé to tell a story of innovative projects tied into clear-cut results and customer engagement.

All the change taking place in the technology field was obvious, but we needed to put Kayla on the winning side of the change with new ideas and solutions for potential employers.

The focus of Kayla's message was her innovative social media programs for the eighteen- to twenty-four-year-old, tech-oriented market. We wanted potential employers (including the new management that came with the merger) to know that Kayla had a lock on how these consumers think and act. We linked the marketing initiatives she had spearheaded that were outside the social media area around core ideas related to new media marketing and showed how they increased customer life, frequency, and profits.

The final shift Kayla needed to make was to create a visually and verbally memorable résumé. The layout should look inviting, and the copy should capture readers' attention and compel them to read more.

Most résumés list accomplishments in the most general way. A long list of skills and responsibilities presented in vague language doesn't get noticed. A résumé that sells you must focus on a message and use action words to bring your self-brand story to life.

## Cascade Your Achievements

A clever way to set your résumé apart from the pack is to place a one- or two-page *achievement addendum* at the back. It's a must for a senior executive but can benefit everyone; it's often the clincher in the sale.

An achievement addendum is the something more that sets you apart and encourages an employer to choose you and not the other guy. (And something more is mandatory in a tough job market.)

An achievement addendum allows you to showcase the most powerful parts of your personal story with more detail and excitement. Use a case study format such as problem, solution, and results or challenge, action, and accomplishment.

Tell the story of the project or initiative so that people can participate in the challenge and the steps you took to succeed. Use the active voice and action words and describe specifics as if you were telling a colleague about the project. Avoid business or technical jargon.

If you worked on an important project outside the office—in your community or with a political campaign, for example—the achievement addendum is a great place to capitalize on it. The next brainstormer will help you get started.

**BRAINSTORMER: Creating an Achievement Addendum**

Think of any project to which you contributed in an important way at work or in your community.

What challenge did you face?

How did you approach the project in an innovative way?

Were there any novel solutions or unexpected problems?

What actions did you take?

What were the quantifiable results? The emotional results?

Describe the results as visually and vividly as possible.

## Create Endorsement Buzz

Great résumés have another extra, a surprise element that makes the reader want to learn more about the person. In order to separate Kayla's résumé further from the pack, we needed to create a different *brand experience* for people who came in contact with her résumé. We took a tactic from the advertising playbook and used *customer testimonials*.

Of course, Kayla didn't have customers in the traditional sense, but she did have two former bosses, a manager, and several clients who were happy with projects she had spearheaded. We put together case studies of these projects in the achievement addendum and featured a quote from a former boss or client at the top of each one. One of her former bosses had moved on to a prominent job, and we placed his "celebrity" endorsement first.

These endorsements of Kayla's abilities created buzz and helped her score more interviews. It allowed her to showcase her successes through someone else's words.

 **If you say it, it's bragging.**
**If your boss or colleague says it, it's expert testimony.**

The achievement addendum gave Kayla a reason to call up former colleagues, not to ask for a job lead, but to ask for a quote for her addendum. (In the course of their conversations, however, these people often came up with suggestions for people Kayla could meet with.)

## Dazzle the Interviewer

Kayla, like most people, always went into a job interview feeling powerless. She boned up on possible questions and the company itself and went to the meeting expecting a formal interview.

Wrong, wrong, wrong! With that kind of mind-set, it will be hard to feel genuine and comfortable in your own skin. You'll be too worried about how you are going to answer the questions. What you need to do is take control. Create a more relaxed experience so that a conversation takes place. You want to make the meeting more informal and conversational as quickly as possible.

The first impression you create is critical. The way you look, enter the room, and explain yourself in the first thirty seconds will make or break you. Part of how you communicate your brand and what you think of yourself are your clothes, your posture and your hair. You must prepare your *elevator speech*: a pithy story about yourself that you could tell in the length of time it takes to travel several floors in an elevator. (See chapter 9 for a detailed account of how to craft your elevator speech for a job interview.) It should be an interesting narrative that positions you and dramatizes the benefit you bring to a project or a company. Practice it out loud. See the brainstormer on the following page to get you started.

You should also be able to tell interesting stories about your professional adventures. Think in terms of cascading your message and capabilities around various themes, such as the following:

Rags to riches
The turning point
Against all odds
Hero to my client

 **BRAINSTORMER: Creating Your Thirty Seconds**

Set a timer for thirty seconds. Practice your self-brand opener. What hooks, connections, or stories can you add that will make your opening more powerful and relevant? Write your response in the space below.

## Turn the Tables

As a self-brander, you have your agenda too. So as soon as you can, ask your interviewer questions. Interview them. And listen more than you talk.

 **The more an interviewer talks, the more interested in you the interviewer will be.**

It is a very powerful tactic, because if you work a series of questions into the conversation, you immediately level the playing field.

In place of a one-way dialogue and a one-way relationship, you've created a two-way dialogue and a two-way relationship.

Ask about key initiatives and projects. You want to know more about the culture. When you take this approach (in a friendly way), you will come across as a person with options. You'll find that your worth will skyrocket in the mind of the interviewer. Likewise, if you try to sell yourself too hard or want quick feedback on how you stack up compared to the other candidates, your value will plummet.

Ask questions and listen. Listening is an art. You'll create a great impression and learn a lot at the same time. When you listen rather than talk, you flatter your audience. Listening says that you think the other person is smart and worth listening to.

Because you're not trying so hard to sell yourself in the interview, what usually happens, as Kayla found out, is that the interviewer starts to sell you on the company and the job. When an interviewer starts to feel comfortable, she might even share war stories about the company or industry. When the balance of power between two people is more equal, it is much more likely to result in a job offer.

When you create more dialogue in an interview situation, you come across as confident and not needy. You give the impression of a person with options who's not just going to grab the first thing but is looking for the right thing.

It's a fact of branding that people want something all the more when they think it is not so easy to get. (Why do you think luxury goods manufacturers produce small lots so that there are waiting lists?) You want to create the perception that you are a brand that is in demand, even if you would give your firstborn for the job. Always remember that people will buy because they want to, not because they're being sold.

## Think and Act Smart

There is no one *right* brand identity, benefit, or message, although some will be much more successful for you than others will. Find the things about you that are remarkable enough to meet real needs in the marketplace. Focus on your different idea, create a different brand experience, but above all, do something.

Avoid the urge to procrastinate or talk yourself out of doing something because you're not ready yet. The best and only time to do something is the present.

We all are dealt different hands in life. Your hand is all good as long as you use it in the right way.

Make use of everything. You have experiences; these are brand assets. You have a point of view; that too is an asset. Make the best use of the assets and resources you have and realize that we all have hidden assets that we need to uncover. Successful people often make use of what others view as worthless or insignificant. Be one of them.

Become the expert on Brand You and your target markets. Do your own market research and keep your own scorecard. The foundation of a self-brand is self-knowledge.

 **IN A NUTSHELL:** The third secret of self-brands: Look for the sweet spot. Uncover hidden assets that meet a real market need: You—fresh, unique, powerful.

# CHAPTER 4

# Find a Great Self-Brand Strategy to Get Great Results

*Some are born great. Some achieve greatness.*
*Some have greatness thrust upon them.*

William Shakespeare
*Twelfth Night* (II, 3)

S trategy is the brains of branding.

A good self-brand strategy is similar to a brand strategy for a company or a product. Strategy is developing a *winnable position* in the marketplace with a smart game plan and tactics for achieving it.

The successful people around you may or may not be the smartest or the most talented, but I'll wager they each had a strategy (whether they called it that). Smarts and talent are important but overrated. We all know lots of smart and talented people who are not doing well professionally.

Even luck is overrated. Sure, luck helps. But most successful people *create* their own luck. Then they give their stories a more romantic spin by saying it was luck and not hard work that got them there.

Strategy is underrated and much more valuable. As the marketing consultant David Beckwith has stated, "All strategies are not created equal.

Terrific strategies and tactics more than beat good ones; they work hundreds of times better."

 **SELF-BRAND STRATEGY: A crisp positioning statement that defines your "brand idea" or unique selling proposition (USP)—what's different and special about you in comparison to others and why it matters.**

I agree with Beckwith, but don't wait until you figure out a killer strategy. Get started now. You're ready for strategic development after you've done the research, analyzed the competition, and completed your analysis of strengths, weaknesses, opportunities, and threats (SWOT).

Having a strategy gives you a lot of advantages. Developing a strategy forces you to think, and that in itself will start to give you an advantage over many people. Strategy also compels you to think big picture and long term.

## Develop a Self-Brand Strategy

Your self-brand strategy should be short and focused.

It should be short enough to write on the back of a business card. If you can't say it briefly, your strategy is probably muddled. As the Bard said, "Brevity is the soul of wit."

Your strategy should dramatize a benefit. And it should be distinctive enough to intrigue people and make them want to know more.

The verbal counterpart of your self-brand strategy is the elevator speech. The elevator speech articulates your strategy—what you stand for and the distinct value you bring—in a brief, conversational way that you can use when meeting new professional acquaintances or at job interviews and the like.

The ability to articulate what your brand is about is important. After all, if you can't articulate it, how can you expect anyone else to get it? You need to create the focus and the sizzle.

Ad agencies use a simple format for brand strategy statements. They aim for a punchy statement of the *positioning* that sets the brand apart from its competitors. They follow the positioning with *proof points*—concrete examples—or credentials that support the positioning strategy.

Another way of putting together a self-brand strategy that defines your brand value is though analogy. Try to put two different ideas together to express your brand, such as "I'm a cross between _____ and _____," or "I'm like _____ meets _____." For example, Tazo defined the brand strategy for its tea as "Marco Polo meets Merlin."

Here are two examples of self-brand strategies from the client stories in chapter 3.

### Anthony's Self-Brand Strategy

*Anthony is a rare bird: East meets West.*

Here are the credentials Anthony used to support his strategy:

Dynamic Western-trained business executive with Indian family heritage

Understands emerging elite class in India through pilot market research study

Asian business ties through family heritage and research project

### Kayla's Self-Brand Strategy

*Kayla creates social media marketing programs that make young customers stick around.*

Here are some of the proof points Kayla used:

Innovative social media marketing initiatives expanded her company's share of wallet by 23 percent last year

Internet game/competition brought in 15,500 new customers and expanded share of spending by existing customers by 28 percent

## Strategize Differently

Truly great self-brand strategies often meet resistance at first, as many new ideas do.

When you take a different stance, you are, well, different, and that may cause discomfort at first. Your brand strategy might not appeal to everyone, and that might make you uncomfortable. But if your brand strategy does not have a bit of an edgy quality, it is probably a strategy that a lot of people are using.

Remember, if the way you talk about yourself and what you can do doesn't have some sizzle, chances are that people will peg you as a commodity. You have to be intriguing enough to stand out in your category.

## Be Authentic

Your strategy must come out of who you are.

Remember, the sign over the entrance to the Delphic oracle's temple read "Know thyself." You'll never make it by copying someone else's strategy or image. Your quest is to uncover yours.

One way to start is by eliminating what is superfluous, what is not intrinsic to who you are. When Michelangelo carved a statue, he believed that the sculpture was already there in the rough piece of stone. His job was to eliminate all the superfluous stone and reveal the *David* or *Pieta* hidden within.

Your job is similar. Eliminate things that are not unique to you. Focus on what is authentic—your human truth—and what resonates with the people you are targeting.

In short, here are the four essentials of a self-brand strategy:

1. *Be different:* Imitation will make you only a B player.
2. *Focus:* Limit yourself to a dozen words or less so you can bore into the essential idea in a quick, punchy way.
3. *Be authentic:* Your strategy must be based on who you are and the assets and experiences you can claim. (Of course, you may create some new experiences.)
4. *Resonate in the market:* If you don't get a reaction in the marketplace, go back to the drawing board.

## Bone Up on the Big Brands

One way to figure out the best self-brand strategy is to look at brand strategies from the commercial world.

Start by devouring good books on individual companies and products. Successful brands always attract analysis. Or read about how brands develop winning strategies. (My favorite marketing authors are Al Ries and Jack Trout, my bosses in my first advertising job.)

Once you start studying the world of commercial branding, you'll see how branding strategies and tactics have lessons for you, too.

Following are ten positioning strategies from the commercial world that clients have used to build a strong self-brand. Do the brainstormers for each self-brand strategy. Don't rule out any: when you start exploring, you might be surprised to find out what works for you and your life.

## Self-Brand Strategy 1: The Innovator

*In my mind's eye.*

William Shakespeare
*Hamlet* (II, 2)

Innovators are the first to create something new or revolutionary, and everyone knows being first is an advantage. The first mover generally ends up the leader in the category. Because it's the leader, everyone believes it to be the best in its category, and so it is often the one we keep in mind.

Being the innovator who is first to do something is a formidable advantage. Michael Dell was the first direct seller of personal computers and is still a dominant player. Jeff Bezos created the first online retail book marketplace, and it is still number one. Steve Jobs was a serial player with firsts in multiple categories, including music players, tablet computers, and mobile phones. The list goes on and on.

You're probably thinking, "These are business giants, and this kind of accomplishment would be impossible for a mere mortal like me. How can I be number one in anything?"

There are two ways to be first: the hard way and the easy way. In the hard way, you (or the brilliant partner you've paired up with) create a whole new category from scratch. This is hard to do and takes a certain amount of genius, but we still continue to see new categories created all the time, particularly in technology businesses. Jack Dorsey and his partners at Twitter revolutionized the way people communicate and share information with their 140-character tweets. Mark Zuckerberg created the first hugely successful social network, and his then-partner Sean Parker advised him to name it Facebook, not The Facebook, to give it a first-of-a-kind distinction.

## ⓉⓂ INNOVATOR POSITIONING: You were the first person who _____ (insert your claim to fame).

There is an easier way to be the Innovator. (Creativity is required, but not genius.) Find an existing product or category and carve out an extension or subset of the category that is new or "first" in some way. This type of first can be a game changer, too. Austrian entrepreneur Dietrich Mateschitz discovered a local Thai drink called Krating Daeng that miraculously cured his jet lag. He introduced the drink in the West with one important modification—carbonation. He named the drink Red Bull, which is a close translation of its Thai name ("Daeng" means red and "Krating" means water buffalo in Thai).

Mateschitz's real branding genius was in positioning the brand as a first in a new category. He didn't market Red Bull as refreshing or energizing (attribute positioning), for young men (user or target market positioning), or as a Thai beverage (heritage positioning). Mateschitz took the "innovator" route to create a first. He didn't simply introduce a new beverage brand, he invented a new category he called "energy drinks."

The *innovator strategy* is very successful for entrepreneurs, but executives can use it, too. Enterprising employees or intrapreneurs often create new products and services or new market niches—whether the niche is for a new type of product, service, or customer. These firsts may end up being enormously profitable for the company and for the employee's self-brand.

As an innovator, you might not be the first person to do a remarkable feat like climb Mt. Everest or another accomplishment, but you might be able to claim a first just the same. Mountain climber Alison Levine has climbed the highest mountains on every continent, an incredible claim, but still one that many others could make. Levine found her first just the same as the team captain of the first American Women's Everest Expedition. She uses her first claim to promote a speaking career connecting successful mountain climbing to successfully climbing the corporate ladder.

There are lots of different ways to slice up a category and find an area to be an innovator in. One client, who works for a well-known global financial services company, talked to key clients and came up with a new type of research report that met client needs better than the reports churned out by competitors. While not a breakthrough invention, it was innovative all the same and brought her recognition with her clients and her management.

The key ingredient for the Innovator mind-set is creative, open-minded thinking. Ask, why not? What about? Say yes to possibilities. Then make time to allow creative ideas to ferment. Try the brainstormer to see if you can come up with a way to position Brand You as an Innovator.

**BRAINSTORMER: Becoming an Innovator**

**Look at your areas of interest, what isn't working well and crying out for an innovative solution?**

**Is there a new category that you can be a first-mover in?**

## Self-Brand Strategy 2: The Leader

*Would you have me false to my nature?*
*Rather, say I play the man I am.*

William Shakespeare
*Coriolanus* (III, 2)

When you have a leadership claim you can appeal to people who want to do business with the principal player in an industry, the person recognized as a leader. You can take advantage of the *leadership premium*. Leadership, in and of itself, gives you a halo effect. As the leader in your category, people will assume that you are better than others who are the number two, number three, or number ten players.

You must be better, or why else are you the leader? You've got proof, too. You've got a track record of accomplishments and arenas where you've played a leadership role.

There are many ways of creating a *leader strategy*. You could be the leader of your department, your company, or your favorite charity. Or you might be the leader in sales at your company or the leader in sales in a segment of the market. You can be the leader who's a change agent known for reviving dying businesses, or the leader who is good at managing large, traditional businesses.

Even if you are just starting out as an entry-level employee with no followers, you can position yourself as an emerging leader. Don't just focus on your tasks, but show an interest in the bigger picture. Ask your boss and your colleague's questions about their work. Raise your hand to volunteer for new projects. Learn to communicate your ideas well. Stand tall and look the part. Pretty soon people will start to see you as the leader you will become.

Many professionals have leadership claims and feel that they are acting like leaders, yet they are not perceived as leaders. To be *perceived* as a leader, you must *lead with ideas* and *lead by example*.

Bill Gates set out to be the leader in computing with this mission: "A computer on every desk and in every home, all running Microsoft software." It was a bold leadership statement for computing in 1975, when few people had a computer or could see a use for one in their personal lives. Gates's vision was that the PC would be cheap, utilitarian, and everywhere. Contrast this with the vision of his contemporary Steve Jobs. The computer envisioned by Jobs was expensive, elegant, and elitist. Both men had a leadership vision that revolutionized the computer industry.

(TM) **LEADERSHIP POSITIONING: You're a leader in** _____
**(list industry, job function, or basis of leadership claim).**

As a leader, you'll want to do leadership things, like speak about the industry in your blog, post white papers on your website, be visible at industry meetings, and be cited as an authority in the trade or business media. And there's good reason for trade associations and journals to select you to speak at industry conferences or quote you in the media because you have something important to say. After all, you are a leader in your industry.

When you are a leader, people will pay more attention to what you have to say, too, than they will to the rank and file. Take advantage of the opportunity by saying something interesting or visionary. Try to come up with a fresh idea, or have a new twist on an old idea, or even brand your idea by giving it a name and visual image.

Leaders have to play a defensive role. There will always be upstart competitors—most likely Innovators or Mavericks—trying to topple you from your leadership perch, but it won't be easy for them to do unless you lose the edge that got you the leadership position in the first place. You need to constantly be at the forefront of what's going on in your industry.

As a leader, you have to be able to articulate ideas that are worthy of being remembered, and you must be able to inspire others. Ideally, you want your employees or target audience to know what your battle cry is. Most important, you must underscore your words with actions, preferably bold actions that demonstrate what you stand for. One leader uses OKR's, Objective and Key Results. Each week he asks his direct reports to let him know their key objective and three key results they plan to achieve that week. It's turned into a good way to get everyone focused on what's important.

My client Emily, for example, had recently been promoted to head a department at her company. Because she had been promoted over her colleagues and the department had been underperforming, her first task was to rally her team under her leadership.

In order to articulate a department mission, Emily created the mantra "full engagement." She wanted to introduce a new sense of engagement—a passion for excellence, a focus on clients and innovation.

Emily asked each of her managers for a five-page memo outlining key initiatives, including what the company could do to get employees more engaged with clients and with the business itself. She then implemented the best suggestions.

Her group's focus on full engagement landed more business and created a dynamic spirit at the company. It also positioned Emily as a leader.

The key ingredient for the Leader mind-set is confidence, the kind of confidence and direction that builds trust in your followers. Great leaders give their team the courage to do things they didn't think they could do, and get everyone united under the same mission.

 **BRAINSTORMER: Becoming a Leader**

**What can you do to establish yourself as a leader? What's your mantra? What actions can you take?**

## Self-Brand Strategy 3: The Maverick

*Oh, what dare men do!*

William Shakespeare
*Much Ado About Nothing* (IV, 1)

As much as leaders are part of the mythology of our country, so are underdogs. We have a soft spot for the rebel, the lone defier of convention who doesn't follow the established path, the Maverick.

The Maverick strategy is also called reverse positioning because whatever the Leader stands for, you stand for the opposite. Volkswagen put the *maverick strategy* on the map when it introduced the Beetle to the United States in the late 1960s. The brand was positioned as the antidote to the big-car habit, with now-classic advertising headlines like "Think Small" and "Lemon."

Also, for every Microsoft, there is an Apple, a brand that symbolizes the opposite of the dominant leader to its customers. An especially powerful tactic of the anti-leader positioning strategy is casting the entrenched leader as the evil empire. Microsoft's competitors have touched that nerve with technology consumers.

In the self-brand category, many entrepreneurs are mavericks. Independent spirits abound in technology and Internet-based businesses, and they get a lot of press to promote their nonconformist ways. Mavericks like Tony Hsieh at Zappos, Jack Dorsey at Twitter and Square, Mark Pincus at Zynga, and Reid Hoffman at LinkedIn all created something fresh in the marketplace and each has his own philosophy and style.

**(TM) Maverick, or Reverse, Positioning: You are the opposite of the established leader _____ (insert name).**

Writers, artists, and creative people of all sorts are often mavericks by choice and personality. They can look the part so well that they seem straight out of central casting, like the controversial Chinese activist and artist Ai Weiwei, the U.K. and Iraqi architect Zaha Hadid, or the fashion designer, Karl Lagerfeld. In the United States, documentary filmmaker Michael Moore is a classic example. His movies and books tweak the establishment, whether it's the automobile industry (*Roger and Me*), the National

Rifle Association and the gun lobby (*Bowling for Columbine*), President George W. Bush and the war in Iraq (*Fahrenheit 9/11*), or capitalism itself (*Capitalism: A Love Story*).

The maverick position could be risky, particularly if you work in a corporation (although many do have a few maverick employees). It is a self-brand strategy adopted mainly by people who are either confident in their positions or have nothing to lose.

However, taking the anti-leader position may be a great strategy for entrepreneurs. You build your company's point of difference as the antidote to the leader by positioning the leader's strengths as weaknesses, as the list below shows. You and your company symbolize everything the leader is not.

### Leader vs. Anti-Leader Position

| Leader | Anti-Leader |
|---|---|
| Big | Small and nimble |
| Slow | Fast and responsive |
| Out of touch | Cutting-edge |
| Bureaucratic | Entrepreneurial |
| Dull | Creative and alive |
| Impersonal | Personal |
| Inflexible | Flexible |
| One size fits all | Custom |
| Expensive | Good value |
| Unresponsive | Responsive |

The anti-leader position is a brand strategy that generally offers a great PR platform for you and your business. Mavericks provide good ink for the media. (Think Richard Branson and Virgin.)

So, if you like to go against the grain, the anti-leader position may be for you. The strategy is simplicity itself. Whatever the leader in your industry or line of work is doing, think of doing the opposite (within reason). Brainstorm it. You could find a market that is looking for someone just like you.

The key ingredient of the Maverick mind-set is contrarian thinking, an unconventional way of thinking that's not fond of the status quo. It takes guts to go against the grain, but it can be a winning strategy and is certainly more adventurous and exciting than other routes.

> **BRAINSTORMER: Taking the Opposites Test**
>
> Identify the leaders in your company, industry, or selected arena.
>
> Outline what they stand for, their image, and the attributes or adjectives that are associated with them.
>
> For each leader, determine the opposite position, image, or attributes.

## Self-Brand Strategy 4: The Identifier

*Assume a virtue if you have it not.*

William Shakespeare
*Hamlet* (III, 4)

The most common positioning strategy for brands is to *own an attribute*. You identify an attribute or strength that has a clear benefit that sets you apart from others. Mercedes-Benz's brand strategy is built around prestige, BMW's is driving performance, Subaru's is ruggedness, and Volvo's is safety. When the attribute strategy works well, your attribute or word is wedded to the brand like the connection between Volvo and safety.

To implement this strategy, you should select the brand attribute that is credible for *you* to own and gives you maximum opportunity in your category.

For example, when Pampers first developed the disposable diaper in the early 1960s, sales were poor. The marketing was positioned around convenience, a brand attribute that had a clear-cut benefit for busy moms. Moms didn't have to clean and disinfect the diapers themselves or use an expensive diaper service. Convenience was especially beneficial for moms on the go with their babies. They didn't have to carry stinky cloth diapers around with them until they got home. But that attribute positioning didn't resonate with mothers. They felt guilty. Cloth diapers were best for babies, while paper diapers were best for moms. So moms voted with their hearts, and sales were poor.

Then Pampers changed its brand positioning to "better absorbency," which was a benefit for babies. Mothers could buy the diapers and feel that they were doing what was best for their babies, not best for them. Sales took off, and cloth diapers and diaper services went the way of the buggy whip.

### (TM) ATTRIBUTE POSITIONING: You are known for _____ (list attribute).

Every category is associated with attributes that are important to customers and prospects. And you can slice your industry, profession, or job category to find the best fit for the attribute you want to own and the category in which you want to do it. This is true regardless of your industry, whether it's financial services, manufacturing, marketing, law, medicine, academia, or what have you.

Your job as a self-brander is to stake your claim to the attribute that is best for you and is not owned by a competitor in the arena where you will have the most impact.

One client, Benjamin, had just been promoted to president of his company. The good news: it was a great job. The bad news: it was a difficult job. Sales revenue was down, and his industry was in a serious slump. Benjamin's first task was to rally the troops and unify the company, particularly the division heads, most of whom were strong personalities with a tight grip on their fiefdoms.

We built Benjamin's personal-brand strategy around the attribute of "accountability." It was an important attribute, one that many colleagues and employees associated with him because of his track record. Other executives might have great creative skills or people skills, as Benjamin did, but none matched his sense of accountability and follow-through.

Accountability was an important attribute for the company at this juncture. In Benjamin's estimation, the company's problem was not a lack of innovative ideas but the inability to follow through internally (by getting all the various departments to work together) and with clients (by focusing on being a real business partner, not simply on closing).

Benjamin wanted to lead by example in terms of accountability with colleagues and clients, and he also took positive action to embed the attribute in the company culture. One of the first things he did was broadcast his management philosophy to all the employees: his rallying cry was "Everyone's accountable, everywhere, all the time."

The key ingredient of the Virtuous or Attribute mind-set is focus, unrelenting focus on your attribute as your value proposition.

 **BRAINSTORMER: What's Your Virtue?**

If you described your brand with one adjective or attribute that expresses your personal or professional truth, it would be _____.

What attributes or characteristics are important in your line of work or in your business?

What attributes are already owned by competitors, either other people or other companies?

What's available for you?

## Self-Brand Strategy 5: The Engineer

*Double, double, toil and trouble;*
*Fire burn and cauldron bubble.*

William Shakespeare
*Macbeth* (IV, 1)

The Engineer re-imagines and re-engineers things in new ways. It could be re-engineering a process. It could be putting new ingredients or components together in a novel way. It could be developing a new computer code that works better.

Don't think the Engineer strategy is just for people out of engineering school, this strategy works well for consultants, doctors, researchers, scientists, chefs, designers, computer programmers, and other professionals if value added comes from what they use or how they go about their work. In this strategy, marketers often position their brand as having a "magic ingredient" or "special process" that sets the brand apart. You can do that too.

The occupation of chef once tended to be rather mundane. Chefs were closer to working stiffs than sought-after celebrities. That is, until some chefs adopted this strategy and emphasized their unique way of cooking and combining ingredients, and the celebrity chef was born. (Think of Julia Child, James Beard, Wolfgang Puck, Mario Batali, and "Naked Chef" Jamie Oliver, for example.) Today, in top restaurants, the chef is often more of a marquee attraction than the well-known customers are.

Whether you're in product development or not, innovative employees are what companies are looking for, and finding a new ingredient or process can be your claim to personal and business fame. Intrapreneur Zanna McFerson works for agriculture giant Cargill, and her "magic ingredient" was the stevia leaf, a natural sweetener discovered in Paraguay over one hundred years ago. She got excited about the opportunity for a natural no-calorie sweetener. The product, Truvia (sounds like true plus stevia), contains a magic ingredient that is paying off at the cash register.

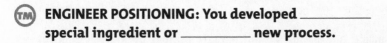

**ENGINEER POSITIONING: You developed _____ special ingredient or _____ new process.**

Beverage makers are always looking for "magic" ingredients that imbue their beverages with special health properties (or create that perception). One of the latest is coconut water, the slightly sweet, clear liquid from coconuts, which is rich in electrolytes, particularly potassium.

If a new ingredient isn't feasible, think of creating a new process that gets better results than what's out there in your field. Tony Horton is the fitness guru who created the successful P90X series of fitness DVDs. It's become the ultimate cross-training exercise series and gained a following with professional and Olympic athletes as well as the rest of us who want to get into shape. Horton's "new process" isn't really new per se; instead, he creatively combines and explains rigorous exercises in a fresh way, juxtaposing aerobic moves with yoga postures like chaturanga, and he's branded his system as P90X.

Any innovative executive or professional can use the *engineer strategy* by reexamining a process or procedure and engineering a new approach with his name tag on it. The key ingredient of the Engineer strategy is the ability to re-engineer and re-imagine what exists into something better.

> **BRAINSTORMER: Searching for a New Mousetrap**
>
> What are the shortcomings in the current way things are done and what frustrations do they cause?
>
> Is there a new component, ingredient, or process that could solve the problem?
>
> What could customers really like to have that they don't get now?

## Self-Brand Strategy 6: The Expert

*Ignorance is the curse of god,*
*Knowledge the way.*

William Shakespeare
*Henry VI, Part One* (IV, 7)

Being a jack-of-all-trades is not a smart strategy. It is smart to be an expert in one area.

Focus is powerful. The narrower the focus, the more powerful the brand. This is an era in which specialists thrive and generalists do not.

In executing the *expert strategy*, it helps to be able to interpret something in a new way. One solution is to choose an area that is not already crowded with experts so that you can be dominant. Or you could choose an area where the current experts are not doing a good job of communicating. Look for arenas where there is a need for better information and interpretation or a fresh point of view. Seek out opportunities where you can leverage your knowledge, experience, and passion.

 **EXPERT POSITIONING: I am an expert in _____.**

The expert strategy propelled Barbara Corcoran into the stratosphere in the New York City real estate brokerage community. With fewer than a dozen real estate sales to her name, Barbara Corcoran created a marketplace report called *The Corcoran Report* and sent it to newspapers.

Formerly a nobody, Corcoran became *the* real estate expert in New York City when the first issue of her report landed on the front page of the Sunday *New York Times* real estate section.

Corcoran recounts this and other tales of how she outsmarted the ladies in mink (the establishment brokers) and even Donald Trump in her book *Use What You've Got, and Other Business Lessons I Heard from My Mom*. (Corcoran rebranded the paperback edition of the book with a sexier title, *If You Don't Have Big Breasts, Put Ribbons on Your Pigtails*. Her publisher had talked her out of using this title for the original hardcover edition.)

So consider carving out a niche where you can be the expert. Remember, the media is always looking for a new face, someone who will interpret something. The makeover craze has spawned new experts on the media stage—hairdressers, image consultants, and stylists. The popularity of home and garden improvement has created a strong market for expert renovators, carpenters, and gardeners.

Every industry has areas that are hot and they tend to change over time. In media and advertising, this year it's social media. Who knows what it will be next year. The collapse of the financial markets made experts in risk and compliance hot commodities. As an expert, you'll need to be adept at keeping your expertise up-to-date and relevant.

The expert strategy is perfectly suited to tactics like newsletters, workshops, media interviews, and bylined columns. The book route is another smart way to go. If you have written a book, you are instantly an expert. And your book tour is a great way to promote your expertise, your business, and your passion.

The key ingredient of the expert strategy is knowledge and expertise in a specific area.

 **BRAINSTORMER: Becoming the Expert**

In what subject are you particularly knowledgeable?

Who are the authorities on the subject?

How does your point of view differ from those of other experts?

What can you do to become more of an authority? To be perceived as the authority? (For example, you could convince your company to fund a research study, or you could write an article on the topic.)

## Self-Brand Strategy 7: The Client Advocate

*They that thrive well take counsel of their friends.*

William Shakespeare
*Venus and Adonis*

Appealing to the identity of a specific target group of customers—to their quirks, preferences, and attitudes—can be a powerful positioning strategy. Also known as *user positioning* or *target market positioning*, you build your brand around the core group of customers you serve. They're your preferred customers and they prefer you to handle their business. You connect to people emotionally at their core, with who your customers are as people. Often marketers go after a target audience that is aspirational in order to attract the "in crowd" but also all of us wannabes, as in the old "I'm a Mac and You're a PC" campaign. Who did you identify with? The hip Mac guy or the conservative PC guy?

 **USER OR TARGET MARKET POSITIONING: You are preferred by _____ (name target group).**

A surefire winner is to be the preferred choice of an elite group. Examples are the financial consultant who manages high-society money, the investment banker whose smartphone is filled with the direct phone numbers of CEOs, and the plastic surgeon who works on celebrity faces. To protect their clients' privacy, names often aren't publicized but are leaked to the press or passed along by word of mouth. Stealth PR like this further enhances preferences among the cognoscenti.

In developing the *user strategy* for yourself, the hardest part is getting the first high-profile client. Once you have done this, that client is a powerful lure for others.

Jake "Body by Jake" Steinfeld was the first celebrity trainer to build an empire off of Hollywood A-list clients, so he brands himself as the "trainer to the stars," a phrase he copyrighted and uses to communicate his preferred target market positioning.

Daniella Helayel is the fashion designer behind the Issa label, but it was a brand known mainly among fashionistas in London and Rio. Then

Kate Middleton selected an Issa dress to wear at the announcement of her engagement to Prince William, and a celebrity tsunami hit the brand.

The user strategy can be for any type of client or customer segment. In chapter 2, we introduced Alexandra, who had a generic executive coaching business that began to flourish when she narrowed her focus to a particular client group: difficult people and the people who work for them. By focusing on the subgroup that she enjoyed working with and with whom she was most successful, Alexandra expanded her business. She also appeared on cable TV talk shows to comment on coping strategies and the like.

The key ingredient of the Client Advocate mind-set is a clear-cut client or customer focus on a specific target audience who you identify with and who identifies with you.

The following brainstormer will help you pinpoint your key target audience.

 **BRAINSTORMER: Who's Your Tribe?**

Have you had consistent success with a specific group? Could that group become the focus of your self-brand identity? Name or describe the group.

## Self-Brand Strategy 8: The Elitist

*He is well paid that is well satisfied.*

William Shakespeare
*The Merchant of Venice* (IV, 1)

Being hard to get and setting a high price on your services or products are good strategies for standing out and garnering business. Creating faux scarcity is often a compelling part of this brand strategy. Look at the way luxury goods manufacturers produce a very limited run of hot new handbags, so that fashionistas have to have to get on a months-long waiting list. Of course, they could produce more of the hot items, but scarcity creates a sales frenzy pushing demand sky high and keeping prices high.

For many people, high price equates with superiority. It seems obvious that $400-an-hour consultants *must* be better than $100-an-hour consultants (or lawyers or doctors or creative directors). How else could they charge that much? And the CEO who is paid $20 million must be better than the one who is paid a mere $1 million.

The strongest brands have *pricing power*. You want to have pricing power, too, or people will think of you as inexpensive Brand X.

When something is available only to an elite group and expensive we think it's better than something that's cheaper. This may or may not be true. Look at a wine taste test in which volunteers were asked to evaluate five wines. Each bottle was labeled according to price: $5, $10, $35, $45, and $90 a bottle.

(TM) **ELITIST POSITIONING: I'm hard to get, expensive and worth it.**

Naturally, everyone liked the most expensive wines best. In reality, the wine labels were deceptive. The most expensive wine, at $90, was also presented as a cheap $10 wine, and the $5 wine also was behind the $45 label. Brain scans were done as the tasters sipped the wine, and it turns out that the brain was fooled too; brains registered less pleasure when people thought they were drinking cheaper wine.

High price gives people an image boost, too. Customers and prospects will assume you are better than someone who is paid less. Of course, high price is a very elitist standard. It appeals to the desire for prestige, and being able to afford high prices encourages a feeling of superiority. This elite status might be manifested by a pricey new sports car, a mansion, or an expensive business adviser.

Anyone who uses this strategy must be able to demonstrate in some way that she is worth the price. In some cases, having a high profile is enough for implementing this strategy.

Many high-priced consultants, lobbyists, and bankers come from prestigious government positions that enable them to cash in when they enter the private sector.

The *elitist strategy* is a tough act to pull off. You've got to have the confidence to push away some desirable opportunities if the price or the client isn't right. You need to have a reputation for turning down business that isn't prestigious enough for your brand. Otherwise, you won't convey the impression that you are "hard to get" and for the elite. For example, you may only accept new clients through high-level referrals, or maybe appointments have to be made months in advance. It's not for everyone; but that's the basis of this strategy.

The key ingredient in the Elitist mind-set is an unwavering belief in your superiority—that you are indeed an elite product that is hard to get and worth it.

---

 **BRAINSTORMER: Elitist Power**

Explore these possibilities for justifying a high price strategy:

Do you have a superior track record, special accomplishments, or a special background that would justify a high price?

Do you have the self-confidence to pull it off?

---

## Self-Brand Strategy 9: The Heir

*A good wit makes use of anything.*

William Shakespeare
*Henry IV, Part Two* (I, 2)

Being heir to a certain breeding or heritage can be a strong selling point. Think French cuisine, Swiss watches, German engineering, Belgian chocolates, Russian vodka, or Persian rugs. The fact that Veuve Clicquot is from the Champagne region of France gives it authenticity because of its special heritage. Its heritage gives it cachet and social capital that creates branding magic.

Julia Child didn't discover her brand until middle age, when she was stationed in France with her diplomat husband. Bored, with not much to do, she studied French cooking at Le Cordon Bleu and introduced French cuisine to the American public with her debut cookbook, *Mastering the Art of French Cooking*. Nine months later, at fifty years of age, Child appeared on the public television show *The French Chef*.

Integral to Child's heritage positioning was her training at Le Cordon Bleu. What's amazing, one writer pointed out, is that her training at Le Cordon Bleu was rather short, measured in months, not years, and she didn't apprentice in a restaurant, as is typical for French chefs. Yet she got a lot of mileage out of her heritage positioning, and her warm, zesty, slightly bumbling television personality made her a brand beloved by millions of aspiring cooks in the United States.

### (TM)  HERITAGE POSITIONING: You're the best because of your _____ heritage.

If your last name is Bush, Kennedy, or Rockefeller, you have not only the money but a special heritage that is brand heaven in terms of the leverage it gives you. Offspring with a family-name brand are often able to start out at third base while the rest of us have to begin at home plate.

Even if your name doesn't appear in the social register, you could leverage the *special heritage strategy* through national origin, a prestigious school, apprenticeship in a well-regarded training program, or a stint at a well-known company. For example, earlier in this chapter, you met Anthony. He didn't have a famous family heritage, but he did have his Indian heritage, his grandfather's business reputation, and a void in the market.

I had no family heritage connections, but I took advantage of my educational heritage when I was unable to obtain permission to view paintings in private collections for my Ph.D. dissertation in Japanese art. I had a business card printed up in English and in Japanese listing my educational credentials: Ph.D. student, Harvard University; foreign exchange student, Tokyo University; recipient, Japanese Ministry of Education Fellowship. Was it a little over the top? In America, yes; in Japan, no. Did it work? You bet.

In addition to school pedigree, there is company heritage. Employment with some companies is like having a stamp of approval associated with your name. In consulting, it's McKinsey. In packaged goods, it's Procter & Gamble.

Top company brands attract the best and the brightest. (At least, that's the perception.) So people will assume that you are, too. Top company brands put their new hires through a rigorous training program and keep them on the cutting edge of best practices. So people will think you know your stuff. Company heritage gives you a formidable advantage. Think of all the Fortune 100 CEOs with a General Electric heritage.

A lot of people who achieve fame in one career are able to leverage their heritage to achieve success in a new endeavor. For example, many prominent politicians or government officials go on to head up companies.

Or prominent people in business or entertainment go into politics. (Think Michael Bloomberg in New York City and Arnold Schwarzenegger in California.)

Sonny Bono told the story of how he knew his entertainment career was over when he mispronounced a name on *Fantasy Island*. Of course, he felt like a has-been when the other guests started ridiculing him. In that moment, Sonny decided that that was it for show business. He went on to open a restaurant and enter politics, leveraging his celebrity heritage to rebrand himself successfully.

Being part of an elite group or training program also taps into the heritage strategy. Look at Teach for America, which attracts the best and the brightest college graduates to teach at some of the most challenging schools in the United States. It's a badge of distinction often used as a way to contribute to society and gain real-world experience before applying to a prestigious graduate school.

Of course, the heritage strategy plays upon stereotypes, but in a positive way by tapping into the positive advantages our heritage gives us. The key ingredient in the Well-Bred mind-set is a strong sense of identity with your heritage credentials to propel your career identity.

 **BRAINSTORMER: Exploring Your Heritage**

> What connections could you leverage from your family, schools, training programs, country of origin, awards or distinctions, political office, or company heritage?

## Self-Brand Strategy 10: The Crusader

> *To business that we love*
> *we rise betime and to't with delight.*
>
> William Shakespeare
> *Antony and Cleopatra* (IV, 4)

For many people, doing something meaningful and significant is much more important than achieving the standard definition of success. Look at TOMS Shoes: for every pair of its iconic cloth, rubber-soled "alpargatas" sold, the company gives away a pair to someone who needs it. Instead of a business with a charity tie-in, the whole concept is to buy one pair of shoes today so TOMS can give one tomorrow. That idea led company founder Blake Mycoskie to the name, Tomorrow Shoes, which he shortened to TOMS Shoes. The brand's tagline, "One for One," communicates the brand's shoe giveaway mission.

 **CAUSE POSITIONING: I am synonymous with _____ cause.**

To reinforce the brand's positioning, Mycoskie spends most of his time on the road making shoe drops to poor children in developing countries and spreading the TOMS gospel and the value of social entrepreneurship.

Speaking of shoes and philanthropy, the Boot Campaign was started by five women in Texas who branded themselves "The Boot Girls" to support returning American soldiers by selling its signature Give Back combat boots. The campaign has been wildly successful aligning celebrities, hip boots, and edgy marketing to raise awareness and money for an important cause. The group has recruited a wide range of celebrities from Hollywood and politics to the stars of *Sons of Anarchy*, country music, and the UFC, to put the boots on and be photographed.

Aligning with a cause can be smart branding for crusaders inside a company. A client, Elizabeth, volunteered to be co-head of a women's initiative in her company, promoting leadership development, mentoring, and a more women-friendly culture throughout the company.

Elizabeth is passionate about furthering women in business, but championing the cause has been great for her career visibility as well. With her team, she launched new initiatives such as a women's speaker's bureau to give women at the company a platform to speak at regional and national conferences and events. She has developed a great network with all the dynamic women who work there as well as with women leaders she's met at other organizations who share her passion for promoting women's leadership.

Being synonymous with a cause or creating a new cause has propelled many people onto a bigger stage. Think of Martin Luther King Jr. and the civil rights movement or Gloria Steinem and women's liberation. In his remarkable quest to alleviate Third World debt and poverty, Bono has taken his rock star power to the United Nations, the G-8 summit, the World

Economic Forum at Davos, and the White House (just to highlight a few of his venues).

Through his work for Habitat for Humanity, Jimmy Carter rebuilt his image. He went from a former president who ranked low in the court of public opinion to a leader who was admired for his hands-on work helping the poor and brokering peace deals around the world. His humanitarian and peace initiatives earned him the ultimate accolade for a self-brand with strong humanitarian goals, the Nobel Peace Prize. And Bill Clinton has kept his brand relevant with the Clinton Global Initiative, whose mission is "to inspire, connect, and empower a community of global leaders to forge solutions to the world's most pressing challenges."

The key ingredient for the Crusader mind-set is passion for a cause, a quest to make a difference in the world.

**BRAINSTORMER: Finding Your Crusade**

Is there a cause or issue that you are passionate about? Is there a cause that you would like to create and champion?

## Get Great Results With a Self-Brand Strategy

In this chapter, you have explored ten self-brand strategies:

1. The Innovator
2. The Leader
3. The Maverick
4. The Identifier
5. The Engineer
6. The Expert
7. The Client Advocate
8. The Elitist
9. The Heir
10. The Crusader

Try each on for size to see if it fits. You might be surprised to see which one has potential for you.

To be fully free to develop your self-brand strategy, you must find the confidence to let go. You have to let go of what worked in the past. Let go of your assumptions about what will work in the future. Let go of feeling powerless and small. Often, the strategy you reject the quickest is the very one that has enormous promise for your career success.

Earlier I introduced Anthony who used the heritage or heir strategy to position his brand, enabling him to leverage his family's strong business reputation in India and his grounding in Western business. Kayla, the social media maven, took the expert strategy route moving away from her broad marketing backing to position herself in the fast growing area of social media marketing. Alex, the executive coach I talked about in chapter 1, used the client advocate or user strategy, positioning her business around a type of client (difficult people and the people who work for them). Each self-brand strategy came from that person's passions and met an important need in the marketplace.

A great way to conduct your strategy exploration is to create the kind of creative brainstorming room used by ad agencies and marketing boutiques. You might find it easier to jump-start the process and pluck the winners from the losers if you can see the different strategies you are considering displayed on enormous stickies on the walls. Then, one by one, take down the weaker contenders. The one that's left will be your winner—your self-brand strategy.

Use the online assessment in the next brainstormer as a complement to your personal analysis to determine the best strategy for you.

 **BRAINSTORMER: SelfBrand Online Assessment Tool**

**Go to http://selfbrand.com/tools/assessment/ personalstrategytest.html**

**After you take the online assessment test, compare the results with your personal analysis. Which positioning strategies hold the most promise for you? Which one strategy is the best?**

**Write down your brand positioning strategy followed by proof points, or reasons why your target audience would believe this brand is true of you.**

**My brand is**

**Because**

On a basic level, your self-brand strategy statement represents a promise. It's a promise of what your brand has to offer its target audience. The support points are the reasons to believe that promise, why *you*—and not others—can deliver on that promise.

## The Creative Brief

Now that you've settled on the best strategy for Brand You, take a page from the account planner's playbook and develop a *creative brief* before you go any further.

The creative brief is the bible for creative development. It's a succinct document that pulls together the strategic work you've done so far. You need to simplify the brand to its essence, to what is crucial and authentic, and doing a creative brief is a great way to force yourself to crystallize your thinking.

Most advertising, marketing, and design agencies have their own version of the creative brief but the goal of all of them is to provide clear, concise, and insightful direction for the people working on creative and marketing projects for the brand. Even if you're doing all the creative work on Brand You yourself (and most of us don't have personal assistants, stylists, and copywriters on our personal staff), you'll find it helpful as you develop your leadership style and career identity. The Creative Brief ties together all the personal brand work you've been doing so far in one succinct document so you'll be ready to explore creative development of Brand You in the next four chapters.

The key elements of the creative brief are:

▶ **Business snapshot:** This is an in-a-nutshell overview of your industry, its key players, and its dynamics—all in a three-to-five sentence Cliff Notes–style synopsis of what's driving things and who the key competitors are. Pick an "enemy," the key competitor that you want to beat or be distinct from in the minds of others.

▶ **Brand promise/reasons to believe:** Define your *brand promise*, your brand positioning strategy in a sentence. This is your dominant selling idea—the compelling, measurable, relevant value that you and only you bring. Under the brand promise, list two or three crisp *reasons to believe* the promise statement. For example, FedEx's brand promise is: "Your package will get there overnight. Guaranteed." Why should people believe this promise? FedEx could include in its reasons to believe its money-back guarantee on next-day delivery and its remarkable on-time delivery record. Your own three reasons to believe could be specific accomplishments that support your brand positioning.

▶ **Brand personality:** Define the brand personality with four or five descriptive adjectives or phrases as if the brand were a real person. This will help you in determining whether certain visibility tactics, messages, marketing activities—or even clothing styles—are right for Brand You.

▶ **Customer persona:** The *customer persona* is a portrait of your ideal or typical customer. Think of your core groups and the individuals you are trying to appeal to. Is there a thematic description that captures their mind-set and preferences?

▶ **Consumer insight:** Convey in a short sentence an important or surprising insight about your business or industry that might unlock branding options for you. What are the tensions in the marketplace that can inspire a breakthrough creative idea for Brand You?

With your creative brief in hand, you're ready to move from Part I Brand Strategy and embark on Part II Creative Development, the creative journey in which you bring your brand strategy to life through a powerful visual identity, verbal identity, and brand personality.

 **IN A NUTSHELL:** The fourth secret of self-brands: Develop a self-brand strategy that gives you a winnable position, a strategy that gives people a reason for choosing you and not your competitor.

# PART 2

# Creative Development: "Packaging" Brand You

# CHAPTER 5

# Use the Principles of Visual Identity to Create a Powerful Self-Brand Package

*Apparel oft proclaims the man.*

William Shakespeare
*Hamlet* (I, 3)

It may seem superficial. It may be unfair. We may not like it. After all, why should you be judged by your looks?

Self-presentation—your visual identity—is important because of the *link* people make between what something looks like on the outside and what is on the inside. This attitude has a long history. The ancient Greeks and Romans felt that beauty of the body was synonymous with beauty of the spirit.

We do this even today despite all the familiar admonitions, such as "Beauty is only skin deep" or "Don't judge a book by its cover." The fact is, looks have a profound influence on our judgment of a brand or a person.

Good looks also have what social scientists call the *halo effect*. Because something is attractive, we assign many other positive attributes to it that have nothing to do with looks.

## The Attractiveness Principle

The way something looks is often the point of first (and lasting) impact for a brand.

Product design, packaging, and brand images are quick ways of communicating the brand message. They make an item (or a service) more interesting and memorable. Although they are wordless, a brand's packaging and design speak to us in color, shape, and material. Brands speak through imagery and symbols in logos, packaging, and advertising.

A great look may even clinch the sale.

A strong visual is a better memory magnet than words, studies show. (Guess that's why they say, "A picture is worth a thousand words.")

That's why brand managers are masters of visual identity.

 **Visuals speak a universal language.**

Visual identity helps differentiate a brand among all the other brands vying for attention in the marketplace. And, like art, great design or an arresting image slows us down to admire and savor it and want the brand for our very own.

Visual identity is such a powerful competitive tool today that even manufacturers and retailers of low-priced brands are turning to well-known artists, architects, designers, and celebrities to spiff up their products. And fashion designers are eager to do low-cost versions of their fashions, housewares, and other designs to increase their brand awareness. Target has Isaac Mizrahi, Michael Graves, and Missoni on its roster. Martha Stewart started with Kmart and moved on to merchandising relationships with Macy's and JC Penney. Walmart has Mary-Kate and Ashley Olsen. Fashionista Kate Moss partnered with Top Shop to bring her style esthetic to the masses. H&M used Karl Lagerfeld, and Stella McCartney, daughter of Beatle Paul McCartney, signed on to design clothes for the retail chain too. It's now chic for well-known designers and celebrities to maintain a low-priced line.

## The Beauty Premium

Whether we like it or not, it's human nature to notice good-looking things. Even newborns react differently to an attractive face compared to an unattractive one. And as we grow older, our eyes lock on to the beautiful people in a group, studies show. Lovely things have a way of breaking through.

Two economists proved the beauty premium with a study based on a mock labor market in which students were employers and job seekers. The "job" was solving mazes. Some "employers" considered only the résumés of potential employees. Others saw a résumé and a photograph. Some received a résumé and did a telephone interview. Others got a résumé, had a telephone interview, and saw a photograph. The last group received everything—a résumé, a telephone interview, and an in-person meeting. Meanwhile, a separate group categorized all the "job seekers" as either attractive or unattractive.

You won't be surprised to hear that the people with good looks were no better than less attractive people at solving mazes. (Whew!)

But what was surprising was the power of looks. Attractive people got the jobs, were offered bigger salaries, and were expected to be more productive. This isn't the only study to show that, like it or not, attractiveness gives you a career boost. The connection between looks and positive attributes is an old idea. In the ancient world, Romans talked of "virtutem forma decorat" (Beauty adorns virtue); clearly, the bias has deep roots.

## Package Yourself

Everyone can be "packaged" to be attractive. It's all about making the most of what you have. Besides, today, we have a much broader definition of what's appealing visually. Looking interesting and having a distinct personal style is attractive. The tech whiz with the large black-rimmed glasses is now more likely to be viewed as hip than nerdy. Even weight is no longer a barrier to looking good. High-profile people with fluctuating weight, like Oprah, are adept at packaging themselves attractively. Nor is age a set back to being appealing as ninety year old actress Betty White has shown.

Everything communicates visually—from your shoes to the watch you wear, your hairstyle to your smile (or frown), your home address to the car you drive. All these things say something about you and contribute to the perceptions people form about you.

Visual identity tells us whether a brand is expensive or cheap, fun or serious, unusual or commonplace. A brand's visual presentation sells to us as adeptly as any salesperson does, sometimes even more so, and it's the same with people.

## Seize the First Two Seconds

We are pegged in a matter of seconds: good/bad, hire/don't hire, hip/stodgy, successful/loser, like/dislike.

It all happens in a couple of seconds—or less. We've all been there. The job candidate is barely in the door and is already sized up. Maybe we've even eliminated that person as a contender.

It's based on snap visual impressions: how people enter the room, how they look, their clothes, how they carry themselves, their facial expressions and body language. We make up our minds about who they are and what they are like (even what they are worth), and they haven't said a word.

In *Blink*, Malcolm Gladwell talks about these snap judgments, which social scientists call "thin slicing." The interesting thing is that the instantaneous thin slice is usually the same as the impression we have after longer exposure.

Gladwell cites the research of professor Nalini Ambady as proof. Ambady has focused her research on the snap judgments people make based on nonverbal clues such as gender, appearance, personality, and relationships. She's found it takes only *two* seconds for people to develop a strong first impression.

## Make a Good First Impression

For most of us, our hasty first impression will be indelible.

First impressions are so powerful in business that one client, Susan, has built a successful business as a fashion coach, writer, and speaker around the importance of a first impression not only in establishing *who* you are but also in selling how *good* you are.

We're all guilty of snap judgments based on looks. We're programmed to respond better to good-looking people. When shown pictures of people they view as "attractive" compared to those they label "unattractive," most people are biased toward attractive people.

Attractive people have the advantage of the halo effect. People with good looks are consistently deemed smarter, more likeable, talented, successful, and better in so many ways. The good news is that ideas of "appealing," "attractive," and "successful" have expanded tremendously today as more people with unconventional looks succeed in spite of, or because of, unusual features. Different looks can be a powerful branding device, particularly if they are packaged as "interesting."

## Accentuate the Difference

A strategy of playing up different looks does not work in every industry, but in certain fields it will not only get you noticed but may be smart brand positioning. Today, we face a sea of choices dominated by sameness in so many areas that an unusual-looking brand is very fetching.

Originally, Absolut's ad agency considered a heritage strategy for the Swedish brand's launch in the United States. Then, the creative team opted for a campaign based on the brand's distinctively shaped bottle. The ad campaign won tons of creative awards, and Absolut entered the big time. The brand went from a small contender, selling 12,000 cases a year in 1980, to the market leader in imported vodka, selling 2.7 million cases a decade later.

Many spirits and beverage manufacturers use a bottle with an unusual shape as part of their brand identity. For many customers and prospects, the shape alone is sufficient to identify the brand. Coca-Cola brought back its curvy bottle after having abandoned it for many years. The bottle was originally designed so that its shape could be recognized by touch in a dark refrigerator in the middle of the night. New beverages such as POM Wonderful pomegranate juice give the hourglass bottle shape an important role in advertising and branding. And Red Bull puts its energy drinks in narrow cans that were smaller than cola drinks to convey that there was powerful stuff inside. The image of the two red bulls and a sun lock in the brand's name and message.

Entertainment and sports celebrities often adopt an unusual look so they will stand out. Lady Gaga is the poster child for using this strategy to drive her personal brand, but Michael Jackson, Elton John, and Liberace also spring to mind. Look at the popularity of Elvis look-alike contests. First thing, you need the hair—Elvis's trademark blue-black pompadour hairstyle. Then get a white fringe jumpsuit, and you are on your way. There are lots of less extreme but equally successful examples of people with a distinctive visual identity: Barbra Streisand, Andy Warhol, Diana Vreeland, Alfred Hitchcock, and Arnold Schwarzenegger all dramatized their unusual looks, features, or shapes.

## Harness the Magic in You

Unlike new products, none of us can create a self-brand from scratch. We have to build off of who we are and what we look like. This is true whether your visual identity is lacking or strong. But everything has potential. Many brands languish until someone comes along with the smarts and creativity to revive the brand image and maximize its assets. Look at the renaissance at Apple Computer, where a strong visual identity and satisfying user experience helped revive the brand.

So to start, you have to focus on yourself. Don't begin by copying the visual identities of people you admire. It is good to be inspired, but you'll never be remembered if you are a clone of someone else. Your visual identity should come out of your personality and preferences.

A good way to start developing your visual identity is by doing a personal visual inventory. What is your best feature? Worst feature? Explore what's different about you (height, shape, hair, features, expressions). What should you emphasize? Or de-emphasize?

## What Is Your Visual Identity Saying?

Visual identity is about visually communicating the message you want to convey. And when it really clicks, visual identity and message are one.

Look at your wardrobe and how you put yourself together. What do you want your entire package to say about you? Is it consistent with your self-brand strategy? Is there a signature feature or trademark accessory you could use to heighten your visual identity?

These are all questions you will want to deal with if you intend to maximize your visual identity. If you don't communicate the right message, or send out confusing messages, or fade into the wallpaper, you are undercutting your effectiveness. As one way of identifying the messages their brands trigger, brand managers conduct visual association tests in focus groups. Do the following brainstormer to do a visual association test for Brand You.

**BRAINSTORMER: The Visual Association Test**

Try doing this test yourself. Then ask a few friends to participate so that you can find out what visual associations they make with you. The purpose is not to copy but to get creative inspiration for your brand identity.

If you were a famous person, who would you be? Describe that person's visual identity: look, style, clothing, accessories, etc.

Why is that person right for you? Probe the association. How can this person inspire your visual identity?

If you were a car, what type of car would you be? Describe the car in as much detail as possible. Why does it symbolize you?

If you were an animal what would you be? Why?

## Create Visual Excitement

An intriguing visual identity greatly accelerates the value of your brand in any kind of business. Sofia Coppola first came into the public spotlight, and was panned, in her father's movie, *The Godfather, Part III*. When she changed her brand category from actor to independent director, her self-brand took off. And she capitalized on her accomplishments with a distinctive, cool visual style, becoming the designer Marc Jacobs's muse.

The great fashion sense and hip image of tennis players like Venus Williams, Serena Williams, and Andre Agassi probably didn't help them win more games. But they did help these athletes build powerful brand identities that translated into more bucks in endorsement contracts.

Inspiration for a distinct visual identity could come from anywhere. In the conservative financial services industry, Tom Gardner and David Gardner stole inspiration from the medieval fool when they launched their highly successful personal investing company Motley Fool. The financial show pundit Jim Cramer stands out with his kinetic delivery style and forceful personality.

Law is another traditional, conservative industry, yet famous American trial attorney Gerry Spence brands himself as a "country lawyer," donning a ten-gallon hat, fringed buckskin jacket, and cowboy boots when he does television interviews.

Spence leaves the buckskin and the big hat in the closet when he's arguing cases in front of a jury, though. He wears a traditional suit so that his image doesn't distract from his case, though he keeps the boots on as a low-key reminder of his brand's visual identity.

The cowboy imagery is not a gimmick without meaning. Spence grew up in Wyoming and his earliest mentor was a cowboy, his Uncle Slim, whose wisdom and advice permeate his philosophy of lawyering. In keeping with his country lawyer brand positioning, Spence speaks from the heart in his courtroom arguments and summations. He relishes the fact that his briefs are done in straight talk rather than in the boring, lengthy, unintelligible prose that most lawyers use. Spence talks to the jury like he's talking to a close friend. He shares his worries and frustrations about the case and about getting justice for his client. His open-hearted talk connects emotionally with jurors and wins cases.

Rodale Press went against the grain in developing a visual identity for *The South Beach Diet* that was different from the serious, almost textbook-like appearance common in the diet-book genre. Instead, Rodale's metallic blue book jacket was inspired by South Beach's trademark Art Deco palette.

## Let Your Clothes Talk

Strong visual identities are a quick read. And clothes are one of the quickest ways to communicate a message about who you are. Clothes often offer more insight than your curriculum vitae.

Clothes communicate what you do for a living and whether you are rich or poor, young or old, hip or square, professional or blue collar. They often express whether you are looking for a mate or a new job or just don't give a damn.

Clothes are such a strong branding device that for centuries there were laws in many regions of the world about who could wear what. Only certain classes could wear certain colors, fabrics, and clothing styles.

Think of the drill you put yourself through for an important meeting or job interview. "What shall I wear?" goes racing through your brain as you tear through your closet. What you choose can help or hinder you in the meeting.

These days there is no simple "dress for success" formula. Today, you have more latitude in using clothes to communicate your personal brand message. The suit is the package for most executives. Suits are practically a uniform for men, although the fabric and fit can be distinguishing features.

 **Clothes can make a difference in job performance.**

**Clothes can make you feel more confident and affect how you are perceived on the job.**

Women have more freedom to brand a personal identity with their clothes at work, since most don't wear a "corporate uniform" like most men do. Women have more variety, giving them more opportunity to stand out successfully or get it totally wrong and brand themselves as non-executive material. If your clothes could talk, what would they say about you? Is there a consistent message? What do you want your clothes to say about you? Which pieces of clothing should you eliminate? Which pieces of clothing should you build on? Choose your clothes and personal style to communicate what you want to say about yourself. Clothes are a visual symbol of who you are.

## Fashion Forward

Chic and modern, Michelle Obama takes control of her brand image and clothing choices. She's too smart not to use the branding power of clothes to her advantage as First Lady of the United States. In the U.S., we haven't talked about a First Lady's clothes this much since Jackie Kennedy was First Lady.

Obama has a high–low thing going on. She wears high-end designer fashions one day and Main Street J. Crew or Target labels the next.

What's interesting about her designer selections is that she tends to favor immigrant American designers like Jason Wu, Isabel Toledo, Doo-Ri Chung, and Maria Pinto, choices that haven't endeared Mrs. Obama to American establishment designers like Ralph Lauren, Donna Karan, and Oscar de la Renta. By choosing ethnically diverse up-and-coming designers along with Main Street or discount fashions, she's sending messages in line with the political philosophy of her husband, President Obama.

Michelle Obama doesn't leave something as important as her visual identity to chance or to the whims of others. She and her trusted style advisers keep control of her clothing and accessory selections, and she is known to bring her own clothes for a magazine shoot rather than wear what the magazine's stylist has arranged. She is clearly in charge of her brand.

## Plaid Hipster

Plaid pants might not appear on your body other than when you're heading to a golf course, but entrepreneur Blake Mycoskie, founder of TOMS shoes, cultivates a hip maverick style. He has a collection of plaid pants and he's worn them to the White House on visits to presidents Bush and Obama. (Guess that made the small talk easy.)

Mycoskie credits his grandmother with introducing him to bright colors and eccentric clothing choices, which she favored because she thought it made her more approachable. And Mycoskie has synced his visual identity and verbal identity to create a personal brand that's a mashup of Indiana Jones and Robin Hood.

Mycoskie brands himself as the "chief shoe giver" to underscore the fact that TOMS donates a pair of shoes to a poor child for every pair that it sells. Most mornings he works in a brightly colored striped bathrobe from his houseboat, a Jeanneau 53 named *Satori*, the Japanese word for enlightenment.

## Send Visual Clues

Remember the gray poncho Martha Stewart wore when she was released from prison? A handmade gift from a fellow inmate, the poncho became the indelible image of Stewart's dramatic departure from prison. Solidifying the garment's symbolism, she also wore the poncho on her first day back at the office.

The poncho was a brilliant branding device because it enabled Stewart to convey the right messages for rebranding herself. Her new image said:

Martha is back on top of her game
Martha made lemonade out of lemons

Martha bonded with her fellow prisoners
Martha can pluck style out of anywhere
Martha is stronger because of this experience

With her prison poncho, Stewart took control of her brand message. Remember how she looked in the months leading up to her conviction? In a word, guilty. She was hiding from the press, often caught looking unglamorous and shielding her face. The poncho put her self-brand back on track.

## Look the Part to Get the Part

Looking good is the price of admission in some careers. In most companies, if your goal is the corner office, you have to look successful.

Often, just looking the part gets you at least halfway there. Looking the part sometimes works like a self-fulfilling prophecy. What you build in other people's minds through images has a way of coming true.

When French president François Mitterand first met Ronald Reagan, he remarked, "Il a vraiment la notion de l'etat" (He really has a sense of the state about him). The *role*—in the case of the president, symbolizing the head of state—is an important part of the *job* of being president. We want people to satisfy a visual image of a key role, particularly the important ones. It is hard to become president of the United States if you don't *seem* presidential.

Not looking the part may be a career buster for people at all levels, as Lauren found out. Without realizing it, she had been branded—and in a way that hurt her career ambitions.

Lauren was a talented account executive at an advertising agency in New York City. She had an image problem and didn't know it. Her drive and hard work had gotten her to the mid-level as an account supervisor, but she was stuck there, and she didn't know why. Lauren had a senior-level workload but not the title, money, and perks that go with it. The situation with her boss had even started to get uncomfortable. He excluded her from new business presentations, although she worked on them behind the scenes, because he didn't feel she was ready. She was clearly good enough to do the work but not good enough to be onstage.

Lauren was from a working-class family in New Jersey. She was a self-made person, but she had never completely left her working-class roots behind. She could create a successful brand-image campaign at the agency, but she had not transferred that skill to her own image. And in today's politically correct workplace, her boss hadn't pulled her aside to tell her that she wasn't dressing like a senior executive, like he might do for a male subordinate. Lauren needed to figure that out herself.

## Tune into the Company Uniform

It may seem superficial, but image reigns in many professions, such as Lauren's.

Each industry and individual company has a culture and a visual identity that can be analyzed. And while most of the rules are hidden and unspoken, they are there just the same.

You need to decode the unspoken dress codes. Look around at work. What is the dress style of your company? What is it on the executive floor? How do these styles dovetail with your style?

In *Who Says Elephants Can't Dance?* Louis Gerstner recounts a telling tale about the IBM company uniform. On his first day as CEO, Gerstner was in a meeting with his key executives, wearing his standard suit and blue shirt. Every male executive was wearing a white shirt, which was IBM's "uniform" at the time. The next day, all the men showed up at the office in blue shirts. And Gerstner was wearing a white shirt!

As the Bard said, "we have our exits and entrances and in our time play many parts." But in Lauren's case, she was doing all the work backstage and had no chance to play a part. In business, meetings are the primary stage on which you perform, and if you are left out of the important meetings, you're in big trouble.

Lauren was doing casual Mondays, Tuesdays, Wednesdays, Thursdays, and Fridays. Low-rise jeans and a hip shirt might be okay every day in the creative department, but not on the account management floor, where trendy was the style and Friday was for dressy casual. The "casualization" of American business has gone overboard, and many companies are reverting to dress codes or more formal attire in an attempt to rein in the flip-flops and denim. Even having chipped or red nail polish can be deemed inappropriate for executive women in some companies.

## Take the Makeover Plunge

Telling a client she needed to upgrade her look was not fun, nor was the message well received at first. Gradually, however, Lauren came around and embraced a makeover and a visual identity that suited her, the advertising business, and her agency.

Lauren's makeover wasn't about spending a lot of money. Though she needed to jazz things up a bit for the agency biz and have some of what the French call *bon chic, bon genre* (good style, good attitude), the style upgrade was about looking good in order to promote confidence in what she was saying.

It was about creating a visual identity that communicated "powerful, dynamic woman on the move," which was what she had wanted to stand for all along. It was about self-actualization, becoming more herself, without letting irrelevant things hold her back.

The better Lauren became at looking and acting the part, the more confident she felt about her business abilities, and the more high-profile assignments she got at the agency. Then, at some point, no one even remembered the dowdy Lauren except the ones who were jealous of her career rise. But that didn't affect her one bit.

Lauren even framed a picture of the modest, white frame house where she had grown up in New Jersey and displayed it prominently on one of the walls in her office. She was proud of her origins. She had made it through her own hard work and talent (with a little branding dust thrown in). After all, she wasn't holding herself back with a poor visual identity anymore.

## Don't Look Perfect

Perfection is not as appealing as a more approachable look. I have worked with some people who had that problem. A perfect visual identity conveys "slick" or "unapproachable." Most people find perfection a barrier to likeability. And that, no doubt, is not what you want to achieve.

 **Perfect reads as plastic. Overdone reads as trying too hard.**

You always want to come across as real. If you decide to try for perfection, leave something imperfect, like a carefree hairstyle or a slightly worn briefcase, so that you appear accessible and likeable. Wearing jeans with a dress shirt helped Mitt Romney appear more approachable in the 2012 U.S. presidential election.

## Don't Ignore Your Hair

Like clothing, hair used to be a branding device in many parts of the world. Your hairstyle indicated your status in society or what you did for a living.

Even though there aren't the proscriptions of the past, hair is still a terrific branding device today. Think of Lady Gaga or Rihanna. These two singers frequently change their hairdos and hit the dye bottle, and their creative, daring hairstyles are idiosyncratic and inventive. In Lady Gaga's case, the hair and headdress are high concept, to complement her inventive clothing and visual identity.

Hair is particularly important as a branding device for women. Many women in Arab or Islamic cultures still cover their hair completely with a scarf or veil, so powerfully is hair connected with a woman's beauty.

If you are a high-profile woman in business, politics, or the media, expect your hair to be scrutinized. Dee Dee Myers, the first female presidential press secretary, remarked that people can't hear a thing a woman says until they first decide whether they like her hairstyle or not! Sarah Palin came onto the national political scene in the United States when she ran on the Republican ticket for vice president in 2008. Her distinctive updo, along with her glam glasses, became signature elements of her visual identity, and made her easy for Tiny Fey to mimic on Saturday Night Live.

In the United Kingdom, there's the bouffant hairstyle of legendary Prime Minister Margaret Thatcher that underscored her brand identity as the "Iron Lady." Today, the wavy locks and glossy sheen of Kate Middleton's locks created the up-to-date "it" look that many young women around the world have copied. Indeed, having an old-fashioned hairstyle as a woman brands you as out of date or, even worse, old. Make no mistake, hair says a lot.

## Gleaming, Steaming, Flaxen, Waxen Hair

There isn't usually a lot of commentary on men's hairstyles, even those of high-profile men. Most men don't have the range of lengths, colors, and 'dos that women experiment with. They play it safe with a traditional haircut similar to the way they use the traditional dark business suit as a uniform for work.

But there are exceptions. Look at Justin Bieber, Conan O'Brien, and Donald Trump. All three men have hair so distinctive and recognizable that their hair has become a media story itself.

*The Late Show* host David Letterman showed a picture of the top of Trump's hair on his show, and everyone in the studio audience knew immediately who it was. In his interview on *60 Minutes*, O'Brien even explained that he came up with his distinctive whipped topping–like pouf as a hook to stand out in the business, because he didn't think his first name Conan was enough to get noticed. Bieber's swish has been wildly copied by the teenage set.

Each man's hairstyle has become a trademark of his visual identity. So make fun of it or not, hairstyle is a powerful and memorable feature of each man's brand.

## Have a Trademark

Developing a signature item as a trademark of your visual style is a good tactic for self-branding. You're creating a branding element that identifies you, like the logo on a product. Having that element will set you apart from the crowd. Chosen well, it will convey a brand message to others and even change the way you see yourself.

During his first trip to Europe, Benjamin Franklin followed the fashion on the Continent and wore a wig and a brocade jacket for state functions. Ever one to understand the value of self-promotion, Franklin later bucked the trend and donned simple American broadcloth when he went to France as the U.S. representative after the Revolution. He didn't wear a wig, and his loose gray hair under a marten fur cap became his signature look.

(TM) **A trademark or signature accessory creates a visual identifier that works as a branding device.**

Franklin's memorable image and coiffure only heightened his popularity and fame. He was hailed as a homespun philosopher and became the most famous person on the Continent.

Is there a signature item that can brand your visual identity? Examples of signature items are endless. Jackie Kennedy had her pillbox hats and, later, oversize sunglasses. Margaret Thatcher had her helmet hair and her purses. Larry King has his suspenders. George W. Bush has his cowboy boots. Katie Couric has her big smile. Barbra has her nose. Bono has his tinted wraparound sunglasses, as vivid a symbol for his brand as the golden arches are for McDonald's.

Your trademark could be an item you dispense with that everyone else wears. Katharine Hepburn eschewed skirts, and pants became her trademark in an era when most women didn't wear pants.

Sartorially, John F. Kennedy's trademark was his hatlessness. He did without a hat at a time when men wore hats everywhere, even to casual activities like baseball games. Neil Steinberg, the author of the book *Hatless Jack*, writes, "Kennedy was lauded as this dashing, hatless guy whose adoring public followed his example and tossed away their hats."

---

 **BRAINSTORMER: Creating Your Trademark**

Here are some areas to explore in developing a signature item.

Is there a family heirloom or something personal from your family?

Do you have different taste in accessories (bow ties, suspenders, hats)?

Is there a feature or accessory you can emphasize (hairstyle, glasses)?

---

## Read My Pins

Former U.S. Secretary of State Madeleine Albright used a trademark accessory to brand herself and her diplomacy. After a difficult negotiating session with Saddam Hussein in Iraq, Albright was described as a "serpent" in the Baghdad newspapers. The comment reminded Albright that she had a snake pin in her jewelry collection and she thought it would be fun to wear it to the next negotiating session.

Albright's snake pin was such a hit that she started wearing pins to signal how the diplomatic process was going. If she wore three turtles, negotiations were slow, very slow. If she donned her butterflies or one of her American eagles, then headway was being made and talks were finally moving along. When reporters would ask her how negotiations were going, Albright would point to her pins and say, "Read my pins."

Because she became known for her pins, heads of state from around the world would give her pins, expanding her repertoire of pins and messages. And she would collect pins on her own, often inexpensive brooches she found in airport stores.

Pins became a branding device for Albright, literally. In her book, *Read My Pins*, Albright recounts how she used to be confused sometimes with Margaret Thatcher or Helen Thomas until her pins became her unmistakable branding device.

## Power Presence

What makes you take notice when certain people enter a room? It can be the way they move or carry themselves. It can be a spark, an energy that's mesmerizing. It can be a naturalness that seems so authentic and appealing. It's that hard-to-define and hard-to-duplicate quality we call presence.

So how do you project presence?

It always helps to smile naturally, what social scientists call a Duchenne smile. It's the kind of smile that lights up your whole face and uses the muscles around the mouth and the eyes, too. It's the smile that's an invitation for others to connect. When you smile, others are likely to smile, and that will help everyone relax and enjoy the pitch.

Posture can go a long way in projecting presence. Researchers have studied *power poses* that can give you authority. There are two poses universally linked with power—taking up more space and openness. Expansive postures such as open arms project power. Closed, contracted poses, such as when you cross your hands in front of your body, communicate low power.

## Forever Young

It's going to happen to you. It's already started to happen to me.

If you're like me, it's a subject that you don't like to talk about, but you think about it more than you care to admit.

Aging.

Even though I had done fairly well in the branding and advertising business, I realized that I was getting older in a business that had no use for people who were getting older. (In the advertising business, approaching forty can be viewed as old!) So I had to find of way of changing age into a distinct advantage. I didn't just want to survive, I wanted to be relevant and make a difference as well. Launching my own company, SelfBrand, and a writing, speaking, and coaching career was my way of turning my experience into a plus. That's why I admire people from all types of careers who have discovered for themselves the secret of aging gracefully and staying relevant.

From a visual identity standpoint, the secret is to stop worrying about trying to be youthful and to find a look that's contemporary and plays to your strengths. According to '70s and '80s rock performer Nick Lowe, rock is a business dominated by youth, "unlike blues and jazz, where you can never be too old." "My hair color was like my career: on the wane. But even that I thought I could turn into a plus. You gain a little kind of gravitas," he said in a *Wall Street Journal* interview in 2011. "I knew I needed to find a new way of recording myself and writing stuff that suited me. And I wanted to be hip as well. So that young people would say, 'Hey, I can't wait to get old, too!' I think the whole secret is that I no longer had to worry about trying to be youthful."

## Visual Prophecy

Here are ten guidelines to keep in mind as you develop your visual identity:

1. *Think of clothes as packaging:* Use clothes to enhance, not undercut, your brand message.
2. *Have a signature item:* Think of a trademark that people associate with you.
3. *Look different:* You don't want to look like everyone else. You want your own vibe—appropriate but personalized.
4. *Look the part:* Fulfill expectations of your role and the style of the institution or target market to which you are appealing.

5. *Use hair as a branding device:* Think of Dolly Parton, Anna Wintour, and Donald Trump. Each has an unmistakable branded hairstyle.
6. *Make your look consistent:* Don't send mixed messages. Everything should tie together for a consistent visual identity at business, casual, and formal events.
7. *Have a signature color or palette:* Build your wardrobe and brand marketing around a related palette of colors for maximum effect.
8. *Have a strong presence:* How you stand and carry yourself gives you presence and helps make you memorable. Aim for expansive, open poses that communicate power rather than contracted poses that communicate weak power.
9. *Leverage your height, shape, or profile:* Build your visual identity around who you are and look at unusual features as an advantage to emphasize.
10. *Stay relevant and fresh:* Let your brand evolve and stay up-to-date.

The whole point of visual identity is to maximize the nonverbal messages you are sending out about yourself.

Look at yourself as a package. Does your brand's message on the outside match your self-brand on the inside?

> ➡ **IN A NUTSHELL: The fifth secret of self-brands: Visual identity—the way something looks. The way you look and are seen by others is often the point of first and lasting impact.**

# CHAPTER 6

# Tap into the Power of Symbols, Logos, and Design to Imprint Your Brand Identity

*We are the stuff as dreams are made on.*

William Shakespeare
*The Tempest* (IV, 1)

**B**rand builders use a range of visual tools to set a brand apart and create an emotional bond with customers: a logo, a shape, a color, or a design.

Symbols and logos convey meaning and emotions nonverbally. That's why they've always been powerful in translating ideas, establishing identity, and building communities. Religious symbols like the cross and the Star of David are full of meaning. They express concepts and emotions that most of us would have difficulty expressing in words. Yet a religious symbol can do it in a flash.

The word "brand" comes from the burning stick or branding iron used to mark animals (and criminals) more than a thousand years ago. By the nineteenth century, the brand mark began to indicate ownership not just of animals but also of wine, beer, and other commodities.

There is another type of brand identifier or brand symbol that also goes back to ancient times. Visual symbols that represented a trade were placed outside a shop to identify it to passersby at a time when many people could not read. The striped pole outside a barbershop is a remnant of that tradition.

A flag could be regarded as the logo of a country. We salute and rally around the flag as a symbol of the country we hold dear. Coats of arms with family or clan symbols and colors may be looked on as personal or family logos.

You need to use visual imagery, too, if you want to build a strong self-brand. Symbols and design can improve how people respond to all of your business activities, from your presentations to informal meetings, from your Internet presence to your letterhead.

## Tap into Nonverbal Meaning

Life today is rampant with symbols and logos.

When a woman wears a pink ribbon, we know she is expressing a message about breast cancer. Another familiar symbol is a yellow ribbon tied around a tree, or a yellow ribbon decal on a car used by U.S. military families to symbolize waiting for the safe return of a loved one.

Once discreet, logos now loom large on clothes and accessories, especially handbags, belts, and shoes. Events such as the Olympics and even big corporate events have logos. Logos like the Nike swoosh and the Coke wave are as familiar as the names of the products.

A logo is a special sort of symbol—a graphic that stands for something specific. It may seem like a small thing, but it can be very powerful in developing an identity and personality for a brand.

Logos become powerful when they are well conceived in terms of design, color, and inferred meaning. Then, they become symbols that have meaning and identifying power for broad groups of people.

 **A logo may look like a small thing, but it is big in importance to a brand.**

Milton Glaser designed the "I ♥ NY" logo using a symbol (a heart) instead of the word "love." It was so novel at the time of its creation in the mid-1970s and so widely understood that it took on a global life of its own. Now you can see the heart logo used with just about anything on T-shirts, mugs, and souvenirs around the world.

## Strive for Icon Value

Imagery also imbues a brand with meaning. Look at the power of the images in fashion and beauty ads.

When an image is particularly potent among a wide group of people, it can become an icon, a symbol for an entire category or for an important idea that is universally understood. Marilyn Monroe is an icon of female beauty and sexuality. Elvis Presley, the king of rock 'n' roll, is an icon of youth and rebellion. Albert Einstein is an icon of intellectual brilliance. (We may not be able to explain it, but most of us know Einstein's equation for relativity, $E = mc^2$). Icons like Marilyn, Elvis, and Einstein are elastic in the sense that they appeal to many people and they can mean different things to different people. Each has a strong visual identity—a signature hairstyle, look, and way of dressing that is easily recognized and even impersonated. And each has an enduring presence and ongoing relevance—indeed, many icons are more powerful after death than they were in life.

 **BRAND ICON: A symbol of mythic proportions that transcends time and place of origin.**

A symbol or even a small detail of something larger may become universally recognized and understood as an icon if it conveys powerful emotional content to a broad group of people. Look at the famous detail of two fingers touching in Michelangelo's *Creation of Adam* on the Sistine Chapel ceiling. The index finger of God reaches out to touch the index finger of Adam. This detail is such a potent image of man's creation that it has been called the masterpiece within the masterpiece. It has been reproduced so often and has evoked emotion in so many people that it has become almost a cliché.

This visual imagery was unique at the time Michelangelo conceived it. There is no correlation to text in the biblical book of Genesis. Nor were there any painting precedents. The sheer power of the image created a stir when people first viewed it in the sixteenth century, and it is still a powerful image that speaks to us today.

## Design to Differentiate

If you are an entrepreneur, you'll want to think about how a logo, product design, symbols, or color can set your brand apart. The best brand managers tattoo their brand in your mind with what Laura Ries calls a "visual hammer." The visual hammer can be color. (Think of Christian Louboutin's red soles or Tiffany's blue box.) It could be a powerful logo that communicates brand essence, like Nike's swoosh. It could be the product's shape or packaging, like the POM Wonderful container or Coke's contour bottle. It could be the brand's symbol, like Wells Fargo's stagecoach, or a founder associated with a brand, like Colonel Sanders.

Whatever visual hammer you select, you want it to say something about your brand—to convey intellectual and emotional meaning. Design professionals are crucial in this area. If people don't tell you that you have a good logo and good branding, go back to the drawing board.

A logo may be a distinctive type treatment of a name. Type font and color treatment alone can create a powerful brand identity, like the purple and orange FedEx logo or the primary-colored Google logo.

A logo can have a mark, a graphic element like the Pepsi logo, that amplifies the meaning of the brand. Pepsi's iconic red, white, and blue circle logo began as a bottle cap in the 1930s and evolved through the years into its current "smiling" visual design. The cute bird on Twitter's logo was originally crowdsourced on the Internet for less than $10, and amplifies the meaning of the tweeting communication brand. A young California company, Pressed Juicery, that makes an assortment of healthy elixirs such as green and root blends, reinforces its brand message with a logo typeface that looks hand pressed and a graphic of roots. The tagline, "Get back to your roots," ties in perfectly with the company's logo and brand identity.

Usually, a logo design is "carved in stone," and its use is carefully controlled by the company's corporate identity people. Even though theirs is an all-type logo, the inventive people at Google break the consistency rule of corporate identity. Google sometimes changes its logo and decorates it during holidays or for other events. For example, at Thanksgiving, the logo or the website's home page incorporated a turkey and seasonal colors. It's an artful way to build an emotional connection between a brand and its customers through its tangible symbol, the logo.

## Use a Graphic Symbol

Many logos use a mark, or graphic element, along with the name. Sometimes the mark's identity becomes so familiar, like the Apple Computer apple, that the mark alone immediately identifies the brand. No name is required.

For the SelfBrand logo, I wanted to capture the idea of self-branding. The graphic designer I worked with came up with this mark: a big red box with a black dot outside it and off-center.

You could look at the mark as an abstract representation of "I" for self or "I brand." Or you could look at it as meaning "thinking outside the box," which is core to my self-branding philosophy. Or the graphic could be a camera, since branding is about identity.

We also played with the key idea of the transformative process of branding. So in the word part of the logo, we began with the word "self" in lowercase black letters. For the word "brand," however, we used all uppercase, with each letter in a different color, alluding to the transformative power of a branding makeover. (The full-color version of the logo can be seen at www.selfbrand.com.)

A logo or an appealing brand look plays a masterful role in locking in a company identity and attracting an audience. Here are the most important guidelines to live by in developing a logo:

*Keep it simple:* A logo should be easy to understand and reproduce. It has to work in small venues, like a business card, and in medium-size venues such as websites and brochures. It must also be able to step up to the plate and look good on large signage.

*Be different:* Have a look that is distinct from those of your competitors. You don't want the design du jour.

*Have a personality:* Your logo should convey nonverbal cues such as emotion and personality. Think of adjectives that communicate personality and style attributes as you develop the logo.

*Be "stretchable":* A logo should be able to grow as the brand expands its footprint.

*Convey meaning:* A logo should be an icon, not an illustration. It's better to suggest than to describe. Many abstract logos take on a powerful meaning, but if you have to explain your logo, go back to the drawing board.

## Tap into Design Power

With all the competition companies face, design has become much more important. Computers and phones used to look dull. No longer.

Design is a way of adding sizzle to your brand. Even more, design provides your brand with strategic control over competitors. Look at how the design of the Guggenheim Museum put the industrial town of Bilbao, Spain, on the map.

Take the jeans category. Today, there are more than 1,000 jeans brands, according to a media report. For many people, telling the difference between jeans brands would be impossible without looking at the label. So jeans put their brand identities on the back right pockets. Any teenager or twenty-something can identify a designer or hip jeans brand by the stitched patterns or decoration on the back pocket. No brand logo is required.

Tap into the power of visual branding even if you're a corporate executive with no marketing role. Work with your company's graphic design department. You need to think in terms of visual packaging for important ideas or initiatives as well as for new products and services in your group.

Including a distinctive logo and presentation package in your overall pitch positions your project favorably even before you've said a word.

## Visualize Your Strategy

When you're developing your visual identity for business cards, presentations, your office, and the like, look at how successful branding experts have done it. For example, look at Tazo. Tazo did a great job of building a visual identity—logo, packaging, and product design—off its brand strategy.

Tazo was launched in the mid-1990s amid the reincarnation of coffee spearheaded by Starbucks. Tazo's founders were a small group of friends who wanted to launch the "reincarnation of tea." This was no mean feat in the United States, a country where tea was a distant second to coffee and often viewed as a beverage for people who are feeling sick.

In order to build high interest in the tea category, Tazo's founders came up with an intriguing concept for their new tea. They called it "Marco Polo meets Merlin." Tazo created a special logo, packaging, and product design to bring the concept to life. They melded Far Eastern colors and style with magical and cryptic elements. They found an obscure type font for the logo that gives the name Tazo a coded quality, like an alchemic symbol. Of course, it wasn't all branding. The company developed tea flavors that matched the brand concept.

## Savor the Senses

Tazo also capitalized on a new trend in branding, orchestrating a total sensory experience through sight, smell, and touch.

Each tea had a name, color, and design concept. Tazo gave customers a new experience in tea names—for example, Awake—not old standbys like English Breakfast. Each tea had an exotic smell.

The sensory experience was heightened through what Tazo called "the discoverability of the brand." Tazo layered packages within packages and messages within messages so that customers would repeatedly touch and experience the brand.

So how important was Tazo's visual identity to the brand's phenomenal success?

Many retailers were so enchanted with the Tazo packaging that they bought in quantity before they even sampled the new product. In relatively short order, Tazo was one of the top natural foods brands in the United States. Tazo's success got the attention of the megabrand Starbucks, which bought the tea company to augment its expansion in the beverage market.

## Own a Signature Color

A distinctive color makes for smart branding. Color creates a mood and identifies a brand personality for your company or individual product line. There's Tiffany blue, McDonald's golden arches, and UPS brown, just to name a few well-known brands and their signature colors.

Think of how important the pink ribbon is to the Susan G. Komen Race for the Cure brand. In 1991 the breast cancer charity started handing out pink visors to breast cancer survivors running the race, then it began handing out pink ribbons. Now, more than 80 percent of Americans shop pink for the cure in October, buying pink products with a breast cancer tie-in. It's become an incredibly successful brand, and the nonprofit has warned others about adopting pink or using their phrase, "for the cure."

You can make color a dominant theme for your personal brand. Mark Twain bought a whole wardrobe of white suits after he noticed that he got a lot more attention walking down the street or at speaking appearances when he was wearing a white suit rather than a traditional dark suit. The white suit became part of his self-brand identity along with his novels, public speeches, and sound bites. A white suit plays a similar role for the writer Tom Wolfe today.

Using color could be as simple as having distinctively colored stationery. One business acquaintance has chosen this strategy, and when the blue envelope arrives, I immediately know the identity of the sender. Or you could have a signature color for your website or blog.

## Package Your Business Documents

We are all familiar with brand packaging. Just the shape of an ice cream container tells us whether it is a premium brand or a discount brand.

Every business document or communication has a package too. Letters, e-mails, handouts, pitch books, presentations—every document that you create on the job to sell or persuade or inform—can be made special if you view its presentation as packaging. Even your e-mail signature can be made distinctive with a branded look.

When you give a presentation or a talk, always prepare a handout that represents your brand footprint. You'll need a person with good computer skills and a sharp eye for layout and type fonts.

Make the business documents look beautiful or interesting or different. Choose a brand color for all your presentation folders. You could even develop a distinctive layout for your presentation documents, with a colored rule around each page or a logo at the bottom. Or use even more creative approaches, depending on the business you are in.

For the book cover design for *You Are a Brand!*, I wanted a boldly different graphic look that would grab attention and spark sales when viewed on the shelf in the bookstore or when viewed postage-stamp-size in an online bookstore.

Think of ways to put your brand stamp on all your output, even your method of delivering a message. When you have an important message to send—a new business pitch or a job inquiry letter—put your packaging inside a different delivery package, such as FedEx, so that it will be branded as important to its recipient. Or have it hand delivered.

## Wow Them With Your Business Card

Your business card does the heavy lifting in brand building. It is often the first or even the only thing people are presented with. And most people are likely to hold on to it.

Your business card has your name, job identity, and company identity all in a small, compact format. A business card should create excitement for your brand as well as identify it. The card should presell you and your company. To do that, you must convey the company's brand personality through the design, shape, type font, logo, graphics, and verbal messages such as the company slogan.

If you work for a company, your business card is no doubt corporate issue. You might want to create your own business card, one that sets the right image and tone, for personal use.

If you're an entrepreneur and people don't tell you that you have a great business card, go back to your designer. This is not an area to skimp on by selecting a template from an office supply store. It will look like a template design. It's worth hiring a graphic designer to help you develop a corporate identity for your business.

On the front of the card, place a graphic design and message that grab attention and provoke a response. Use the back of the business card to carry your mantra or company catchphrase. (Consider using your signature color as the background color and printing your slogan in white type.) Then use the brainstormer below to test your card's appeal.

> **BRAINSTORMER: The Business Card Test**
>
> Show your business card to five people.
>
> What is the first response you get after handing out your card?
>
> What is your message? Do people get the right message?
>
> How would people describe your self-brand based on the business card?
>
> How could you improve the card?

## Create Experiences

Don't stop with your personal image or your brand-marketing materials when you think of visual identity.

Think of *total brand experience*.

Today, marketers spend a lot of money creating a branded environment at the retail level. The point is to control the way customers experience the brand. Whether it's drinking a latte in a Starbucks or shopping at Victoria's Secret, the whole store environment is one big brand package. Retail employees are carefully selected and trained so that they are *brand ambassadors*. These branded environments are a very effective way of promoting the brand and building a loyal customer base.

That's why you should think of brand experience too. Look at your clients and colleagues as customers. What is your brand experience like? How is your phone answered? Do you send your secretary out to meet a guest, or do you do it personally? Make sure that your brand experience is consistent and represents what you want to be known for.

## Think Brand Environment

Your office is a part of your packaging and brand experience. Your office says a lot, so why not put your personal brand on it?

Even if you have standard corporate-issue furniture, consider accessorizing your office, as many people do. Bring in a handsome lamp, hang your Audubon prints, or even display your baseball memorabilia. I learned a lot about creating a branded work environment when I worked at the ad agency Wells, Rich, Greene, run by Mary Wells Lawrence. The agency's offices were different from the rest of Madison Avenue, just as a sturdy oxford is different from a dainty pump. Wells, Rich, Greene was feminine. As soon as you entered the lobby, you felt the warmth and richness of an elegant Park Avenue manse, with vibrant wall treatments, carefully chosen colors and textures, and tasteful art and antiques. This was not your typical corporate office.

A grand staircase was the focal point of the agency. It would be easy to imagine a 1930s film star sweeping down elegantly in a long ball gown. The staircase, naturally, led to Mary's suite of offices. We would meet with clients in the Jade Room or the Duck Room.

All the ad execs' offices were fitted out with antique or sleek modern furniture, and what you chose mattered to Mary. A very senior female executive made the mistake of selecting without the proper gravity. When Mary came by and saw her simple Parsons table and bare walls, the next visitors were a moving crew replacing the entire contents of the office. Afterward, the senior female leader had a darling French provincial desk, striking paisley drapes, and Andy Warhol sketches of flowers on the wall.

The agency's offices were unabashedly feminine. Their stylishness was appreciated by clients and by all of us who worked there. Our branded environment was part of our edge.

## Paint the Walls or Tear Them Down

If you're an entrepreneur, you have more latitude in creating a branded business environment than you do if you're employed by a company with its own brand in place. The graffiti artist David Choi was brought in by Facebook's then-president Sean Parker to paint edgy murals on the office walls when Facebook was a little-known start-up in California. Parker offered Choi $60,000 in cash for the project or Facebook shares. Choi is a risk taker, so he chose the stock, which was worth over $200 million at the time of Facebook's IPO in 2012.

Some CEOs and other senior executives nowadays take the opposite route and downscale. And that can be very powerful branding and good PR indeed.

Few executive moves can top joining the cube culture if those leaders hope to communicate the feeling of a democratic work environment, where everyone is in it together. Wall Street has long had a bullpen, an open-plan workspace for the trading floor, where managers sit alongside their staffs. New York City mayor Michael Bloomberg, who came from that culture, has gotten a lot of ink by giving up the traditional, large mayor's office and moving into a bullpen-style space.

When technology companies such as Intel adopted the open-plan workspace with the CEO in the midst of the rank and file, they pioneered the trend on a broader scale. This arrangement has become the trademark of the just-folks, down-home, T-shirt culture of many technology companies that want to create a culture of empowerment and innovation. And now to save money, many companies are embracing "office hoteling" where employees don't have an assigned office or cube, but grab what's available. As a brander, you'll want to have a couple of personal touches that you can put up quickly to mark your space.

## Think Advertising

For your most important ideas and messages, you might want to take a big leap forward visually and study the advertising playbook. People aren't interested in messages and propaganda, but they are interested in being entertained or in learning something new that's important and relevant. That's why advertisers disguise their messages to make them entertaining or educational in TV commercials, print ads, advertorials, and web games. Sometimes they even embed their products within the story line of a television show.

Rather than rely on a PowerPoint slide or press release, think about how you can use bold imagery or even film or video to tell a story. Look at the videos that go viral. It's not corporate videos that try to inform, demonstrate, or sell but rather the ones that entertain or strike an emotional chord.

It's the same with online articles that are passed along. One researcher studied 7,500 articles that were on the most e-mailed list in The *New York Times* from August 2008 to February 2009. While the researcher expected to see lots of articles on practical information like the latest diets and gadgets, he found that the most popular stories were the ones that triggered the most arousing emotions, such as awe and anger.

Turns out we don't want to share facts and practical information as much as stories and emotions. This is true whether we're passing along an article, a video, or an ad.

Why? Research shows that we want to share strong emotions because we want to connect and feel solidarity with a group. We pass along things that surprise or move us because they excite us. Emotional content brings about what social scientists call a state of "high arousal."

When we read or see an article or ad that excites us, our nervous system reacts to these feelings. Our hearts start beating faster, our sweat glands open, and we're ready to do something. We respond in this way whether the stimulus is a horror movie or a love story. And when we're in a state of arousal, we're much more likely to pass along and share the news article, ad, or video that aroused these emotions. And the Internet makes it easy to do that.

## Strive for a Focused Brand Identity

Everything—business card, clothing, résumé, presentations, letterhead, holiday cards, office, website, blog posts, social media profiles, even your posture and gestures—conveys meaning, so use everything to your advantage.

What you want to do is burn in a single-minded identity at every touchpoint, producing a consistent brand experience. What you don't want to do is send confusing messages. That will undercut all your branding efforts. Everything virtual and everything real should be in sync with your brand message.

But, remember, consistency doesn't mean cookie-cutter and identical. That's boring and rigid.

(TM) **Branding always involves sacrifice.**

Marketers must always be prepared to give up a design or an attribute that could be confused with that of a competitor.

Eliminating such items enables you to distill the vital points that will give you a successful strategy with a focused message and presentation.

You may have to leave out things that are off-strategy and would dilute or confuse your self-brand message.

What you want is a total brand experience that's consistent and powerful—that's you.

 **IN A NUTSHELL:** The sixth secret of self-brands: Create a distinct visual identity that hammers in your brand message and is consistent at every touchpoint for a total brand experience.

# CHAPTER 7

# Harness the Power of Names, Signature Words, and Phrases to Lock in Your Message

*How long a time lies in one little word!*

William Shakespeare
*Richard II* (I, 3)

The words you use can be powerful and memorable or blow away like a feather in the wind.

Fresh or unusual words and expressions make you pause. You take notice of them. They create visual and verbal connections. They linger in your consciousness and may even work subliminally to create a brand image.

What if President Franklin Delano Roosevelt had not crossed out the phrase "world history" and replaced it with "infamy" in his famous lead sentence, which began "Yesterday, December 7, 1941, a date which will live in infamy"? One little word. But what a difference! The use of this unusual word made Roosevelt's phrase arguably the most famous ever uttered by a U.S. president.

Words can be so potent that what you create in the mind through words and messages often comes true. That's the power of advertising. Or the power of self talk, whether it's positive or negative. Words can have a strong influence on your outcomes.

## Create Intellectual Capital

As a nation, we used to make things. Now we make ideas. We create intellectual capital. You need to make some, too, if you want to get ahead and build a strong self-brand.

When you look at public companies, it's clear that a large part of their value or market capitalization is due to brand. Today, soft things like brand names, slogans, trademarks, patents, and other forms of intellectual capital are often worth more than tangible assets like product inventories and bricks and mortar.

So, how do you create intellectual capital?

Branding shows you how.

Think *productize*. You start by packaging your ideas, projects, or services just as branders package names, messages, and catchphrases. Names and positioning slogans turn an intangible into a product or a brand.

A great name or slogan makes a good first impression, and it might be indelible if it is a particularly good one. Giving your projects or ideas a name and slogan draws attention to them and makes them seem more important.

Your ultimate goal as a self-brand is to achieve *memory lock*. You want your projects, capabilities, and persona to be noticed and get locked in the memory of your target audience.

## Brainstorm in Cursive

When you're trying to create names and coin expressions for your ideas, write down what comes to mind first.

Don't worry about whether an idea is good or whether it makes sense. Doodle with the words. Build one idea off another. Try not to filter your ideas. Your goal is to start creating intellectual capital and creative ideas for yourself.

When you do this sort of brainstorming, try writing down your ideas in cursive. (You should already be doing this for the brainstormer exercises.)

Why?

Writing in cursive spurs the thought process. You actually come up with more ideas. You tend to probe things more deeply and to be more creative since writing taps into your right brain, into your creativity and intuition. (If you type your ideas and responses on your laptop, print them out double-spaced so you can revise and add to them by hand.)

## Make a Name

A great name is a valuable asset. A name is a label that identifies and defines something.

 **From a branding perspective, the first critical decision is the name of the product.**

A great name can practically make a brand. In fact, in some cases, there is not much difference between two products except for their names. The positive and negative feelings people have about a brand often reside in its name.

A name is critical for a brand because of its influence on a brand's image.

Consider these two cars. The Toyota Corolla and the Geo Prizm were the *same product*, manufactured as a Toyota and General Motors joint venture. Both cars were built in the same factory.

The only thing different about the cars was their names. One was branded Toyota Corolla and the other Geo Prizm (later Chevrolet Prizm). One commanded a premium price and sold many more cars each year.

Because consumers feel the brand-name Toyota is superior to the brand-name Chevrolet, Toyota could charge more and sold more even though the only difference between the two cars was the name. The Toyota name alone was worth many hundreds of dollars more per car and drew more consumer interest.

Finally, General Motors had to throw in the towel. The Prizm isn't made anymore.

## Look at Your Name

Do you have a good name?

It may be unfair—after all, we don't choose our names—but your name often creates the first impression people have of you. (This is absolutely true if you aren't meeting in person.) And that first impression has a powerful influence on the lasting impression people have of you.

Names are just as important for people as for products. In one study, a researcher showed pictures of two beautiful women to a group of men. The group voted and ranked both women as equally beautiful.

Then, the researcher told the group that the first woman's name was Elizabeth and the other woman's name was Gertrude. Again, a vote was taken. This time, one woman had a thirty-point lead in the beauty contest. And it sure wasn't Gertrude.

Social scientists call this "expectancy theory" or the "Pygmalion effect." If you have a name that's considered unattractive, people don't expect you to be attractive, despite what they see.

To a large extent, you see the image that the words trigger in you. So a name is either an asset or a liability.

## Be Aware of Name Expectancy

A name may say whether you are rich or poor, native or foreign, likeable or distasteful, attractive or unattractive.

Steven D. Levitt and Stephen J. Dubner did an interesting study of names in their book *Freakonomics*, using California data that included not only each baby's name and vital statistics but detailed information on the mother's income, level of education, and date of birth.

Levitt and Dubner were able to categorize the "whitest" girls' names (Molly, Amy, and Claire) and the "blackest" girls' names (Imani, Ebony, and Shanice), as well as the "whitest" boys' names (Jake, Connor, and Tanner) and the "blackest" boys' names (DeShawn, DeAndre, and Marquis).

One interesting finding was the relationship between a baby's name and the mother's economic status. Another was the tendency of people with clearly black names to have a less advantageous life outcome than people with clearly white names. For example, the authors relate audit studies in which identical résumés were mailed out, one with a name that sounds white and one with a name that sounds like a black or minority name, and the résumé from the supposedly white candidate generated more interviews.

## Create a Brand-Worthy Name

A great last name certainly is worth something in business, your career, or your life.

We've all seen how having a famous last name like Kennedy, Bush, Rockefeller, or Hilton gives a person a big head start. In the case of designer and philanthropist Lauren Bush Lauren, you can peg on two famous last names.

Just look at the offspring of celebrities or well-known people from the world of politics, business, or entertainment who are leveraging the family name to enter the family business or set up a different high-profile endeavor.

But if you're like me and most other people, you weren't born with a family brand name. You have to make a name for yourself. You must build your own brand, whether the realm is your community, your industry, your company, or the whole planet.

You will find it easier to build a self-brand if you have a good name. It's the same for products and for people: a good name is distinctive—not too common or owned by someone else—and is easy to spell and remember. Of course, you also want a name with that something extra that will give you marquee name potential.

The image-making power of names is why a lot of people in entertainment, fashion, or other highly visible fields change their names. So Esther Lauder became Estée Lauder. Susan Weaver became Sigourney Weaver. And Paul Hewson became Bono.

Of course, you've reached the name zenith when your first name alone is sufficient to identify you, like Bono, Adele, or Oprah, or when a single letter of the alphabet, like W, does the trick.

There has been a reemergence of the personal name as brand across all types of products and services. It allows for the development of a *brand character* based on what we think of as the individual's persona. You get two for one. You don't just have the brand; you have the person and the brand. Sometimes it's hard to figure where one stops and the other begins.

### (TM) Different names create different assumptions.

Ralph Lauren is a familiar example. First, there's the name change. Would his success have been the same if his brand had been known as Polo by Ralph Lipschitz? I doubt it. Lauren needed a name with the right pedigree so that he and his designs could symbolize the Polo brand concept: hyper-WASP American aristocracy. And Lauren, the person, is the model for the look, lifestyle, and essence of the brand, symbolizing both the brand and its users.

Or look at Sean "Diddy" Combs, the former hip-hop performer turned business impresario. Combs is also a brilliant naming tycoon. There are the serial personal nicknames: Puff Daddy, Puffy, P. Diddy, and now simply the one word, Diddy. And there are the well-named product lines: Sean John for his clothing label and Bad Boy Records for his music label.

In another example, struggling author Joanne Rowling took her editor's advice and added a dollop of mystery to her persona by using the initials J.K. in place of her first name. (The "K" came from her grandmother, Kathleen.) And thus J.K. Rowling, the creator of *Harry Potter*, was born.

The good news is that our ideas about what is considered a good name are evolving. It used to be a rite of passage for aspiring actors and actresses to change their names if they thought that doing so would be helpful for their careers.

Arnold Schwarzenegger wasn't held back by his name (although it breaks the rules of a good name by being too long, too ethnic, and difficult to spell). And "odd" first names are in vogue. No doubt Gwyneth Paltrow's daughter, Apple, and Julia Roberts' twins, Hazel and Phinnaeus, won't be hampered by their given names. Now it will be much easier for people to have unusual names and succeed.

## Crafting a Unique Name

The idea of a name as an asset to be protected is spilling over into the human brand realm. Beyonce and Jay-Z applied to trademark their new daughter's name, Blue Ivy. While that may be an extreme example of protecting your personal brand, from a branding perspective, there is an advantage to having a unique name: you are more likely to be able to own it on the Internet.

Parents are getting hip to the importance of having a distinctive name in today's searchable world. "Baby names" is one of the most searched phrases on the Internet as expectant parents try to find unusual or unique names that can be owned on the Internet. Having a rare and ownable name is critical for brands, and they go to great lengths to trademark and protect their asset.

Indeed the variety and uniqueness of names has skyrocketed in recent decades. In the early twentieth century, the most favored names were John and Mary, and Americans generally picked from 200 commonly used names. Now, less than 50 percent of girls and about 60 percent of boys have a top 200 name.

## Naming Power

A name is particularly powerful when it is the only thing you know about someone. Throw in a picture or an in-person meeting, and the power of the name recedes.

Yet, as a self-brander, you want to maximize all your assets. If you have a name like Mary Jones or Bob Smith, you have generic name syndrome. You will find it harder to build a self-brand identity than will those who have a more original name.

Here are some ways to make your name a better asset:

*Use your middle name as your brand name:* Ray Charles Robinson became Ray Charles. Thomas Cruise Mapother IV became Tom Cruise. Angelina Jolie Voight became Angelina Jolie (Jolie means "pretty" in French, which gives the name a foreign flair as well.)

*Use a quirky nickname:* An unusual or descriptive nickname is a great branding device. Think of Tiger Woods, Tipper Gore, and Topher Grace.

*Use your full name:* A middle name often makes a generic last name stand out. Sarah Jessica Parker, James Earl Jones, and John Fitzgerald Kennedy are good examples.

*Use a double-barreled last name:* This works best if the last names are short, for example, Catherine Zeta-Jones.

*Use initials:* Initials help you stand out: Jennifer Lopez is a fairly common name, but she also has the brand-name J. Lo to set herself apart. The poets T.S. Eliot and e.e. cummings successfully employed this device, as does J.K. Rowling today.

*Spell a common name in an uncommon way:* Tune up a common name with a simple spelling change. Examples are Barbra Streisand and Suze Orman.

*Modify to add flair or a foreign accent:* Simply changing a few letters often makes an important difference. Gary Keillor changed his name to Garrison Keillor. Stephen Colbert gave a French flair to the pronunciation of his last name.

*Simplify your name:* Many people chop off part of a name that is long or difficult to pronounce. James Baumgarner became James Garner, Antonio Benedetto became Tony Bennett, and Jennifer Anistonopolous became Jennifer Aniston.

*Totally make it up:* This is the favored route of rappers and some entertainers. They give themselves names that are radically different from traditional standards, such as Ice Cube, 50 Cent, and the like.

*Make a "bad" name work.* Today it's easier to break the rules and succeed, especially if the name has a quirky quality, like Renée Zellweger.

*Sound good:* Names that are easy to pronounce and sound good have cognitive fluency: people find them easy to pronounce, easy to think about, and easy to prefer. In one study, people tended to have a better impression of people who have a nice sounding name. Alliteration or repetition can help: Marilyn Monroe, Lady Gaga.

*Own a word:* The ultimate in branding is to so dominate a category that all people need to hear is the one-word name. Think Bono, Beyonce, Martha, Adele, Oprah. Or you name can have a strong identification with a keyword. Think Volvo and safety or FedEx and overnight.

---

 **BRAINSTORMER: What Does Your Name Say?**

Write your name on a piece of paper.

What adjectives or imagery comes to mind when you read or say your first name?

Which other people with this name come to mind?

If you could choose your name, would you choose this one?

If not, which name would you choose?

Is your name distinctive or similar to others? How could you make your name more distinctive?

How could you make your name suit you better?

## Look at Labels

Your name isn't the only word you need to think about. What "label" do you use when you describe who you are or what you do?

A label is an important naming word, too. Labels are names that define and position something in the minds of others. The way you label yourself can make or break you.

 **Different labels carry different perceptions.**

A number of research studies bears this out. Professor Nalini Ambady did a study showing students a two-second video of a professor. One group was given the label "statistics professor." The other was given the label "humanistic psychology professor."

Students described the statistics professor as "cold," "rigid," and "picky." They called the humanistic psychology professor "warm" and "concerned with students."

Both groups of students saw the same professor in the same video; only the job title was different.

So it's not surprising that more people have started looking at the labels they use for themselves. Nobody's a secretary anymore. The description is now "administrative assistant." Hoping to expand the definition or escape the poor image contained in their label, stockbrokers became "financial advisers," used-car salesman began to call themselves "pre-owned vehicle consultants," and computer programmers became "e-business solutions experts" or "systems analysts."

Many high-profile people have been given labels that capture the essence of their personal brands, like Warren Buffet (the Oracle of Omaha), Margaret Thatcher (the Iron Lady), and Frank Sinatra (the Chairman of the Board).

Of course, labels can rise or fall in value. It used to be prestigious to say that you work on Wall Street, and the label "Wall Street executive" branded you as smart, a member of an elite. That all changed with the connection between Wall Street firms, the financial collapse of 2008, and the hard economic times that came afterward. The brand image of Wall Street and the people who work there has nose-dived in value. The fact that you work on Wall Street is today more likely to be whispered than declaimed. In 2011, we've had Occupy Wall Street protests in New York City and other metropolitan areas that testify to the financial sector's reversal of fortunes, at least in terms of its brand image.

## Take Title

Whether or not you get the boss to change the job title on your business card, you should think about it.

Don't think a job title is cast in stone, either.

When I worked on Wall Street, my title initially was senior vice president, director of advertising. During a downturn in the market, which also affected the firm's ad budget, I created a community-based, cause-related marketing program. It had a lot of impact with a budget that was relatively small compared to the cost of TV ads. I approached my boss about changing my title to director of advertising and community affairs. This gave me a label that offered a bigger brand footprint and might open up more options in the future.

The following brainstormer will help you explore your own possibilities.

The corporate title is the other big label in business that ranks you as succinctly as the number of stars on an army general's shoulder. It matters whether you are branded a vice president, a senior vice president, or an executive vice president or have no corporate title whatsoever. Your title affects the perceptions people have about how you perform on the job and what you are worth.

So, as long as you are in a company or line of work that uses title branding of that sort, fight for the best brand label you can get. Or, move into an area where merit is measured in other ways.

**BRAINSTORMER: What's Your Line?**

**What is your job title?**

**Is there a better way to label what you do or who you are?**

## Own a Keyword

Brands try to own a word, or a short phrase, in the minds of consumers. If they succeed, people think of the brand when they hear the word. It usually takes a fair amount of tine to lock in a word with your brand and have it go mainstream. Now, in the Internet era, going mainstream can happen rapidly like the association of "follow" and "tweet" with Twitter, and "search" with Google, and "like" and "friend" with Facebook.

Owning a word is important because it means that your brand is positioned with an important attribute in the minds of prospects. Your brand has meaning in a world where there are so many brands and messages that most do not stand for anything. It's like being the top result that comes up when you enter a keyword in a search engine.

Owning a word helps self-brands too. Your word could be a positive attribute that defines you. It could be a niche in the market that you dominate, or it could even be an idea that people associate with you.

Many people end up owning a word by writing a book, as Warren Bennis did with "leadership," Steven Levitt and Stephen J. Dubner did with "freakonomics," Larry Bossidy did with "execution," Tom Peters did with "excellence," Al Ries and Jack Trout did with "positioning," and Jay Conrad Levinson did with "guerrilla." Guy Kawascki chose the word "enchantment" for a book title with the hope of owning the word. Thought leaders with several breakout books, like Malcolm Gladwell, can end up owning more than one word ("tipping point," "outliers," and "blink").

As a celebrity CEO, Jack Welch didn't need to increase his renown by writing a book, but he did want to lay claim to the word "winning" and wrote a book with that one-word title. Of course, words can be co-opted if someone else uses the word and it captures the zeitgeist. Today, when you hear "winning," you're more likely to think of the actor Charlie Sheen, his public meltdown, and his use of the word. Who knows who will lay claim to it in the future.

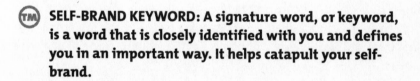

**SELF-BRAND KEYWORD: A signature word, or keyword, is a word that is closely identified with you and defines you in an important way. It helps catapult your self-brand.**

You might choose to own a word that expresses an important attribute you believe in, as my client Benjamin did with "accountability." He used "accountability" in talking about his vision for the company in internal meetings, in memos, and on the company website.

Benjamin also took action to embed "accountability" in the culture and associate the word with his leadership, a classic move for the identifier stategy. He introduced new sales reporting metrics and performance reviews and instituted client feedback mechanisms and similar procedures that tangibly demonstrated accountability in action.

## Name Your Ideas

Business isn't just about facts and statistics. And it's not smart branding if that is the way you approach it. You have to create interest in what you have to offer, not bore people. That's why smart businesspeople, like smart brand managers, brand their ideas by packaging them with a name.

Turns out whether a word or name lives or dies depends on natural selection, studies show. Every year about 8,500 words enter the English language, but the creation of new words is slowing, and the death rate of old words is increasing. A catchier word like "X-ray" was the death knell for its ungainly synonym, "roentgenogram." What's interesting is that new words, especially names of innovations like "Twitter" and "iPod," are becoming part of the vernacular much more quickly than in the past. We're living in a viral era where the word for a hot new idea can travel and take hold fast.

Naming is a good way to create tangible assets for your self-brand. Naming an important idea or project has enormous advantages. When you give something a name, you make a tangible thing out of an intangible. A name will help people visualize and understand your idea or the point you are making.

Names make your ideas and points more memorable. When you name something, you are branding it and giving it the potential to be a "big idea." Names will help you sell your project to your clients, whether external or within your organization.

Nothing is sold until it's branded, whether it's a product or an idea. Talking about his much-criticized health care plan, former President Bill Clinton said, "I did a disservice to the American people—not by putting forward a bad plan, but by not being a better brander and not explaining it better."

Coining your own word or expression gives you a marvelous branding device for both your idea and yourself. If you express your key message in an interesting way, it helps people see your point of view and makes you more memorable.

## Make it Sticky

Give your idea or point an unusual or unexpected name. Quirky words are sticky—they stay in the mind, and people remember them.

Politicians can be adept at mocking their opponents with colorful, sticky names and expressions to frame their opponents in a negative light. And they're more likely to be quoted in the press. In the 2012 Republican presidential primary, Newt Gingrich branded President Obama as "the food stamp president," a stinging, sticky phrase that vividly recalls the bad economy and high unemployment at the time. In the 2004 presidential campaign, President George W. Bush memorably branded his rival John Kerry as a "flip-flopper," a phrase that many politicians adopt to point out opponents who change their opinion.

By naming things, you can frame something in a positive or negative way by the name you choose That's why opponents of the estate tax in the United States brand it the "death tax" to frame the tax negatively in the minds of citizens, just as opponents of President Obama's healthcare plan brand it "Obamacare." You can persuade people to your point of view with the names you give things, particularly options in a series that are under consideration. Henry Kissinger talked about "coloring the options" when he presented various alternatives for then-president Richard M. Nixon to consider.

Give your idea a particularly memorable name or a name with emotional content, and you can create a company mantra or rallying cry. Starbucks coined the word "glocally" to express its paradoxical ethos of trying to think locally and globally simultaneously. Another way of coming up with an unusual word is to steal a word from another field and use it in a business context. Facebook doesn't just want to promote connection with its users, it wants to create happy emotions, what they call "serotonin" after the neurotransmitter that elicits feelings of happiness.

When Jack Welch headed up GE, he used the word "boundarylessness" for the idea of a seamless culture with no silos, a business utopia where employees can find good ideas everywhere and share them throughout the company. Calling the culture "seamless" or without silos wouldn't have been memorable because too many other companies claim that (whether it is indeed true or not). Though awkward and a bit of a tongue twister, "boundarylessness" was unusual and unexpected. It was sticky.

## The Hedgehog and the Fox

Naming proposals and processes, as well as ideas, can be effective branding in business, too. Mark Pincus at Zynga uses OKRs (Objectives and Key

Results) to get his employees focused on one key objective and three key results each week.

Look at Jim Collins and his slew of business best sellers beginning with *Good to Great*. No doubt Collins owns the words "great" and "great company" in the business imagination, as he has "great" in most of his book titles, and his books and ideas have been so influential.

Collins has a research team that helps him compile the research and analysis to back up his ideas. But what makes his ideas so influential and his books compelling reading is his branding ability. For example, Collins talks about "the Hedgehog Principle" to make the point that business success is not about knowing many things but about being able to isolate the one important thing.

The Hedgehog Principle is not an idea original to Collins. It's an old idea attributed to ancient Greek poet Archilochus from a fragment that reads, "The fox knows many things, but the hedgehog knows one big thing." The concept was popularized in 1953 by the British philosopher Isaiah Berlin in his essay "The Hedgehog and the Fox." But Collins had the insight to adopt this wonderful visual metaphor to make his point sticky in his book. (If you're like me, Collins's book may be the first time you became acquainted with it.)

In another book, Collins admonishes business leaders that it's about "clock building not time telling" if you want to build a great company. The businessperson who can tell the time simply by looking at the sky has a skill. But the person who can build clocks and sell them has a great business. Again, Collins uses a vivid visual metaphor to tattoo his idea in your mind.

## Plant a Better Name

You don't have to invent the big idea, as you can see when you're creating intellectual capital, although you should put your own spin on all ideas. If you give an existing idea a great name and spread the word, you'll end up owning it in the minds of others.

For example, the concept of ideas and trends spreading like an epidemic originally came out of the worlds of science and social science. One scientist, Richard Dawkins, called such ideas and trends "memes," a name that gradually took hold and is now a household word.

Malcolm Gladwell wrote elegantly about the concept, coining the phrase "the tipping point" to describe ideas and trends building slowly at first and then dramatically tip and become a mass phenomenon. When his book *The Tipping Point* made the best-seller list, the concept entered the national consciousness. Gladwell's phrase had something going for it that Dawkin's word "meme" lacked; the "tipping point" was a visual metaphor that made the concept easy to understand. And Gladwell gave good names to the people who tip things: connectors, mavens, and salesmen.

Seth Godin put his own spin on the concept. He came up with the term "ideavirus" and wrote a book called *Unleashing the Ideavirus*. (You are trying to create an ideavirus with the names you give your ideas.) Godin took it one step further and came up with the concept of packaging your ideas to make them spread faster.

All three men were exploring a similar concept, yet each laid claim to the idea by giving it a name and their own interpretation.

## Use Your Own Name

The best place to start is often your own name. You make the history books if you get your name to stick to your idea, as with "Moore's Law" and the "Peter Principle." Or your name could become an adjective that describes your intellectual contributions, like "Darwinism," "Pavlovian," and "Freudian."

Look at the diet book category: Dr. Robert Atkins didn't invent the no-carb or low-carb diet. Others came before him; but he used his name for the diet and in 1972 came out with a book, *Dr. Atkins' Diet Revolution*.

Atkins had a fresh USP: if you cut out carbohydrates, the body will react by eating body fat. The USP and branding resonated with the public. Soon the name Atkins became synonymous with "no carbs" and "skinny." In the thirty-three years since it first came out, Atkins's book has sold a whopping 21 million copies.

## Tip An Idea

Atkins ruled the low-carb diet world until Dr. Arthur Agatston came along. (His name may not be as familiar as Atkins, but his diet sure is.)

At first, Agatston named his diet "The Modified Carbohydrate Diet." He promoted it with a booklet in 1996 among a relatively small group of overweight clients in Miami, who started losing weight.

What propelled the Miami diet doctor to great success was a sexy name and packaging. Of course, he had a good product—a good diet—but there are a lot of good diets out there.

The doctor didn't use his own name, Agatston, which is a bit hard to remember and spell. He piggybacked his diet on the name and imagery of a chic part of Miami Beach when he launched his book, *The South Beach Diet*, in 2003. The book went on to top the best-seller list, spawned two spin-off books, and sold 14.5 million copies in two years. It was a phenomenal success.

Would the diet have done as well if he had continued to call it "The Modified Carbohydrate Diet"? Unlikely. Or if he had used his own name and called it "The Agatston Diet"? Again, unlikely.

(TM)  **A good name can make your idea memorable.
A fabulous name can really make the idea break out.**

The words "South Beach" gave the diet a breakthrough handle, like the Scarsdale Diet developed by Dr. Herman Tarnower. Only South Beach has more cachet and sexier imagery than Scarsdale.

An interesting by-product of the South Beach phenomenon was that the label "low-carb" also took off. Soon food companies started putting the words "low-carb" on thousands of products, both foods naturally low in carbohydrates and new low-carb versions of high-carb foods. And their sales also took off.

## Find Enticing Names

Smart self-branders name their ideas all the time. The trend guru Faith Popcorn comes up with fanciful names for her trends, such as "cocooning," that put them (and her business) on the map. Ditching her ethnic last name and adopting "Popcorn" was her first naming feat.

If you are in a service business, avoid generic marketing of your services. Don't list capabilities and features. Package your services and name them so that you create excitement and can sell the benefits of what you are offering.

Look at hotels. Most used to market themselves on price per night. Now, smart hoteliers also use names and packaging to create demand. They offer "Romantic Couples Weekends" or "Mother/Daughter Spa Weekends" or "Fitness and Beauty Weekends." Small bed-and-breakfasts offer "Mystery Weekends" or "Civil War Battle Reenactment Days."

## Encapsulate the Name

One of my clients, Lynn, first began coining words as a sales representative for a large company. When Lynn left the corporate world to start her own sales-training business, she wanted a way to market her workshops that expressed her innovative ideas on how salespeople need to sell today.

We came up with "Sell SMART." It is not a selling system. (Most selling systems are too complicated for salespeople to implement.) Sell SMART is a positioning line and uses an acronym that spells out the key ideas behind its selling philosophy. We completed the transformation by encapsulating the idea in a logo.

$$
\begin{array}{ll}
\text{(S)} & \text{........Find the Sweet Spot} \\
\text{(M)} & \text{........Capture Mindshare} \\
\text{(A)} & \text{........Have Answers and Advice} \\
\text{(R)} & \text{........Get the Right Reaction} \\
\text{(T)} & \text{........Think Tactics}
\end{array}
$$

With the new name and positioning, Sell SMART offers a different value proposition than other sales-training programs.

## And One More Thing

Steve Jobs used his signature line, "And one more thing," to introduce new products each year. An important part of the line's impact was the way he delivered it, almost like an afterthought, when in reality, it signaled the most important part of his presentation. The signature line became so famous that everyone waited to hear it to see what new product Jobs would be showcasing each year.

The signature line is a phrase that captures our imagination. We're all familiar with signature lines from television like "Beam me up, Scotty" if you're a Star Trek fan or Donald Trump's "You're fired." And many hot shows spawn signature lines that take on a life of their own outside the show, such as *Sex and the City*'s "He's just not that into you."

 **Signature line: A catch phrase that everyone knows and associates with you, and waits to hear.**

Signature lines, like Steve Jobs line for introducing new products, are powerful. Everyone knows them and gets the association between the line and who said it. Generally the signature line is said just once in a television show or movie, often at the end like "I'll be back" (*Terminator*) or "Hasta la vista, baby" (*Terminator 2*).The advertising equivalent of the signature line is the tagline at the end of the commercial that tries to lock in the brand's essence, like BMW's "The Ultimate Driving Machine."

## Create Self-Brand Bites

Mark Twain wrote literary masterpieces, but he was also a master of the sound bite. His ability to toss off an interesting phrase on important issues and life experiences brought Twain to the attention of people around the world.

One of the jobs of a politician or pundit is to create catchphrases and labels that frame the debate or debunk naysayers. We're all familiar with Winston Churchill's famous words from World War II, such as "I have nothing to offer but blood, toil, tears, and sweat" and "We shall fight on the beaches." Then there's Margaret Thatcher's signature phrase, "You turn if you want to. The lady's not for turning."

In the United States, we have Barack Obama's "Yes, we can," his catchphrase in the 2008 election, and George W. Bush's "I'm the decider," about the fate of the secretary of defense.

## The Expression *du Jour*

Every year media pundits and others in the news introduce catchphrases that grab the public consciousness. In 2011, we heard a lot about "reaching out," "pushing back," and "taking a seat at the table." (Full disclosure: I use this phrase myself in talks to women leaders.)

We learned to speak in terms of a "narrative" to "frame" the conversation. Indeed, in 2012 President Obama was criticized for lacking a compelling narrative that tied together his accomplishments in his first term and framed his campaign for re-election. Another hot phrase was "viral," reflecting the rise of the cyberworld in our lives. Indeed, even the term "personal brand" is being used more and more. We'll probably keep using these expressions until we get push back and something better comes along.

You should harness the power of defining phrases or catchy slogans for your ideas and your department or company mission. Don't give a presentation, make a new business pitch, or present a recommendation to your boss without a few sound bites on your key points.

Sound bites are memory magnets. They could be surprising, shocking, or funny. They may use word play or other literary devices such as rhyme and repetition. A sound bite creates a strong visual image that brings the idea to life in a novel way. At the very least, a sound bite should be a pithy saying that communicates your essential message.

Often, the devices that make for a great sound bite are the same as those used by marketers in developing great taglines or slogans for brands. In the past, advertisers often put the brand slogan to music and created an ad jingle. Once heard, it was surprisingly difficult to get it to stop replaying in your head. Now, ad jingles are passé, although music or sound may still play a role. McDonald's uses the slogan "I'm loving it" and a five-note melody. The company even created a hit song for Justin Timberlake.

## Tell Stories

Beyond a name and sound bite, you must think of how best to talk about and sell your idea. Most people speak in generic or factual terms about their ideas and projects.

This is a lost opportunity!

You can't influence and persuade someone by boring them. You have to be a masterful communicator. The best communicators use wit and personal charm to connect with you. They say something unexpected or have a story or anecdote to frame their point of view.

Stories have universal appeal. Successful brands use the power of stories and an evolving story line to keep people interested in the brand and its message. You should, too. Stories bring your accomplishments and personality to life for people in a way that gets them involved in the narrative of what happened.

Stories bring characters to life through description and dialogue. They make the challenge and struggle seem vivid and real. Bring in good dialogue (quotes and sound bites). Build suspense in the way you tell what happened.

Look at the following themes from literature and movies and see if there is a way you can talk about your ideas in a more dramatic way:

▶ Against all odds
▶ The comeback
▶ The turning point
▶ Talent wins out

Stories are often built on a narrative construction of conflict, struggle, and final victory. Top-notch business writers like Michael Lewis (author of *The Big Short*, *Moneyball*, and *Liar's Poker*) and James B. Stewart (*Den of Thieves*, *Blood Sport*, and *DisneyWar*) know how to craft a nonfiction narrative so that it reads like a whodunit.

Even if you're giving how-to advice in your area of expertise, your themes will be more interesting to readers if you introduce some backstory. For example, the personal-finance author Robert Kiyosaki could simply have told his philosophy of successful money and life management in his book *Rich Dad, Poor Dad*. Instead, he used a story about the conflict between the teachings of his father (the poor dad) and his friend's father (the rich dad), who gave him the low-down on how money really works in the world.

It turns out there may not have been an actual rich dad, as a reporter later found out. But the story of the conflict made Kiyosaki's book captivating. No doubt, many people could relate to having a poor dad, a loving parent who worked hard and saved but didn't know how to work smart and invest for himself, much less pass these valuable lessons on to his children.

Using stories in a presentation to sell yourself, your ideas, or your company is a type of *emotional marketing*: getting people interested in your ideas not just because of the facts but because they *feel* something about who you are and what you're talking to them about. People will get wrapped up in your story, and it will make your ideas and recommendations not only more memorable but more engaging. And that will help you sell your ideas and recommendations.

## Use a Visual Metaphor

A form of mini story is the *metaphor*. A dramatic metaphor or analogy works like a photo snapshot—it's quick, visual, and gets the listener to engage and see your point of view.

 **A metaphor compares two things that are not alike in most ways but are similar in one important way.**

Famous U.S. defense lawyer Clarence Darrow was known for a visual metaphor that was so powerful it turned his defense into a prosecution. In 1898, Darrow represented striking workers at Paine Lumber in Oshkosh, Wisconsin. Mr. Paine owned the town of Oshkosh in those days. Even the police captain was on his payroll. It was not an easy case for Mr. Darrow to win for the powerless striking workers.

Speaking to the jury, Darrow told a story about how workers were locked in the factory once they arrived at 6:45 a.m. and were kept locked in, except for a lunch break, until the guards turned the key when it started to get dark.

Then Darrow painted a dramatic picture at the end of his pleas to the jury with this metaphor: "Why, gentlemen," Darrrow said, " the only difference that I can see between the state prison and George M. Paine's factory is that Paine's men are not allowed to sleep on the premises."

## Name Your Ideas

If you want to become a successful self-brander, you have to get into the naming game for your ideas, initiatives, and business concepts. Keep these ten naming principles in mind:

1. *Keep it short:* Small names act big when you promote the brand. They are easy to grasp, spell, pronounce, and remember, and being remembered is half the battle in branding. Many brand names have

gone on a diet (Citibank became Citi, and Federal Express is FedEx).
Some top global brands are as short as three or four letters (AAA,
Nike, Ford). Some brands have used one-word taglines ("Always,"
"Enjoy," and "Real" for Coca-Cola), and many top-selling book titles
are made up of a single word (*Drive, Freakonomics, Blink, Unbroken*).

2. *Look for verb, generic, or sound-bite potential:* You hit the jack-
   pot when your name becomes the generic term for the category
   (Scotch tape, Band-Aid) or a verb (Skype, Dropbox, Xerox, Google).
   You could even aim for an expression that enters the vernacular
   ("Where's the beef?" "He's just not that into you").

3. *Use unexpected or quirky words or expressions:* Fresh words and
   expressions are sticky—they are memorable and grab people's attention (axis of evil). Just one unexpected word can make an expression
   sticky ("It's the economy, *stupid.*").

4. *Tell a story or paint a picture:* Words and expressions that suggest or
   describe are very effective. Research shows that people remember
   suggestive or descriptive names because the meaning is embedded in
   the name (cocooning, the tipping point, the world is flat). Baby Einstein, the video and book publisher, has a name that conjures
   up every parent's dream for a newborn. Look how changing the
   book title from *Men Who Hate Women* to *The Girl with the Dragon
   Tattoo* created visual excitement and enhanced book sales. Likewise,
   don't use names that have poor visual imagery. Beaver College in
   Philadelphia changed its name to Arcadia University and doubled
   applicants.

5. *Position the brand or idea:* Position your brand or idea favorably
   against competitors. Look at how the U.S. military chooses names for
   wars and military operations that appeal to people and position the
   campaigns favorably (Operation Iraqi Freedom, Operation Enduring
   Freedom [Afghanistan]).

6. *Employ literary devices:* Look at what has worked in great literature
   throughout history. Alliteration is used frequently to burn in a name
   or idea (Six Sigma, Spin Selling). Other literary devices such as
   rhyme, repetition, assonance, and parallel construction are also very
   effective ("Ask not what your country can do for you, ask what you
   can do for your country").

7. *Connect emotionally:* Try to create a name or expression for your idea or product that resonates and connects emotionally with the people you are targeting ("Just do it" for Nike, "Think Different" for Apple, and "Whassup?!" for Budweiser).

8. *Consider tying in your own name:* The ultimate in self-branding is to embed your name in the idea or cause you're promoting. It can work if you have a name that's easy to say and remember (Moore's Law, Peter Principle).

9. *Make sure it sounds good:* Think of how the name, title, or expression sounds when you say it. Is it melodic? Does it sound right for the brand personality or the idea? Is the word memorable? Does the sound of the word suggest the idea? (The original name for the zipper was "separable fastener" before B. F. Goodrich renamed it.)

10. *Make it stretchable.* The best names and sound bites are elastic enough to grow. Apple uses the prefix "i" for its products as a memorable naming device: iBook, iPod, and so on. Bill Maher's "New Rules" and David Letterman's "Top 10 Lists" are stretchable enough to be used again and again with different examples, even spawning books and imitation.

## Study the Masters

People often ask me, "How can I learn to use the power of words to build my brand?"

Study the new brand names, ad taglines, and expressions that enter the public consciousness. But, if you're looking for real inspiration, read great literature.

For me, as for many others, Shakespeare is the writer who continues to offer inspiration. He never ceases to astonish me with the branding power of words. Shakespeare is so rich that I've relied on his words alone in the quotes throughout this book.

It used to be said that Shakespeare is quoted more than any source except for the Bible. Now that statistic is out of date. The Bible is number two.

Certainly, Shakespeare has risen to the pinnacle because his expressions and use of words are timeless. English would have been a different language without him.

Shakespeare achieved the ultimate in word branding power. His words speak to all people regardless of their status in life, just as when he wrote them some 400 years ago.

>  **IN A NUTSHELL:** The seventh secret of self-brands: Burn in your messages and your brand power with memorable names, words, and expressions.

# CHAPTER 8

# Learn to Speak for Effect, Not Just Facts

*All the world's a stage.*

William Shakespeare
*As You Like It* (II, 7)

**W**e're always onstage.

In business, meetings are the primary stage on which you perform. You're aware, of course, that your performance on that stage, your presentations and your appearance, will shape your business image as either a star or an understudy. Phone calls, voice mail, letters, and memos are also part of the business stage and convey meaning.

What is the point of communicating if you don't have an impact? The ability to sell yourself and your ideas—to communicate to another person, whether it is your boss, employee, or mate—is a critical skill for personal success.

And *how* you say something is just as critical as *what* you say. How often do you go into important meetings or make important calls or give presentations without a persuasive message? Communication means persuading people to choose you for the job, buy your product or service, or promote you to lead the department.

Great communication equals great self-branding. On a basic level, your success in life and in business depends on the art of talking and communicating well. And the higher you go in business, the more public speaking will be part of your job description. A 2005 survey of 100 Fortune 1000 companies by Burson-Marsteller revealed that CEOs receive an average of 175 requests a year to speak at conferences.

## Have Something Interesting to Say

Lack of communication skills holds you back from promotions and relegates you to the B-list at your company. As you move up in a company, the ability to build confidence in your leadership is a crucial part of the job. And being able to articulate and sell your ideas in meetings is your primary method of doing that.

Never go to a meeting without having something to say and knowing how you are going to say it. Remember, there is not a lot of demand for messages per se, but there is a demand for interesting messages.

(TM) **Advertisers dress up their messages by making them entertaining, relevant, or emotional.**

Prepare *three points* in advance of every meeting. These points should offer new information that will appeal to the people in attendance. Whether we're now entering the "Knowledge Age," the "Creative Age," or the "Conceptual Age" (all have been predicted), it's important to empower yourself and add intellectual value in your job, no matter what it is. If you're a salesperson, it's more important than ever to understand your clients' business and bring new solutions. As an executive or professional, you need to help invent the new ideas that will carry the company forward. If you are the president or chief executive, you need to have a vision for where the company is going and why that is important. And everyone at every level needs to be able to communicate these messages and ideas.

## Give Good Meetings

If you're like me and many others, you've often thought, "I could really enjoy this job if it weren't for the meetings."

As a person building your self-brand, you want to be known for great meetings. This is particularly true when you are leading the meeting and have more control. But even when you are not in charge, you'll want to navigate your way through them successfully. To do that, you must understand the hidden rules.

These are the four basic types of meetings that you will encounter again and again in business:

- ▶ The staff meeting
- ▶ The "I want something" meeting
- ▶ The "move the project forward" meeting
- ▶ The presentation meeting

Let's look at what characterizes each one.

## Staff Meeting

We are all familiar with the staff meeting, the team update with your boss and all your colleagues. Prepare beforehand a short synopsis of your three major points on key projects or issues and why they are important. This is not the meeting for droning on about the nine projects in your group or the detail of your call to Harry in legal.

Never introduce an initiative that your boss has not already approved or argue for a project at the staff meeting. The keywords for staff meetings are "brief," "informative," "informal," and "collegial."

## "I Want Something" Meeting

This meeting generally takes place with your boss or a small group of executives when you are seeking approval for something: a new project or initiative, a budget increase, or a promotion.

 **TALKING POINTS MEMO: A bulleted one-pager for your eyes only that prepares you for important meetings and interviews. All the key points should be linked to make a compelling argument for your recommendation.**

This is your time to showcase your persuasive skills and a well-thought-out rationale or plan of action. It helps to prepare a talking points memo beforehand. This memo is your practice sheet with bulleted points. That way you can build a logical rationale and have all the facts at your fingertips.

Don't forget to weave in stories or anecdotes that will help defend and sell your request with passion and supporting facts.

### "Move the Project Forward" Meeting

This is a team meeting pulled together to launch a major initiative and follow it though until completion. Because this type of meeting is cross-functional, one person usually is selected to be the team leader.

If you are the team leader, make your command of this type of meeting a notable characteristic of your brand. Take charge of the agenda by keeping the discussion lively but moving forward without acting like a drill sergeant. (If you do, you'll get the job done, but you won't have any friends.) If you are a team member, be prepared to discuss your progress and provide a handout for the group if there are a lot of moving parts.

### Presentation Meeting

This is the most important type of meeting if you have self-branding aspirations.

At this type of meeting, you will be presenting a proposal, pitching a new prospect, updating senior management on an initiative, or speaking to a large group on an industry topic or broader issue.

## Take a Cue from Performers

A presentation is a performance.

Great presentations (like great performances and branding messages) come about by focusing on your audience. Actors and performers often do a mental rehearsal along with other preparatory exercises before they go onstage. The goal is to get in the right frame of mind to give a peak performance. Take a few minutes of mental quiet. Visualize success before you go onstage to speak. Imagine walking confidently onto the stage. Imagine hearing your voice speaking. Imagine being witty and engaging. Imagine the audience's applause. You might even want to have a personal trigger word or mantra, a special word or phrase that speaks to you.

As you develop your presentation, think as actors do of *becoming the audience*. Rather than worry about yourself, think about the reaction you want to get from your audience. You could even visualize yourself as an audience member who has gotten involved in your ideas. Feel the warmth and energy of the audience. The technique of becoming the audience not only will relax you but will help you figure out what to say and how to say it.

Great presenters engage the hearts and minds of an audience. So speak colloquial English. Don't read your talk. Internalize it. You want to be confident that you know the message so that you can speak from the heart.

If you are to give a great talk, you must say something interesting. Think about hot buttons that will move people emotionally and hot buttons that will move people rationally.

(TM) **A talk is successful not when everyone nods in agreement but when some agree, some don't, and some are transformed by what you say.**

No audience wants to be bored, so don't give your listeners just the facts, with no unexpected or emotional connection. Pull the facts together in a way people haven't heard before. Tell a story that gets people emotionally involved in what you have to say. Bring a prop. Above all, aim for a magic moment that will make your talk memorable.

## Talk Personally, Not Formally

The trick to formal business communication, whether it's oral or written, is to make it sound informal. You need to build a relationship between a brand and a target audience. And you do that by being natural and engaging, rather than formal and businesslike.

It helps if you think of your business communication as a conversation with a colleague. Carry on a conversation in your head as you compose your thoughts. Think in terms of friendly engagement. Break the habit of relying on business jargon and technical terms.

You could tap into various influences in developing your speaking style. Listen to people around you who speak well and might help inspire your style: your minister or rabbi, executives in your company, speakers at networking or industry meetings.

Watch media personalities on television. Pay attention to their techniques and see if you could adapt one or more for yourself. Listen to the rhythm and cadence of their words.

## Bookend Your Best Stuff

The most important part of a presentation is the beginning. You win or lose your listeners in the first twenty seconds.

Display stage presence when you enter. Stand tall with your weight evenly distributed. If you are nervous, a good entrance will disguise it.

Plan your opening gambit. Open a talk with something unpredictable, something that will immediately grab the attention of the other people in the room.

Use contemporary news, stories, anecdotes, or examples to make your points. Pick words that paint a picture. Unusual words will impress your ideas in the minds of your listeners. Great speakers use language artfully to brand their ideas with an audience.

You need to hook your audience with a surprising statistic, news, or anecdote. Whatever it is, it should evoke an "aha!" from the audience. Say something that is different from the usual view (or why bother?). Too many talks are rehashes of what's been said before.

You also want to end on a high note. Keep a surprise or special story for the end, so that you leave your audience wanting more. The end of your talk is as important as the beginning. It's the same in brand advertising. The beginning and end of a television commercial are carefully planned to capture attention and impart the brand message.

## Slow Down and Pause

Leave space around your words by talking slowly and pausing. Just these two things will make a dramatic difference in your presentations or any type of spoken communication.

Pause at important points, such as at the beginning, when presenting key ideas, or while telling a story. When you slow things down, you give your listeners the opportunity to hear your ideas and to comprehend them and become emotionally involved. It will also make you seem more confident if you don't appear to be rushing through your message.

Pausing gives you a chance to take deep, relaxing breaths.

Try to carry these speaking habits into all areas of verbal communication. Most people talk too fast at meetings, on the phone, or when leaving a voice-mail message. As a result, they undercut their effectiveness as communicators.

## Sonic Branding

Sound and voice can be powerful branding devices. Brand managers hire composers to come up with a sonic logo, a sound that signifies the brand like its logo does visually. Most of us can recognize McDonald's "Ba da ba ba ba" *sonic logo* or NBC's three-note chime that it's used since 1929.

Then there's the human voice that represents the brand, generally done by voice-over artists like the English actor Jake Wood, who does the Cockney voice of the GEICO gecko, or Billy Crudup, who does the voice-over in MasterCard's Priceless commercials.

A voice is like DNA; it is unique and recognizable. If voice branding weren't powerful—if you didn't recognize and respond to the voices of Tom Hanks, Ellen DeGeneres, Queen Latifah, Jeff Bridges, Kevin Spacey, and Eddie Murphy—there would be no point in paying stars millions of dollars to do voice-overs in animated films or television commercials.

 **BRAINSTORMER: Recording Your Voice**

Record yourself talking and play it back. Listen to it.

What do you hear?

What does your voice say about you?

Record yourself again. This time, try to put more resonance in your voice by speaking from the diaphragm. Work on your inflection by practicing speaking at a lower pitch. Then think of ways that you could improve your voice and vocal delivery.

## Find Your Voice

The voice is a potent branding device. Your voice brands you as male or female, obviously, but it can also brand you as upper class or working class, from the big city or the countryside, as native born or immigrant, even as a leader or a follower. Studies show that an attractive voice increases your attractiveness. So if you have a nice voice, keep talking!

An unforgettable voice can linger in the mind for decades, like the sexy, whispery voice of Marilyn Monroe singing "Happy Birthday, Mr. President" to John F. Kennedy. A soft, affectless, low-energy voice can brand you as weak, while a deep, low-pitched voice with high energy connotes power. On the other hand, a high-pitched voice can brand you as nervous or excitable.

While many Americans view accented English as charming, if you have a heavy foreign or regional accent it could hold you back in your career. Your voice can be an easy thing to fix by working with a speech coach. And you won't have to worry about people tuning you out because they can't understand you or find you hard to follow.

As a brander, you want a voice that not only is easy to understand, but that projects power, emotion, and your personality. You want a voice that is in sync with your brand. Have you ever met someone whose voice seemed to contradict his appearance? If you've ever done online dating, you know what I mean.

The best voice for each of us is our natural voice—not too high and not too low. Good speakers also alter their speed, volume, inflection, and pitch as they make their points, keeping people engaged in their message.

Listen to your voice on a recorder. How does it sound? Is it too high? Too soft? You use your voice all the time in meetings and in the cell-phone and voice-mail world of your business life. Is it in tune with your visual identity and your self-brand strategy?

People will brand you by the way you speak, sound, and present your ideas, and they will judge you and your ideas accordingly.

If you are not happy with the sound, pitch, or cadence of your voice, work with it. You'll find that people respond to a lower-pitch voice rather than a higher-pitch voice. Try to develop a rhythm that works best for you.

## Cut Back on Powerpoint Bullets

Too many presentations are like trial by PowerPoint: too many slides, too many words, too many points. Better to take a presentation—zen approach with more visual, less wordy slides.

One of the problems with PowerPoint is that it homogenizes your message. Everything looks the same, from headlines to bullet points. Even if you say something memorable, it will be hard for the audience to pick it out and remember it in a sea of similar-looking slides. Here are my pointers for an effective slide presentation:

- ▶ *Make yourself and your message the star, not the slides:* Fight the monotony by limiting your slides to those that dramatize your message.
- ▶ *Follow the 10/20/30 Rule:* In his book *The Art of the Start*, Guy Kawasaki advises people to limit themselves to ten slides, twenty minutes, and thirty-point fonts when making a pitch: "The fewer slides you need, the more compelling your idea."
- ▶ *Use pictures, diagrams, and illustrations:* Don't rely on just words to make your points. Be dramatic visually.
- ▶ *Develop a brand look for your slides:* Put your logo on the master slide, add a signature background color, or have a graphic artist design a branded template that will set your presentation apart.

## Take the Stage

One advantage of cutting back on the PowerPoint bullets habit is that you'll no longer be hiding from your audience.

You'll be able to harness the visual cues of gesture, posture, and appearance that contribute as much as 75 percent to an audience's opinion of a speaker. After all, you must engage the audience if you want to build your self-brand. You can't do that if your listeners don't experience you because they are busy trying to follow slide after slide.

Take the stage and enter the room with energy and confidence. Make eye contact with your audience. If you aren't looking at the audience when you start to talk, you won't get your listeners' attention. The development of a relationship begins with eye contact and full frontal engagement.

John F. Kennedy was said to look at people first in one eye and then in the other, a technique called "planting." In a large group, you can isolate a few people to make eye contact with. You want each person to feel that you are talking directly to him or her.

Don't let paper come between you and the audience, either. Know the message well enough so that you don't need to read it. (You can always put notes on index cards and keep them in your pocket, or use your slides as triggers.) Use gestures or any animating movement that's natural to you. You want to make the audience feel your passion.

It's very powerful to expand the space you take on the stage. Just walking around on the stage will captivate the audience, and the closer you get to the audience, the more impact you will have. John Chambers, the chief executive of Cisco Systems, likes to walk around on the stage and into the audience like a talk show host. People have labeled him one of the most dynamic corporate speakers in America.

Pay attention to the room size. Your aim is to build a relationship between you and the audience, no matter how big or how small. Always ask for a room that is just the right size for the group. You don't want a lot of empty seats, which will drain energy from the room.

## Don't Numb Them With Numbers

Too often, business presentations are a sea of statistics—bullet, bullet, bullet; number, number, number; pie chart, pie chart, pie chart. Unless you're speaking to numbers people, don't cite a lot of numbers. Focus on the important ones if you want them to be remembered. You can also bring numbers to life through several techniques:

- ▶ *Show and tell:* Read a customer letter or relate an anecdote that brings the statistic to life.
- ▶ *Use an analogy:* Compare the number to something tangible from everyday life that people can understand. For example, you could say that the cost of funding a project is less than the cost of supplying the coffee machine on the sixth floor for a year.

▶ *Put the number in a time context:* Use established data in your comparison. For example, explain that savings from technology has cut production cost to one-tenth of what it was just two years ago.

## Tattoo a Visual Image in the Mind

If you tell people something, they will tune out. Involve them in your ideas and who you are with visual stories, metaphors and examples. That way you create a picture in their minds that can be indelible like a tattoo.

Think of how you can make a visual connection, either figuratively or literally, to make a point. A sales colleague, Toni, was applying for a sales job with a company in the horticulture industry, an area where she had no sales experience. But gardening was Toni's new passion. She had even won second place in flower arranging at the county fair. So Toni crafted a cover letter for her résumé that talked of her new passion for plants and included a picture of her at the fair with her red ribbon and winning bouquet. She got a call the next day and landed the job.

## Study the Eloquent President

Need to improve your presentation skills?

Become a student of good speaking. Study good speakers at events or on television or even from history. Then develop and practice your presentation so that you have a powerful delivery. Pay special attention to how your talk will *sound* to the audience.

Abraham Lincoln is one of my favorite mentors in the art of speaking well. In *The Eloquent President*, Ronald C. White Jr. points out that Lincoln was "fascinated by the sound of words." Lincoln "wrote for the ear," while most politicians "write for the eye." Lincoln said the words and expressions out loud as he was composing a talk. And it made a dramatic difference.

Lincoln wrote and spoke in plain talk. He used Saxon words and simple sentence constructions and avoided the Latinate words and flowery rhetoric that were popular at the time.

White points out that, while the average person speaks at 150 to 160 words per minute, Lincoln spoke at 105 to 110 words per minute. Once, when he was unable to get to Springfield, Illinois, to give a speech himself, he mailed the speech with the request "read it slowly."

Lincoln kept his talks and letters short. He was always editing to condense and shorten them. His second inaugural address still clocks in as the second shortest. There's a wonderful story about the photographer setting up to take a picture of Lincoln speaking at Gettysburg. Lincoln got up, spoke, and sat back down, and the photographer was still setting up his equipment. (The Gettysburg Address was about two minutes long.)

Lincoln incorporated many literary devices in his talks, such as parallel construction, alliteration, and assonance. He used the device of organizing in threes, or triplets ("of the people, for the people, by the people," and "We cannot dedicate, we cannot consecrate, we cannot hallow this ground"). He used words to create vivid visual images ("bind the nation's wounds").

**BRAINSTORMER: Video Study Hall**

Study great speakers on the Internet, on YouTube, or in the TED Conference talks at www.ted.com

## Practice, Practice, Practice

Another story about the Gettysburg Address offers a valuable lesson. We have all heard that Lincoln wrote the Gettysburg Address on the back of an envelope while he was riding the train to the battle site.

It is true that Lincoln was the last person to be invited to speak. He received the formal invitation just three weeks before the Gettysburg dedication. But, according to White, Lincoln may have been asked orally before that.

Nonetheless, Lincoln worked on his remarks for at least three weeks. And he kept working on his Gettysburg remarks until the final minutes before he spoke. Some of the most memorable parts of the address, such as "of the people, by the people, for the people," were phrases Lincoln had been exploring earlier in his writings and talks.

The Gettysburg Address was not written spontaneously on the back of an envelope in a flash of brilliance.

No one, not even a person known for eloquence, like Lincoln, writes and delivers memorable talks without lots of preparation and practice. It's the case with all great speakers and presenters. Winston Churchill's secretary said that he spent one hour in preparation for every one minute of a speech. That means he would spend thirty hours preparing for a thirty-minute talk!

While you do want to practice, you don't want to overwork yourself just before your talk. Use that time to slowly get warmed up like actors do. The actress Sissy Spacek says she thinks of it like catching a train. You want to build up your energy so that you and the train gain speed together and you hop on and give your performance.

## Give Riveting Backstory

Perhaps the most engaging thing you can do with an audience is share personal stories and anecdotes about your struggles and triumphs. Steve Jobs told three stories at the commencement address he gave to the 2005 Stanford University graduating class.

The first story was about "connecting the dots." Jobs talked about being adopted and about dropping out of Reed College after six months, as well as about auditing courses that gave him inspiration later when he founded Apple. The second story was about "love and loss." Jobs spoke of losing his job at Apple, the company he had founded and loved. His initial anger gave way to a new period of creativity as he founded NeXT and Pixar, and met his wife.

The third story was about "death." Jobs told how he had been diagnosed with pancreatic cancer earlier that year. He thought he would have just months to live, but the cancer turned out to be a rare form that could be treated surgically.

Jobs talked about how each of these experiences turned out to be the best thing that could have happened to him at the time. He learned that "your time is so limited, so don't waste it living someone else's life."

At the end of his talk, Jobs left his audience with an image and a wish. He talked about the *Whole Earth Catalog*, "one of the bibles of my generation." He described the cover of the final issue, a picture of a country road, "the kind you might find yourself hitchhiking on if you were so adventurous," with the words "Stay Hungry. Stay Foolish." "And I have always wished that for myself," he said. "And now, as you graduate to begin anew, I wish that for you. Stay Hungry. Stay Foolish."

In his address, Jobs tapped into the power of telling authentic stories, personal stories that were right for this audience since they were about identity and life choices, and success, failure, and renewal. Jobs framed the speech using the device of three—"just three stories." His words were so compelling that people started talking about the speech, and it spread by word of mouth. (I read it when it was reproduced in its entirety in *Fortune* magazine.)

## The Power of Three

The power of three is an important principle to remember when putting together a talk or story. Stories usually have a three-act structure. Classic stories and fables have three obstacles that must be overcome, three wishes granted, or three main characters.

There are "The Three Little Pigs," "Three Blind Mice," "Goldilocks and the Three Bears," *The Three Musketeers*, and the list goes on and on. Even today, how many stories have you heard about the rabbi, the priest, and the minister?

When you're presenting options in a pitch, three is the right number, not five or ten or twenty. One or two is too few, yet four or more will lead to confusion and the lack of a decision. Studies show that it is easy to grasp three points or elements, but when you throw a fourth in, the mind gets confused and wanders. Make it easy on your audience and stick to three.

Three is often a good internal structure to use in a talk for expressing an idea or to simplify the logic around an argument or point of view. The U.S. Declaration of Independence speaks of "Life, liberty, and the pursuit of happiness," and France's motto is "Liberty, Equality, Fraternity." The number three has a sense of completeness that is powerful.

## Fuse a Style

The lesson of great speakers is to study great orators and presenters who "speak" to you and use the inspiration they give you to create something uniquely your own.

After his keynote address at the 2004 Democratic National Convention, Barack Obama explained the sources of his speaking style to Anna Deveare Smith: "I tap into the tradition that a lot of African Americans tap into and that's the church. It's the church blended with a smattering of Hawaii and Indonesia and maybe Kansas, and I've learned a lot of the most important things in life from literature. I've been a professor of law. I'm accustomed to making an argument. When I am effective, it's coming from my gut."

Humor is a great way to make your presentation indelibly your own—not using canned jokes, but telling about events in a humorous way. If you can make them laugh, you can make them buy your ideas. Laughter builds rapport. Humor is a hard thing to do well, but like any presentation skill, the more you observe people who use humor in their speaking and the more you do it, the better you will be.

Fuse your own speaking presence out of your strengths and the stylistic devices and speaking styles that work for you.

## Sharpen Your Point of View

In professional communications, it's important to bring more of yourself into the equation. People will be excited by your take on the facts and how you present your ideas. When you bring more of yourself and your ideas into the equation, chances are that your audience will not only understand what you are talking about but will listen and respond to what you are saying.

An effective way of standing out is to have a defining point of view (POV)—your own "voice," a self-brand POV. Great self-brands create a philosophy. And the bolder and less conventional your point of view is, the more riveting it will be.

 **SELF-BRAND POV: Your own mental angle on the world, with a set of values and a narrative that ties it all together.**

Your self-brand POV could be a point of view on your industry, where it's heading, and what needs to be done to attain future success. It could be about your customers and what you or your department could offer them that they are not currently getting. It could be about anything.

We all need to hear viewpoints that help us frame the debate on topics of interest. That's why many of us turn to certain commentators, columnists, or news outlets, particularly to news sources with a point of view that supports our own. People want more than accuracy, they want an opinion that makes sense of all the facts. And news producers can use a defining point of view as branding and marketing tools.

It will help you in your career, too; you will be viewed as a person with a point of view—a brand—someone who is different from the norm.

## The Sparkling Introduction

Every time you give a presentation or introduce someone in a meeting you have an opportunity to move the group emotionally. Try to include an element of surprise, a nugget that's fresh, or a revelation that's unexpected so your audience has an "aha" moment. Or use humor, which is the best way to get the group aroused.

At the Women in the World Summit in New York City in 2012, the Oscar-winning actress Meryl Streep introduced Secretary of State Hillary Clinton. Now, Clinton is perhaps the most scrutinized woman in the world, so what new twist would Streep come up with? She began her introduction with a setup and punch line much like comedians use. Streep first mentioned their shared history. Both were raised in middle-class families by strong, warm-hearted mothers. Both went to public schools and to prestigious women's colleges. Both went on to Yale. But, Streep revealed, while she was a cheerleader, Clinton was the president of the student government. "And there, the two paths in the woods diverged."

Streep went on to deliver an emotional tribute to Clinton, emphasizing that it's "not a simple job to be a role model." She continued, "But while we are busy relating to her, judging her, assessing her hair, her jackets, supporting her, worrying if she's getting enough sleep, she's just been busy working. Doing it. Making those words—'Women's rights are human rights'—into something every leader in every country now knows are a lynchpin of American policy."

Then, Streep waved her Oscar in the air—showing off the trophy she won in 2012 for *The Iron Lady*—as she said, "This is what you get when you *play* a world leader, but *this*," gesturing toward Clinton backstage, "is what you get when you *are* one."

## Brand It

You could use a provocative stance and personality as a defining stamp. Or introduce a signature element that becomes a trademark of your presentations. At the State of the Union address, the president acknowledges everyday American heroes who are present in the audience. It's become a branded element of the address.

Whatever your personal style, here are ten guidelines for moving your presentations from good to great:

1. *Start out strong:* Your opening lines will make or break your presentation. So begin with dramatic news, a tie-in with a current event, or an amusing story that will grab attention. (President Kennedy surprised his audience when he began his talk at the Berlin Wall in German: "Ich bin ein Berliner!") Don't forget to make a strong entrance and show some stage presence. (Standing straight and evenly on both feet will go a long way toward building presence.)

2. *Use stories and examples:* Bring each point to life through an anecdote, a story, or an example. People remember stories. That's why parables and stories have been used throughout time. Give your audience backstory that fills in behind-the-scenes details or your personal struggles.

3. *Control the message:* Think strategically about the substance of your message. Develop a few key themes around a central point of view. What is the best way to affect this audience emotionally with what you want to say? What is the best way to persuade them rationally? Weave in both as you develop your themes.

4. *Brand it with your brand:* Let your personality and point of view come through. Make your talk indelibly your own through your presence, style, and way of speaking. Develop a branded element, such as a show-and-tell prop, to strengthen your point.

5. *Finish strong:* The ending is as important as the beginning. Think of a memorable takeaway phrase for your idea and leave your audience with it. Always end on a high note, so that the audience will want more. Use the question-and-answer period to repeat your message in a new way, not to get into new themes. Even if you're hit with a trick question, stand firm and answer with one of your key messages.

6. *Coin words and sound bites:* Harness the power of names and sound bites for key ideas and concepts throughout, so that what you say is unforgettable.

7. *Use the branding power of your voice:* Your voice can have a dramatic impact or undercut your message. Put resonance in your voice by

speaking from the diaphragm. Speak in as low a tone as is natural. Practice your speech out loud, record it, and listen to your delivery. Use emotion in your voice to underscore a point.

8. *Talk (don't read) to one person:* Think in terms of talking to one specific person, and you will be less likely to pontificate or to be overly formal. Don't let a written speech or slides come between you and the audience. Likewise, use the simple words and colloquial expressions that you would use in conversation.

9. *Pause and slow down:* Don't rush through a talk. Leave air around your key ideas so that you don't reduce or eliminate the impact of your lines. You should always feel that you are speaking too slowly when you are giving a speech.

10. *Offer something new:* How often have you sat through a presentation and thought, "I've heard all that before"? Always bring some fresh content to your talk. Having a surprise—something bold the audience didn't expect—is even better.

## Master Difficult Talks

Not every business talk will be a motivational pitch filled with good news, nor will every talk be given to a group of adoring fans. A difficult conversation involves communicating a message that you don't want to deliver and the other person doesn't want to hear. Or it's finding a way to connect with a person or group who has a different mind-set or point of view from yours.

The vast majority of managers say they have trouble giving a negative performance review to an employee, and many find pitching themselves to be a difficult conversation. (If you're reading this book, you should be on your way to mastering the personal pitch.) How do you master the art of difficult conversations, so that you end up with a more or less positive outcome?

The key is delivering the message honestly, fully, and with empathy. Show that you understand the other person's point of view and then share yours or give the bad news you have to deliver.

As much as you might prefer to delay a meeting where you have to convey bad news or do it over the phone, difficult conversations are best done in person and always privately. When Yahoo! CEO Carol Bartz was fired in 2011, she immediately sent an e-mail to all employees that began:

"I am very sad to tell you that I've just been fired over the phone by Yahoo's Chairman of the Board." The way she was fired—over the phone—became the media story rather than her job performance.

## Negotiate and Ask

Use your personal-branding skills in negotiating and in the follow-up to every pitch you make. The key is not just discussing *what* the other party wants but finding out *why*, so you can frame your response effectively and persuade the other person to your view. This will bring you closer to what you want.

You will uncover more options in the negotiation, some of which may not have even occurred to you. For example, if there is a stumbling block over salary or your fee, the "why" may be the P&L budget line. Maybe there are perks or other benefits that can make up the difference and that are accounted for differently.

Of course, you are in the best negotiating position when you are willing to walk away or have other options. That's why it's important to determine before a negotiation what your bottom line is. And if you don't get that, you have to walk. Otherwise, you just made a bad deal for yourself.

Asking the right questions can make a big difference: Ask, "Can you explain how you got to that number?" Understanding the other side's rationale gives you valuable information and a way to apply the principles of empathy in your response. Another tactic is, "I need to talk this over with my team." Stalling gives you time to slow things down and think things over.

One of the smartest tactics is to ask, "Would you consider. . . ?" It sounds inviting and undemanding, and can work like magic. And you can always play dumb and ask, "Can you explain this again?" Making the other side talk more often leads to options.

## Beware of E-Mail!

Not long ago, I sent a prospecting e-mail to a woman I'll call Sally, an executive I didn't know very well. But I wrote the e-mail in a somewhat chatty style, since we had worked together briefly at the same company some years back.

Now, when you are making a business pitch, a lot of your effort comes to naught or takes a while to develop. But because I had known Sally casually at a previous job, I wasn't prepared for her curt, one-sentence e-mail reply.

Frankly, it stopped me in my tracks. It sounded so strident and impersonal. I got a totally different impression of her.

And it's not surprising. New neuroscience research shows that communicating by e-mail is an emotional wasteland. We don't see the other person, as we do when we meet in person. We can't convey our emotions as we can over the phone. Even letters tend to be rich in content, nuance, and emotion.

There's something so quick and efficient about e-mail that we dash them off quickly, without flourishes or any warm and fuzzy feelings at all. It's easy to rush responses off to get through your e-mail backlog and lose touch with how you're coming across. That's why e-mail can increase the likelihood of misunderstanding. That's why my philosophy is to use e-mail only for positive messages. You can use e-mail for a polite brush off (PBO), but if you need to deliver a negative message, try to do it in person.

(TM) **E-mail is an emotional wasteland.**
**Add something personal before you hit "Send."**

With e-mail, it's also easy to forget how something we've written can come back to bite us. E-mail messages can have a long life even after you've erased them, as many people have regretfully discovered.

E-mails can be dredged up in dismissals and lawsuits, upending your promising career. So be careful not to send anything that could come back to haunt you, like this e-mail from a top corporate executive to a direct report that got sensationalized in the business news: "I think about us together all the time. Little moments like watching your face when you kiss me." Once you hit "Send," it's out of your control.

Observe good e-mail etiquette. To me, that means avoiding "urgent" flags (unless the matter truly is); breaking the cute habit of using emoticons, those little faces made up of punctuation symbols; or employing the annoying "notify sender."

## Craft Your Voice Mail

With voice mail, people can't see you but they can hear your voice, which is a very potent branding device. Think of how quickly you can identify a friend just by hearing a word or two, or recognize a celebrity doing a voice-over in a TV commercial or an animated movie.

Take a moment to put yourself in a confident, positive state of mind before you speak. Put a smile on your face as you leave the message. It will make a big difference in the way you are perceived.

Above all, keep voice-mail messages short and to the point. There's nothing more annoying than a rambling message. So, resist the temptation to go into a lot of detail explaining the whys and wherefores of your call. For example, a good message might be, "Sidney, I hope you can attend the meeting on the X project next Thursday. I'm going to recommend a new vendor and I know you've been dissatisfied with the last company as well. With your support, I'm confident we can get the project back on track."

## Mend Your Speech a Bit

If you're ambitious and want to take your brand somewhere in the world, communicating and speaking well are skills you'll need to master. The higher you go, the more you will be asked to speak at industry meetings and give presentations to the executive committee, the board, or employees.

You'll know it when your way of communicating clicks.

There will be that wonderful moment in a meeting when you feel at one with the audience. You know it when you're connecting—both the content of your message and the way you deliver it is breaking through. You're fully present and looking at your audience. Some are smiling. Others are signaling that they have a question. You can feel the energy in the room.

That's when you'll know what it feels like to be a powerful communicator. That's when you'll know it was worth the effort to develop your verbal edge.

Personal communication is a crucial skill for anyone embarking on the journey toward becoming a self-brand. It's a skill that few of us are born with. But we can all develop a wonderful personal style through practice.

After all, if you're not selling your recommendation, yourself, or your product, you've got to learn how to do it, fast. Otherwise, you're wasting everybody's time. You'd be better off just cutting to the chase and mailing in what you were planning to say. And that will have very little self-branding power.

---

 **IN A NUTSHELL:** The eighth secret of self-brands: Cultivate a powerful communication style, a voice that is heard because of what you say and how you say it.

# CHAPTER 9

# Master the Art of the Elevator Speech and Pitch Yourself Anytime, Anywhere

*Glendower: "I can call spirits from the vasty deep."*
*Hotspur: "Why, so can I, or so can any man;*
*But will they come when you do call for them?"*

William Shakespeare
*Henry IV, Part One* (III, 1)

You got the interview. It's the perfect job, so you spent the last week researching the company and fine-tuning your résumé. But you blew it in the first few minutes because you planned everything but the most important thing—making a great first impression when you're asked an open-ended question like "Tell me about yourself."

The most important story you'll ever have to tell is the one you (like most of us) are probably most uncomfortable delivering—your own.

You have to believe in your value or you won't be able to compete with others who are adept at the elevator speech, a short personal commercial told in a minute or two that perfectly summarizes the value you bring. And you have to believe in your value in order to say it so others do too.

After all, if you can't market yourself and your professional abilities, who will? The promoter-in-chief for Brand You has to be you!

 **The best personal branders have a knack for promoting themselves without seeming to promote themselves.**

Smart branders realize that they always have to be selling themselves and their value, and the best do it with a lot of finesse. They're so good that they don't seem to be tooting their own horn. It doesn't feel like a pitch but a natural conversation that seamlessly and artfully weaves in positive business stories and credentials.

Masters of self-promotion also realize that opportunities abound for variations on the elevator speech, even in the elevator, as one of my clients discovered.

## Going Up, Please

Marisa is an ambitious, hardworking executive.

Every morning she takes the elevator up to her office, and most days she goes in early to get a jump on her projects. And sometimes the CEO of her division pops into the elevator with her.

Marisa was scared to talk. But she was also scared not to talk. So she would talk about the weather.

Then, after being introduced to personal branding, Marisa started paying more attention to business dynamics and her performance.

Lo and behold, Marisa again found herself in the elevator with the CEO. Then a colleague, Bob, entered the elevator. When Bob saw the CEO, he jauntily said, "John, great to run into you. I'm Bob Jones on the ABC team, and you'll be glad to know that we had a wonderful meeting with the new client. We came up with a novel solution that will save them money, and we did an even bigger deal than we expected."

The beaming CEO said, "Bob, you just made my day." And he didn't stop with the proverbial pat on the back, either. The CEO actually patted Bob on the back as he was getting out of the elevator.

Now, Marisa was already thinking about personal branding power and how to be perceived as a leader, but there's nothing like a little reality show to convince her. Marisa felt like she had been slapped in the face with a fish.

Later, in my office, she became reflective. "I just saw firsthand what you're talking about, Catherine. Bob is branding himself as the next VP. And what am I doing? I'm branding myself as the weather girl."

Bingo.

Not knowing how to brand ourselves in business is an obstacle that many of us need to overcome.

## Take a Seat at the Table

When you're not able to participate in the business conversation or market yourself or your group's activities and accomplishments, like Marisa, you risk branding yourself as lacking confidence or not up to a bigger job. It's a missed opportunity to brand yourself for success and build important business relationships.

Of course, you could look at Bob as a self-promoter. On the other hand, why brand it that way? Bob shared positive business news that the CEO was eager to hear. Both are on the same mission to grow the business, after all.

Marisa got on the branding bandwagon and learned how to talk about her team and projects when she bumped into senior managers or colleagues, or in more formal situations when she was pitching herself for a lateral move or stretch assignment.

Marisa later told me that mastering the elevator speech made a major difference in her career. No longer seen as the weather girl, she was part of the business conversation and part of the company team. Later, the CEO recommended her for the company's high-potential program. Today, she has a senior position at the company.

## It's Never Carved in Stone

Your elevator speech is something that you will be working on, tweaking, and perfecting for the rest of your life. It's like your résumé but better, because it's more casual, more nuanced, and has more of your personality in it.

Your aim is to find a way of saying who you are in a unique way. You want to let your personality come through.

The words you use to introduce yourself and tell your story can be powerful and memorable, or instantly forgettable. Many people tell a long-winded story that's incoherent in terms of a selling message. Or they use corporate jargon and insider acronyms so people are left wondering who they are and what they do.

## Prepare an Elevator Speech Template

There are so many things in life you can't control, the economy and the unemployment rate, for example. But you can control how you come across in your elevator speech and on your résumé. Yet, many clients worry about the things they can't control rather than focusing on those they can: developing a great elevator speech and job marketing package.

Never is an elevator speech more important than when you are interviewing and networking for a new job, a promotion, or a stretch assignment.

Remember, when someone says in an interview, "Tell me about yourself," what she is really asking is, "What can you do for us?" So the elevator speech is never really about you, but about the other person and how you can help her. Even in a networking situation, when someone asks, "What do you do?" what she wants to know is, "Do I want to get to know this person?" A compelling elevator speech needs to answer the real question behind the question.

Here's how to do it.

The best elevator speeches are crafted in three parts, a beginning, a middle, and an end.

### The Beginning: Grab Them at Hello

The beginning of your elevator speech is the most important part, so try to make it as memorable as you can. One way to do that is with a hook that locks in your self-brand idea. Try to express your brand idea in a personal brand sentence, a differentiating line that positions you differently and succinctly defines your brand.

 **Your brand sentence is your differentiator, a line that captures the essence of your brand identity.**

Your brand sentence is the core idea you want people to remember about you. It should describe your value proposition—the value you bring that's different from what others bring. In other words, it should convey the impact or key results that you produce.

Often, the best brand sentences take a page from the advertising playbook and are memorable, visual, and catchy, like an advertising tagline in a television commercial. For example, the brand sentence used by a New York City market researcher who specializes in the female market is "I'm the Oprah of Madison Avenue." Or a game-changing finance executive could say, "I'm the Steve Jobs of finance."

If you're a business development executive, you want to emphasize how you build revenue. For example, a sales executive in new media defined her brand this way: "I reimagine underperforming assets across the converging worlds of Hollywood, Silicon Valley, and Wall Street."

If you're in a field like accounting where there is an alphabet soup of credentials you can acquire, lead with a value proposition that includes your credentials and Big Four accounting experience. It will differentiate you from candidates who don't have blue-chip credentials.

To differentiate myself from other business coaches, I often say, "I'm a personal brand strategist—a cross between a P&G brand manager and an executive coach." Then I might add that I have a background in product marketing and advertising and make the point that I help people apply principles and strategies from the commercial world of branding to themselves.

(TM) **The first fifteen seconds and first fifteen words of your elevator pitch are the most important.**

The reason metaphors and analogies work so well in branding is that they give us something visual and unexpected to associate with a product or person. A metaphor compares two things that are different in most ways but alike in one important way. So it locks in your brand in a clever fashion.

Brand copywriters use other literary devices like alliteration, rhyme, and repetition to construct memorable brand taglines and catchphrases, and you should too. Think of the way the words sound when you say them. Do they sound pleasing or unusual? If they do, you're on the right track.

Remember, your brand sentence should contain a metaphor, keyword, or phrase, and a value proposition that defines why you are different, or even better, than others. It should encapsulate the one thought that you want people to associate with you. Here's a brainstormer to help you draft the brand sentence that will kick off your elevator speech, and to give you ideas for other sound bites you might be able to use in your elevator speech.

---

**BRAINSTORMER: Developing Ideas for Your Brand Sentence, Your Differentiator**

What specific qualities or abilities make you different, even better, than others?

Unlike others in my field, I . . .

I am a cross between _____ and

_____.

My job title says _____ but in reality, I'm

_____.

My tagline (philosophy or mantra) is:

A metaphor for my career identity is:

My brand sentence is:

(Underline the keyword or phrase that you want people to remember about you.)

---

## The Middle: Develop a Brand Narrative

Your opening brand sentence sets up your value proposition and the narrative of your elevator speech. The core narrative should take people on a journey, a journey that uncovers your career story and the distinct value that you bring in business. Your core narrative must answer these questions, "What do you help people or businesses do?" and "How do you help companies win?" And it should do that in an interesting and coherent way.

In crafting the core narrative of your elevator pitch, put yourself in the mind-set of the person you are talking to. The core story in an elevator pitch for a job interview will be more formal than one for casual encounters with your company's executives, and should include credentials, accomplishments, and projects that would appeal to the person you are meeting with.

Think in terms of a plotline that tells a coherent story. It should reinforce your value proposition that you established in your brand sentence. It should make clear why you and your accomplishments are relevant in the current market.

If you're worried about sounding like you're bragging about yourself, tell your anecdotes in the third person, through the eyes of your client or your boss. For example, rather than saying, "I executed the project in half the time we expected it to take," you could say, "My boss couldn't believe we pulled it off in the time frame we had. In fact, he bet me $5 that we couldn't. It was very sweet collecting that bet."

There's nothing more powerful than third-party endorsements. If you've been thinking like a brand, you should have letters of recommendation from bosses and clients, and hopefully they're passionate letters from people with gravitas. If you don't have letters, reach out and ask. Most people are willing to help. Try to weave into your brand narrative a quote from a boss or colleague about a project that you worked on or how your performance was an asset to the company. You can include the letters of recommendation in your follow-up letter to the person you are interviewing with.

Remember, good elevator speeches have to make a compelling business argument for Brand You, one that is relevant for the job and person you are meeting with.

It's your story. You're both the author of your elevator speech and the storyteller. It's your job to craft the right story that makes the best case for a specific opportunity, not the other person's job to find out if you're a fit. Most people won't do the work unless you make it easy for them by crafting the right narrative.

Good branding always involves ruthless editing. In the commercial world of brands, a lot of effort is put into crafting the right message and making sure the right media buy is made to reach the right target audience. A lot of options are eliminated in the process.

You have to do the same. Tell the story that you want tell. Leave out the parts that are negative about companies, former bosses, and bad luck, unless they led to a turning point in your life. For example, the network workplace commentator Tory Johnson describes how she was fired unexpectedly from

NBC; she relates how "the permanent scar from that experience inspired her to shift from employee to entrepreneur and in 1999 she founded Women For Hire from a corner of her New York City apartment."

Only include examples and stories that relate to your brand positioning, where you want to take your career next, and the career opportunity you are pitching right then. Otherwise, you're likely to confuse people or, even worse, unsell yourself.

Early in my career, I decided to make the dramatic switch from Japanese art historian to advertising executive. It was a big leap, not for me as much as for the people I was interviewing with, so selling myself with a great elevator pitch was essential.

In interview after interview, my elevator speech bombed, and I wasn't getting any interview callbacks. As weeks went by and my money dwindled, I got frustrated and then started to panic.

In looking at my approach from the interviewer's perspective, I realized that I was not connecting the dots to where I wanted to go. The main focus of my résumé and elevator pitch was my academic achievements as an art historian, accomplishments that had little connection with a branding career. Rather than impressing my interviewers, my achievements branded me as an academic who wasn't right even for an entry-level job.

I decided to downplay my academic achievements and focus my elevator speech and résumé on my marketing experience at the Seattle Art Museum, limited though it was. In my new elevator speech, I positioned myself as a marketer for difficult products, noting that successfully promoting Asian art exhibits—a "difficult product"—to a U.S. audience demanded breakthrough marketing skills.

I also drew parallels between my academic experience and the process-oriented thinking needed in branding: understanding a client's business and the ability to distill information into what's essential, as well as the ability to move between the big picture and small details. Armed with a relevant elevator speech and résumé, I got traction and a job offer.

It's crucial to connect the dots for people and eliminate experiences that lead them in the wrong direction. It always has to be a true story, but you don't have to tell people everything you've ever done. You have to tell the right brand story for the situation.

Here are some brainstormer exercises to help you come up with examples for your core narrative in your elevator speech.

---

- 💡 - **BRAINSTORMER: Your Best Story**

List 3 memorable projects or accomplishments and why they are relevant.

The best or most challenging business experience I ever had was _____ because

_____.

Describe a peak experience and why it was so powerful:

---

## The End: Engage in a Conversation

You not only want your elevator speech to sound conversational, you want to have a conversation. So don't end your narrative with an emphatic conclusion or period. End with a question that will keep the conversation going.

If you're in a job interview, your question could be about the company, such as, "How would you describe the company culture?" If the company has been in the news, you could ask a question about that. Or you could take the conversation in a totally different direction and ask the interviewer how he got started in the business. You could also ask something specific about the job you are interviewing for, such as, "What are the three major things you want the person in this job to accomplish?" Even better, you can ask for the job: "I'm so excited about this opportunity. When can I start?"

If you're in a networking situation, you could say, "I am looking for X opportunity. Do you have thoughts on other people I should talk with?" If you ask for something vague, you are likely to get a vague reply. Most people want to help, so make it easy.

If you're trying to build a relationship with a mentor, your question could be, "I've always admired the way you've navigated your career through different business areas. I would love to talk with you about how you did that, because I would like to do that in my own career." The key is to get a conversation going and get the person talking. It's a cliché, but true: the more you get the other person to talk, the more he will think you are a great conversationalist and a great fit.

**BRAINSTORMER: Conversational To and Fro**

What are your questions?

## What's Your Pitch?

Here's a kickoff elevator speech used by a business executive at a networking event:

> *I'm Tom Smith. Growing things is my passion, but my green thumb is with nurturing small businesses into bigger businesses through cyberbranding. I'm a growth agent for corporations. For example, I led the effort to develop a web-based platform to market our company's business advisory services.*
>
> *Our primary market is mid- to large-sized companies serviced by our sales reps, so my boss didn't believe it would amount to anything. "You can't sell business-to-business over the Internet," he said. But now, he's a believer. We're getting 26 percent of our business from small companies we service over the web. I finally found my calling. My personal sweet spot is leveraging the Internet to expand the market for my company's products and services. How are you using the Internet to grow your businesses?*

Tom used a visual metaphor—gardening—to lock in his brand idea of being a growth agent. Then he gave a specific example of an initiative he spearheaded at the company—leveraging the Internet to open up new markets cost efficiently. And he brought the story to life with his boss's warning. Tom ended with a question to get a conversation going with the other person.

**BRAINSTORMER: Your Elevator Speech**

Looking at the work you did in the three previous brainstormers, draft your elevator speech.

## A Self-Fulfilling Prophecy

The way you replay specific memories shapes your life story, shapes your destiny even. That's why articulating your life and career in a drama is not just memorable branding, it will also help you understand who you are and will be.

There is a strong connection between the stories people tell and actual life experience, studies show—what often is called a self-fulfilling prophecy. The way we visualize and tell our life stories has a profound impact on how we think about ourselves, how we act, and even whether we succeed. The narratives we tell shape our experiences, so make yours positive and authentic, and try not to sell yourself short.

Changing the way we see ourselves and the stories we tell about ourselves may help us alter our narratives in a more positive direction. Always accentuate the good that came out of an experience rather than the bad. In studies, people who had sad stories but told them in reverse order, so that the sad story was linked to a good outcome, were more positive and grounded. (For example, positive people said, "I was able to discover an exciting new career for myself as a result of the downsizing at my company," rather than "I lost my job but finally I was able to get a job in a new career.")

What you don't want to do is tell a happy story marred by a dark detail. ("The job was a great opportunity in a good company but my boss is demanding and likes to micromanage.") A good way to move beyond painful memories is by thinking about these experiences in the third person. (For example, "Losing his job was a setback, but he's moved on now." But, of course, this is your mental self-talk not to be shared with others.) This will help you reframe the story for yourself and distance yourself from the experience so you're not stuck there.

 **Don't focus on what went wrong.
Focus on what you learned.**

In telling our stories, we learn what our experiences meant, even who we are and who we will become. That's one of the reasons I like telling stories so much. I finally can make sense of all of my different experiences.

If you tell stories about your ability to succeed, you are more likely to succeed in the future. Not that you don't have to take action, too, but it pays to get good at recasting memories so that you see the silver lining. It will help you reshape your bigger life story.

Good stories have a way of coming true if you focus and act on them long enough.

## The Emotional Power of Story

Story is the ancient secret of communication, and gives meaning to the facts and the figures, to the accomplishments and events you talk about in your elevator speech or, indeed, in any presentation. People remember things better when those things are presented in a narrative rather than as a list or in an expository paragraph. So don't give a catalogue of job functions in an interview or read a list of statistics from a slide during a presentation. Break away and tell a story. Stories persuade in a subtle way, because the listener gets involved in the story. The listener is pulled into what is taking place and what the underlying meaning is.

When you tell a story, you don't tell the other person that you are better or that your product or service is superior, you tell a story that leads her to that conclusion herself, so that she owns the decision.

The best storytellers, like the best actors, tap into sense memory, the memory of a specific emotional experience, so the audience can have an honest reaction to the emotions in a story. You want to take your listeners on an emotional journey with your story, even if it's the thrill of achieving your sales numbers in a tough economy.

## Create a Story Bank

As someone committed to personal branding, you'll want to have a roster of "for example" business stories and anecdotes that show what you're all about. You can include a story about getting your first big client. You can include one about a letter you received from a particular client that demonstrates your company's deep connection with its customers. You can include one about a career failure that led you to become a leader.

Begin by building a story bank of three to five business stories about one to two minutes in length. Obvious places to begin are with major challenges and accomplishments, but bring them to life in a short story that is visual and emotional.

Good storytellers simplify a story. Too many characters and subplots confuse people. Of course, you do want some colorful details so that people can visualize and "live" the experience.

 **Think like a movie director. Make your stories visual.**

You can use your stories in interviews when you're asked to talk about challenges and accomplishments. You can use them at networking events to bring your career identity to life. You can use them in presentations when you make a point, to break away from the numbers and stats and share how you achieved those numbers or solved a specific client problem. To learn more about how to give a great talk and use story, read Nick Morgan's book, *Give Your Speech, Change the World*, a book that influenced my approach to speaking and story, such as the quest story.

## The Quest Story

The quest is the hero's journey. It is an ancient tale type and is the most common story format. Many stories from around the world, like that of Ulysses, feature a hero who goes out from his everyday world on a journey into the larger world. He is tested with obstacles and hardships. Finally, he wins a decisive victory and comes back stronger and wiser as a result of his journey.

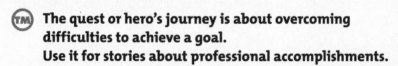 **The quest or hero's journey is about overcoming difficulties to achieve a goal.
Use it for stories about professional accomplishments.**

Business is all about setting and reaching goals, so the quest is a great format to use for a situation where it took time to achieve your goal and you had to overcome a lot of obstacles. Your story could be about overtaking your key competitor in the market, landing an important client, or fending off a new competitor. Emphasize your expertise, courage, and resilience in overcoming difficulties and highlight the thrill of achieving your goal.

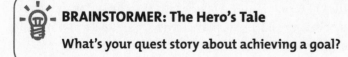 **BRAINSTORMER: The Hero's Tale**
**What's your quest story about achieving a goal?**

## The Leader's Tale

The leader's tale is the story of how you became a leader, discovered your purpose, and inspired others to achieve great things under your leadership. Throughout history people have been fascinated by stories of the rise of great leaders, the kings of kings, the maharajas, who led their people to a golden age.

The leader's tale is not about overcoming obstacles but about leading others to a peak level of achievement, an age of superior performance. It's about a leader with a leadership style that attracts followers who trust them and are inspired by their leadership.

 **The leader's tale is about the rise of a leader. Use it to talk about your purpose and mission.**

Every period in history and every country has its leader tales. Film director Francis Ford Coppola called *The Godfather* "a romance about a king with three sons . . . a film about power." The leader's story not only tells who you are and why you became a leader, it highlights your purpose, values, vision, team, and customers. It's a great format for entrepreneurs who are pitching investors, rallying employees, or attracting clients to their company and its vision. But it's also a great format for leaders at all levels of an organization because it allows them to talk about what molded them and their leadership style. The leader's story has a linear format and is in essence a coming-of-age story.

 **BRAINSTORMER: The Leader's Tale**

What's your story about you as a leader?

## David Versus Goliath Story

David versus Goliath is the up-and-comer's tale. It's a great format to use to show how you bootstrapped and achieved great things with a miniscule budget or a small team and surprised everyone by coming out on top.

In the biblical tale, Saul promises to reward any man who defeats Goliath, and David accepts the challenge. David's initial plan was to fight a conventional battle with swords against Goliath.

 **David versus Goliath is the classic story of the underdog. Use it to talk about how your ingenuity led you to success in bootstrapping a project or a business.**

David realizes, however, that he can't win against Goliath using conventional methods and armament. "I cannot walk in these, for I am unused to it," David says. Inspired, he takes a secret weapon, a slingshot, and five smooth stones from a brook.

Using his wits, our hero defeats the giant. He hurls a stone from his sling that hits the giant squarely on the forehead. David takes his sword and cuts off Goliath's head. The hero, through pluck and inventiveness, defeats the giant.

David and Goliath is an excellent format to use for any achievement where you succeeded against all odds. In the basic plotline there are two uneven foes, then a reversal takes place. The mood in telling the story should be suspenseful, reflecting the uneven battle. Then, in the reversal, the mood shifts from tension to insight and courage.

 **BRAINSTORMER: The Bootstrapper's Tale**

**What's your story about a project or business that you bootstrapped to success?**

## If You Can't Take the Elevator, Take the Escalator

While many situations will be right for variations of your elevator speech, there may be times when it's more appropriate to have a brief, more casual business conversation, what I call the escalator speech. The escalator speech is a short, ten- to fifteen-second icebreaker that you can use in business situations. It's smart to prepare some ideas in advance so you won't be tongue-tied like our former example, Marisa, who talked incessantly about the weather.

You could share some business news like, "I don't know whether you know it or not, we met briefly last year but I'm now part of the team working on the company's new initiative . . ."

Or you could share positive news about a recent meeting, such as, "I just came out of the most extraordinary meeting with the ABC client. It was a marathon meeting, but they ended up doubling their business with us. The whole team is elated."

Alternatively, you could comment on news about the other person you bump into, such as, "I read on the company website that you've just launched the company's office in China. That sounds like an exciting opportunity for us." Then give the other person the chance to share what that experience was like.

When you have some different angles for approaching the escalator speech, you'll be less likely to avoid useful networking when unplanned opportunities to connect come your way.

## Click Click

Super salespeople and networkers do something very powerful when they meet with people. They "click." It's a way of rapidly connecting with another person. Either consciously or intuitively, clickers tap into the social and emotional rhythm of the other person or the group. It's a very powerful way of connecting with others and something that you can learn to do.

We've all had the experience of meeting someone new and really hitting it off, whether it's in a business meeting or on a blind date. A mutual syncing takes place, studies show, so there is a kind of mind meld. Often, this effect goes beyond the areas of the brain and people even start to imitate each other.

But what a lot of us don't realize is that there is a secret to this clicking business, a secret that we can learn, and one that will encourage a clicking experience. Clickers, social scientists observed, look for similarity and connection with others, often by subtly and unconsciously imitating the other person.

Quick social bonding comes from mimicry! Ouch. It may seem unappealing and inauthentic, but it's true. It's usually unconscious, but you'll need to start consciously at first, until it becomes second nature.

(TM) **To "click" with another person (or group), use similar words and display similar interests, movements, facial expressions, and even similar breathing patterns.**

Of course, clicking is easiest to do in small meetings or in one-on-one conversations. Clickers use similar words, gestures, and movements when they are with others, and that creates a vibe of goodwill.

Here's how it works. If another person is concentrating his eyes on you, do the same. If he is fidgeting and glancing around, do a little of that after a one- or two-second pause. If the person is laid back, take the meeting slowly and casually.

If the person is brusque, get to the point efficiently. Studies show that expert clickers even take on the breathing rhythms of the other person!

To be effective you have to perform your mimicry slowly and imprecisely. For natural clickers, it's totally unconscious and intuitive. It's a way to relate to another person that comes to them naturally.

## Mirror, Mirror

Studies found that people who mirror other people when they meet with them or give a pitch get cooperation and a positive response, even from complete strangers, within minutes. It may seem contrived, but clicking can help you connect with others and be more persuasive.

It even helps to be similar to other people in the way you dress. You don't want to arrive in a bespoke suit for your sales pitch in most places outside of world-class cities. Nor do you want to underdress, because that shows a lack of respect. You want to be appropriate but have a personal flair. (You're trying to promote a personal brand, after all.)

## The Persuasive Power of Connection

Another way to speed up clicking is by being open and revealing about who you are as a person. We're so used to being formal and trying to appear flawless in a business setting.

In reality, self-disclosure and showing vulnerability are powerful in jump-starting relationships with other people. That's why a lot of business leaders tell self-deprecating stories. It cements the bond. Of course, choose the vulnerability you will display with discretion. Real masters of self-deprecation manage to simultaneously humanize and promote themselves. For example, "Imagine how I felt. I tripped on the stairs on my way to receive the sales leadership award at our annual sales meeting."

 **In terms of quickly connecting with others, vulnerability is a strength not a weakness.**

Many clickers do some planning to make sure they click; they often research clients before important meetings. Their goal is to figure out what they share with the client or what the client's hidden agenda is. They try to determine the client's business problems so that when they meet, they can weave into the conversation a story about having a similar problem, which creates rapport. It may seem contrived, but it can be very effective.

One reason subtle mimicry and self-revelation works is that it activates the part of the brain connected with feelings of empathy. It's the same area that successful salespeople activate when they relate a challenge that is similar to the one the client is facing. In fact, it's an area that is stimulated any time you share challenging experiences with another person.

Each of us has mirror neurons in the brain that enable us to understand and connect with others through simulation. We have emotional and audio mirror neurons as well as many mirror neurons for modeling physical behavior. When people tune in to others in this way, they feel a strong sense of connection.

When you practice the secrets of clickers, you'll find it easier to establish rapport with others. You're in tune with each other. And the more comfortable someone feels around you, the likelier it is that he will agree with what you're proposing. It's emotional branding.

## To Choke or Not to Choke

Some of us, well prepared though we might be, choke during an interview or an important presentation. According to experts on performance anxiety, there's usually a single moment, a distraction, that triggers a mental switch.

The good news is that there are tactics you can use to reduce the chance of choking. Some experts recommend writing a feelings journal to work through interview or performance anxiety emotions just like you would prepare for tough questions you might be asked. When you do that, your negative emotions are less likely to pop into your head at the critical moment.

Because something unexpected triggers performance anxiety, prep for interviews with different people and in various environments so that you won't be thrown by something unforeseen happening. When you do a practice session, encourage people to ask you "gotcha" questions.

It also helps to mentally prepare with positive self talk. You can do preinterview breathing exercises to develop a calmer rhythm, too.

If you are worried about remembering specific points, write them down on an index card and carry it with you.

## Internalize Not Memorize

You have one shot to make a great first impression. Your elevator speech has got to be short and compelling and must get people to care. You want your elevator speech to seem natural and conversational, even spontaneous, like you just thought of it at that moment.

Even though I'm telling you to put it together in advance, don't memorize it. Your elevator speech shouldn't seem wooden or rehearsed. The key is to practice, but to avoid memorizing it. You don't want to sound scripted.

You just need to know your speech well enough so you can internalize the message. It doesn't matter if you don't follow your written script word for word. In fact, it's best if it is a little different each time. No one will know but you.

By being prepared, you'll be able to weave in appropriate business stories and anecdotes, depending on where the conversation goes. Above all, you want your elevator speech to convey who you are, what you've done, what you can do for the other person, and why it matters. You must be able to deliver your speech quickly, clearly, and distinctively.

## Pitching Pivot

The more you pitch yourself and your ideas, the better you'll get at it.

Sometimes you'll face rejection. It happens a lot in a bad job market. My philosophy is, persist. When an interviewer, client, or prospect you're pitching says no, pretend that you can't hear her.

Look surprised. Say, "What about . . . ?" Suggest a new option or another reason why you're a good fit.

As a personal brander, you don't want to give up until it's hopeless. Ask questions. Keep the conversation going. You'll be surprised how many things can be turned around by persisting and finding a way to move forward. Plus, you'll have a new quest story to talk about!

Another technique to master is the *pivot*. When you're asked a difficult question like, "Why did you leave the company after only six months? Were you fired?" Have in your back pocket some key pivot phrases to take control of the question. Let's assume the worse and the answer is yes, you were fired for poor performance (in their opinion). Answering "Yes" would certainly doom your candidacy. The best way to answer is to pivot. In the pivot, you seem to be answering the question, but you pivot into your talking points. For example, you could candidly say that the company was a great experience, outline what you accomplished in the brief time you were there, and that it became clear it wasn't a good fit. Then, pivot into the strong points of your career history and what you can do for them as an employee.

 **A good rule of thumb in business is to act strong when weak, and act weak when strong.**

Everyone talks about persistence, but the truth is that most people give up too soon. The winner in business keeps on. Winners act confident and bold when weak, and are accommodating and self-deprecating when strong.

You need to keep knocking on doors, delivering your elevator speech, tweaking your pitch and your business stories, and pivoting when the going gets rough until you knock one of those doors down.

The key is to never, ever give up.

**IN A NUTSHELL:** *The ninth secret of self-brands: Learn the art of the elevator speech and clicking with others. After all, if you can't pitch yourself and tell your story well,* who will?

# PART 3

# Marketing Brand You: Building Visibility and Connection with Your Target Audience

# CHAPTER 10

# Take the "Work" Out of Networking

*Be wealthy in your friends.*

William Shakespeare
*Timon of Athens* (II, 2)

Successful people nurture a network of contacts. Ouch! This sounds calculating and heartless. So let's go past the words and look at an example we all know.

> *Once upon a time, there was a dynamic businessperson who didn't know he had something wonderful. He was just a small-town banker although he could have been more.*
>
> *Business can be ugly, and an unscrupulous rival took advantage of a simple mishap to ruin him. Not realizing that he had tremendous assets, the banker fell into despair and decided to end his life.*
>
> *After a failed suicide attempt and a very strange night, he arrived back home to find that his assets were there: his family, his contacts, his friends. His network had rallied to solve the problem.*
>
> *Everyone cheered when his brother lifted a glass and toasted him: "To my big brother, George. The richest man in town!"*

## Adopt the George Bailey Model

Real networking is about building relationships, genuine relationships. The best way to network is to adopt the George Bailey model: help others and be genuinely interested in what they do and care about.

It's all part of what's known as *emotional branding*. You build relationships through an emotional connection with others like George Bailey did. When your motive is connecting with and helping others, you'll find your networking is a lot more rewarding in every way.

There is a close connection between empathy and likeability. We like people who are empathetic, people who we feel understand us and seem to be like us. And we repay them with a mutual feeling of connection.

Empathy is the ability to step into another person's shoes and quickly pick up their pain, joy, or other feelings and respond with a similar emotion. Expressing empathy can break down barriers, including differences in point of view, age, and social status. There's the famous story about a guy in overalls who stood crying as FDR's cortege passed through a small West Virginia town. A reporter asked, "Did you know him?" and the man said, "No, but he knew me."

Finding similarity is a driving force in human behavior. We are attracted to people who are similar to us in some way: people who have similar beliefs, similar looks, even similar names and birth dates. When a person is similar to us, we give him special status, like wanting to do business with him or help him out.

 **EMPATHY: Finding a comfort connection with others through a *sense of similarity*.**

So in business networking and relationship building, don't look for differences from others, look for similarities. Use your power of empathy to find things to like about them, and you will be surprised at the result.

Scientists only recently discovered a new class of brain cells, called mirror neurons, that help us understand the minds, actions, and intentions of others. Mirror neurons aid us in seeing similarities with others and even in mimicking actions we see others do. One neuroscientist predicted that "mirror neurons will do for psychology what DNA did for biology."

The brain has multiple mirror neuron systems for reading people, mimicking actions, reading intentions, determining social implications of an action, and reading emotions. The same brain areas that are active when a person feels pain or pleasure also are activated when that person imagines someone else feeling the same pain or pleasure.

And it all happens very quickly, in a fraction of a second. It's these unconscious perceptions and identifications with what others are feeling that helps us click with them.

## What's Your Q Score?

In branding, being liked and being well known counts a lot. That's why marketers look at a brand's or a celebrity's *Q Score*. The Q Score is a numerical ranking of the familiarity and appeal of a celebrity. People with high Q Scores are *well known and well liked*. We feel a rapport with them, almost as if they were friends of ours. They have strong *brand equity*.

Marketers use celebrities in commercials because they want a rub-off of the celebrity's likeability onto their brand in order to create an emotional bond with consumers. Julia Roberts and Tom Hanks get paid top dollar for starring in movies not just because they are famous or are great actors. One could argue that they are not even the "best" in terms of acting ability, but they do have very high Q Scores, and are not only well-known but extremely well-liked by lots of people.

It's as if the celebrities with high Q Scores bear a resemblance to the person we see in the bathroom mirror each morning. We feel an emotional connection with these celebrities, even see them as sharing our values and life experiences. It's all a part of emotional branding. We buy things most often because of the way a particular brand makes us feel not because of rational analysis.

 **The secret of popular people is being emotionally available to others.**

**Begin by liking others and see how they repay you by liking you.**

We've got a "Q Score," too, though it's not the kind you can look up on a ranking list, like a celebrity can. We get sized up in terms of authenticity, personality, and likeability by others in business all the time giving us a virtual Q score.

Likeability can make a big difference in your business success. When I worked on Wall Street, I gave an important presentation that I had worked hard preparing. Afterwards, my boss took me aside. "Great presentation," she said, "But did you get input from any of your colleagues beforehand?"

"No, but," I stammered. "You're making your colleagues feel that you don't value their advice, and that's not smart. Some are not going to like you as a result, and you'll need their support to implement your ideas," she warned. I had been so focused on coming up with ideas and putting together a great presentation, that I blew the most important thing, bonding emotionally with my colleagues and getting their buy-in beforehand. It was a lesson I never forgot.

## Go Big and Selectively Deep

Power networkers realize that you need an army of different kinds of contacts on the road to success. If you're building an army, you will only be able to know most people superficially, but those people have value just the same. You'll find that the more varied your network is and the more people you know, even casually, the more opportunities will come your way and the more help will be there when you need it.

Networking stars also spend time developing a strategic network of allies, close business associates, mentors, and advocates. These are people who talk you up and you talk them up. It's a mutually beneficial relationship built on trust and friendship.

## Build Four Key Networks

Here are the four key networks that can play a significant role in your professional success. The two on the left, your *core network* of business associates inside and outside your company and *weak links network*, acquaintances that you don't know very well, are your wide/shallow networks. The two on the right, your *strategic network*, or tight allies, mentors, and sponsors, and your *grassroots network*, your close friends and family, are your narrow/deep networks.

Here are the special kinds of people who play a significant role in your professional networks.

## FOUR KEY NETWORKS

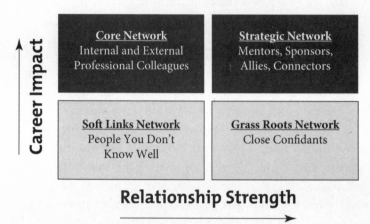

1. *Strategic Network:* This is your strategic network of influential allies, mentors, and sponsors, an informal "board of directors." It is, no doubt, your most important network because these people are influential and can impact your career success dramatically. Most mentors and sponsors are high-level executives at your company or elsewhere who you can count on for advice, connections, and putting in a good word for you at critical junctures in your career. The best are *sponsors* who actively advocate for you. (There's nothing better than that!)

   There are two other types of people who are important to have in your strategic network: *allies*, professional colleagues who help and talk up each other, and *connectors*, plugged-in people who know a lot of people. Connectors may or may not be powerful in terms of job title, but they are powerful in knowing influential people. Doctors, financial advisors, and even hairstylists often are valuable connectors because they interface with so many different types of people. Bloggers and tweeters are strong connectors, and cyberworld is a great place to tap into virtual connectors.

**BRAINSTORMER: Allies to the Rescue**

List your allies, mentors, sponsors, and connectors.

Is there new blood you could add?

2. *Core Network:* These are your business associates inside and outside of the company. Most people think of networking as building contacts outside of the company and neglect to build an internal network inside their company, which is often the most important. When networking within your company, don't focus only on your department and functional area, try to build relationships throughout the company and at every level. Volunteering for committees, charity fundraisers, and task force assignments is a formal way to expand your contacts at work. You can also join relevant employee resource groups but don't forget there are dozens of casual opportunities every day in the cafeteria or hallway where you can reach out and strike up a conversation.

**BRAINSTORMER: Strengthening Your Core**

What specific things can you do in the next three months to increase your internal contacts at your company?

What can you do to increase your external contacts?

3. *Grassroots Network:* These are close friends and family who are your confidants. They are people who you trust and who know you well. What they may lack in prestige, they make up for in the support they provide.

**BRAINSTORMER: Career Confidential**

Who are the people who you can really count on? Do you need to add someone new to the mix?

**4.** *Weak Links Network:* The people in this network are weak links because you don't know each other well, but don't ignore them. A weak link is often the source of a fresh job lead or introduction because you don't travel in the same circles. When I look back on my career, most of my job opportunities came through weak links, people whom I had just met through friends or at networking events. It's often the connections outside your usual networking circles that provide the entrée to the new company or new arena you want to enter.

The bigger your network gets, the more it will multiply and the more valuable it will become. Business is about accessibility, and networking gives you accessibility. But you have to realize the value of building and nurturing a network and make time for it.

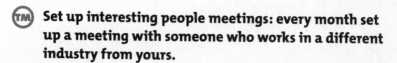 **Set up interesting people meetings: every month set up a meeting with someone who works in a different industry from yours.**

Robert is a busy executive in New York City, but he sets aside ten minutes a day to call or e-mail business colleagues and acquaintances. Just ten minutes first thing in the morning or between meetings. "My day is pretty much wall-to-wall meetings," he says. "Then there are the dozens of e-mails on my computer or phone. But I make the time because I can't afford not to. When I lost my job a few years back, I found a new position though a networking contact. My network helped me rebound much quicker than other colleagues who were caught up in the economic meltdown."

## The Networking Economy

While networking is about building relationships, that doesn't mean that it doesn't have transactional components. Done right, networking results in the best kind of business transaction, one where there is a win-win. Both sides feel good about the exchange because both sides feel that they benefit.

Think of networking as an economy, an economy of favors. Just like any healthy economy, you want to have active trade back and forth. In the networking trade, there is the expectation of reciprocity.

For some, thinking this way may seem too transactional or manipulative. But there's another way to look at it, what psychologists call "reciprocal altruism." You'll find that if you do a lot of favors and participate in the networking economy, you'll have a reputation for helping others and people will want to help you.

You'll discover that doing favors and giving small "gifts" are assets that attract others to you. The gift could be an article you e-mail that you think might be of interest. It doesn't have to have monetary value at all to be appreciated by someone. It just has to show thoughtfulness. Being generous in this way will give you a strong network of contacts that will be career capital you can practically take to the bank, that's how helpful it will be in serving your career.

While there isn't a formal quid pro quo system in the networking economy, favor givers are attracted to those who reciprocate and punish those who take favors and don't reciprocate. Believe me, word will get out if you're a taker and not a giver, too!

## The Secret to Attracting Mentors and Advocates

Today, just about everyone has a mentor or two. Many companies have formal mentoring programs and will assign you a mentor. Smart personal branders don't stop there. They find their own mentors, the more the better.

Building a strategic network of mentors takes some finesse. Don't make a bold request, like "Will you be my mentor?" I've had complete strangers ask me that. It feels like a big commitment, and few people will respond favorably unless there is an established relationship or the introduction comes through a trusted friend.

A more natural approach is, "I've admired how you've navigated your career and done different jobs. I'm trying to figure out how to broaden my experience in the company, and I'd like to hear more about how you did it." Then, if you both hit it off, the relationship can turn into a mentor relationship.

What separates the networking A-listers from everybody else is their ability to attract and nurture sponsors or advocates. These are people who don't just give you advice, like mentors do. They actively advocate for you, calling the CEO or other influential people to talk you up.

**Sponsors are CEO whisperers, people who talk you up to the CEO and other influential people.**

Let's look at the story of a client, a woman I'll call "Gemma," a talented lawyer at a large firm in Washington, D.C. The firm created a new position that Gemma thought would be perfect for her abilities, experience, and personality.

She interviewed with a committee of five partners at the firm. The interviews went so well and her background was so spot on that Gemma felt she had the job in the bag. Of course, we know how this movie ends. The job went to Tom, a colleague who didn't have as compelling a record in the position.

When I first met with Gemma she was understandably angry. I asked her, "Why do you think you lost out to Tom?" You're probably thinking, law is a male-dominated field, it must have been a sexist thing. But Gemma felt her firm was pretty gender neutral (and two of the lawyers on the interview panel were women).

What Gemma found out was that Tom had networked his way into the job!

What tipped the committee in favor of Tom was that several partners had called committee members to recommend him. Tom had called those partners about his interest in the job and they offered to lobby for his candidacy (or maybe Tom politely asked if they wouldn't mind calling on his behalf).

So I asked Gemma, "Do you know other partners who think highly of you that you could have approached?" "Sure," Gemma said, "But I didn't think of it. I played it straight."

 **There's nothing more powerful than positive word of mouth, particularly when it's from someone influential.**

Then Gemma said something interesting, "Gee, it doesn't seem fair."

Of course it's fair. That's how the business world works. As a personal brander, you want to marshal all your assets. Don't feel, as Gemma told me, "My work should speak for itself." In an ideal world, perhaps it would have. But wouldn't you have been swayed to Tom's candidacy, too, after receiving those endorsement phone calls if you were on the committee?

## The Allied Forces

There's another group in your strategic network that can be even more powerful than mentors and sponsors. These are your allies, a small group of your peers who are ambitious and want to succeed like you do. You and your allies are committed to helping each other on your career journeys.

What makes a person an ally? Allies are people you can call regularly for advice; you realize that they've got your back, and vice versa. This evolves into the most powerful business relationship, because your allies are people who sing your praises and who you talk you up (or defend, as the case may be). And you collaborate and share opportunities.

In his book *The Start-Up of You*, LinkedIn founder Reid Hoffman calls his allies his tribe and describes the lengths that tribe members go to help each other. When Bret Taylor launched his company, FriendFeed, Hoffman gave him a detailed critique of his product strategy and that made their business relationship stronger. When Digg founder Kevin Rose was told that there was no room for additional investors in the initial funding round for Jack Dorsey's new company, Square, Rose didn't just walk away. He noticed that Square didn't have a demo on its website, so he prepared a high-definition video. And he got into the initial funding round.

Remember, a key part of strategic networking is doing unexpected favors and giving little business "gifts," not necessarily with the expectation of gain. It's an informal quid pro quo system that can strengthen relationships. It's all about sharing mutually beneficial opportunities, ideas, and contacts.

## Let Me Introduce Myself

One of the best ways to introduce a new brand is to use a celebrity spokesperson, a satisfied customer, or a third-party expert in the ads. An introduction by a trusted person is very powerful because the person you are trying to meet will be more likely to respond. According to one study, 84 percent of salespeople got a call back when they were introduced by someone at the company.

When you have been introduced by someone, it means that you have been vetted. It says that you are a person who should be considered before the long line of other candidates.

So how do you ask for an introduction? It pays to be specific, but think in terms of a value proposition. Think not of what you want, but of what you can offer the other person. So if you want to be introduced to Clay, and your friend, Robert, knows him, don't say, "Robert, I think you know Clay. I'd like to meet him because I'm trying to break into the consulting industry." That's about you. Say, "I'm interested in meeting Clay because his company has a fledging practice in technology and I think I can play a major role in building that business for them." That way Robert will feel more comfortable making the introduction since it will be mutually advantageous.

## Network for Ideas

Since so many feel uncomfortable networking, I suggest that you move away from the idea that your goal in networking is to make useful contacts. Instead, decide that your goal is to expand your thinking, get new ideas for your work or life, and maybe make some lifelong friends in the process.

Just this shift in emphasis makes a big difference. You'll be much more successful at networking if your motive is to learn and get to know a wide variety of people, rather than to hustle contacts or business.

People can sense when you're genuinely interested in discussing ideas and experiences and when you're interested in knowing them just because they can help you.

That's why I say, *network to learn*. Don't network for contacts who will help you, but for what you can learn from them in a networking conversation. You'll find it easier to build friendships and alliances that lead to more, whether it's an introduction to someone at a company you're targeting or a referral for a board seat.

When you take this approach, you'll also discover the value of knowing people with different backgrounds and from different areas of the world. You'll also become "information central" in areas of interest to you, an important role for any networker.

 **If your motive is to learn and be involved, not to make contacts, you'll end up with more contacts.**

## Think in Terms of Building a Community

One of the branding buzzwords today is building a *community*. That's what blogs and social media are all about. You want to build a community, too, of like-minded people who share areas of interest. That way you'll have a network in place long before you need it. You may invest more than you get back in the early years, but over time the payback is enormous, emotionally and tangibly.

Having a community is especially important today. Whether it's job security or job progress, you can't count on the company. Recruiters can't open as many doors as a good network can, either. A recent Bureau of Labor Statistics study showed that more than 70 percent of executive jobs paying $100,000 or more were obtained through a friend, relative, or business acquaintance.

You have to rely on the people you know and the people who know you—your community. This is true no matter how talented, smart, and experienced you are.

## Hunting Grounds

Putting your network together will take some ingenuity at first, and then it will take some effort to keep it alive when you are busy. Like any ecosystem, your network needs to be kept healthy with new blood coming in on a regular basis; continue infusing your network with contacts you meet in person as well as those you find through virtual networking, which we'll explore in chapter 11.

These are the best in-person networking places.

- ▶ *Industry conferences:* Go up to speakers and panelists and tell them how much you enjoyed the talk and exchange business cards. This can be a great source for new people in your strategic networks. The best networking takes place in the hallways, so make sure to move around during coffee breaks. Make it a goal to meet at least three new contacts at each conference you attend.
- ▶ *University alumni groups:* There is something very connecting about school ties. There is a willingness to help that many other professional network groups don't have, so get involved in alumni networking groups in your town or over the Internet.

▶ *Networking groups:* Explore different groups until you find ones that are the right fit. These groups can be daunting if they are large, so consider going with a friend and breaking up to network separately. Then come back together again from time to time. Master the art of the elevator speech that we discussed in chapter 9.

▶ *Gender- or ethnicity-based networking groups:* Take advantage of the shared interests of these groups, and the natural bonding that takes place.

▶ *Nonprofit activities:* Meeting others who have a common goal can be a great way to connect with people in your community or across the country because you share values and a commitment to making a difference in the world.

## Build a Two-Way Street

A network is a relationship. It's a two-way street.

Some people view a network as a one-way proposition—something that you use when you need help. We've all had to deal with people who call only when they are looking for a new job or who give you a business pitch right after meeting you. That is not networking. That is using people. A network has to be mutually beneficial. Both parties need to feel that it's a win-win. Here's how great networkers build a relationship and keep their community alive:

▶ *Find common ground:* In order to take a relationship you make networking to the next level, you need to connect in more than a superficial way. Find linkages and areas of mutual interest with people of different backgrounds. This is what schmoozing is about, but your goal is to take the conversation beyond small talk to something more personal and engaging so that there is a reason to connect again in the future.

▶ *Act like a host:* It can be daunting to go to a big event where it's hard to get an hors d'oeuvre, much less meet people you would like to meet. That's why a number of master networkers advise acting like a host yourself. Rather than waiting for someone to introduce you, go up to a group or an individual and introduce yourself. Most people will be wearing name tags, so it will be easy to break the ice by referring to their organizations or companies. And individuals who are standing alone will no doubt love you for it. Likewise, back home you can create events like a small dinner gathering at a local restaurant to bring together diverse people in your network.

▶ *Help someone first:* Make the first move to help the new people in your network, even if it's just forwarding an article via e-mail. Generosity pays. The benefit of giving first plays into what social scientists call the "reciprocity rule." People feel a need to do something for you when you do something for them first.

▶ *Take your business cards with you everywhere:* Most people make the mistake of not carrying business cards. Consequently, they don't have one to offer when they meet someone they want to get to know better. It's hard enough to remember a person's name and particulars—don't make it impossible by not having a card.

▶ *Keep the embers alive:* Send a short note or e-mail to new contacts right after you have met them. The embers will die if they aren't tended in the early stages of a relationship. Never let someone completely disappear from your network unless there is a good reason. Have touchpoints like periodic e-mail, holiday cards, and a surprise phone call.

## Enter the Inner Sanctum

As we all know, there is a hierarchy of networking events and organizations. The by-invitation-only events and clubs are more powerful than organizations that are open to everyone.

At the pinnacle are private clubs or meetings like the World Economic Forum Annual Meeting at Davos, Switzerland, which attracts top CEOs and heads of state from around the world. Many elite organizations charge a hefty admission fee or require that new members be nominated by members. Even book clubs in some major cities are highly exclusive.

These are power networking events and organizations where the elite meet.

So how do you get in?

 **Strategic networking requires planning and homework.**

Through networking, of course. Strategic networking enables you to get to know people who know members of elite organizations. Then, you must network to build a relationship with the person who holds the key. Find common ground with the people you want to meet by researching their interests and backgrounds. You'll also need to research the organization and think about how you can bring value to it.

> **BRAINSTORMER: Getting into the Sanctum Sanctorum**
>
> **Who in your network could be a link to an elite organization's gatekeepers?**

Even going to important gatherings and conferences entails strategic planning or you won't connect with the people you want to meet. If there's a project or area of mutual interest, e-mail or call the person to suggest setting up a one-on-one meeting beforehand. Most people will be flattered by your interest and respond favorably.

Make it a point to read the bios of the speakers and panelists provided at a conference or event. See if you have anything in common or have a mutual business interest that you could bring up during the cocktail hour. Or approach them and comment on their talks. You'll not only learn more, you might form a lasting friendship.

## Use, Don't Abuse, Your Network

Once you have your network, there are hidden rules to follow so you will not wear out your welcome. Many people ask for too much. Here are ten top networking dos and don'ts to keep in mind:

1. *Ask for one contact:* Don't say, "I'm looking for a job in marketing. Do you know anyone?" The better way is to say, "I'm targeting the X industry or Y company. Can you suggest someone I could talk to?"
2. *Ask for something specific:* Don't be vague or too general. It's hard to respond to sweeping requests. Ask for help on one company, or ask the person in your network to do something specific (such as write a letter) and provide a time frame, if there is one.

3. *Ask for advice or a point of view:* Everyone loves to give advice, and this is always a great way to approach your network. It is a good way to lead in before asking for something more, such as an introduction.

4. *Tell the person you have everything lined up except for X:* Don't overwhelm your contact with too many requests. For example, tell a contact that you have written your project proposal and now just need to locate X or figure out Y.

5. *Keep the conversation upbeat:* Don't depress your network with your fears and problems. Don't share your anger about your company or boss, or your financial problems.

6. *Do your homework:* Find out the interests and backgrounds of the people in your network. Let them get to know who you are and what you're like, but do your homework so that you get to know them as well.

7. *Thank people immediately:* Saying thanks at the end of the phone call isn't enough unless you have made a simple request. When people go out of their way to make an introduction, let them know how special they are for helping you by sending handwritten thank-you notes or letters.

8. *Keep people informed on the results:* Remember to tell the people who helped you that you got the meeting or the job you wanted. (Lack of follow-up is a complaint I hear frequently from people who went out of their way to help someone and never heard back about what happened.) Send periodic updates on your progress.

9. *Stay in touch:* A warm contact will grow cold if it is not nurtured. Keep in touch periodically through e-mail, phone calls, lunch, notes, or letters.

10. *Reciprocate:* Don't neglect to help people in your network. Stay tuned for things you can do to help your network. And, if someone asks you for help, follow through.

Networking and community building are skills that anyone can learn. Self-branders learn it because they know they can't succeed on their own. And having a community of friends, colleagues, and advisers around makes the journey a lot more fun.

**IN A NUTSHELL:** The tenth secret of self-brands: Whatever you want to achieve, whoever you want to know, wherever you want to go on your journey, use your network to get you there.

# CHAPTER 11

# Learn the Art of Cyberbranding to Build Your Brand Online

*And we must take the current when it serves,*
*or lose our ventures.*

William Shakespeare
*Julius Caesar* (IV, 3)

Cyberworld gives us the best of times and the worst of times. The career identity you've worked hard to create in person can be made more valuable through cyberbranding on the Internet and via social media. Or it can be damaged in a nanosecond if something bad about you spreads online.

What's more, you're a part of cyberworld whether you want to be or not, or whether you do anything online or not. You have a virtual brand, either a strong one, a mediocre one, or a weak one.

People want to know about you, and they're going to use the Internet to find out about you. That's true whether you're lobbying for a job interview, a date, or a seat on the community board. Your story—the one you want to put out there, one that has been created by others, or one told by the total lack of an online presence—is just a Bing or a Google away.

## Getting Social

Your brand—your image and reputation—is valuable. That's why you need to take charge of building and nurturing it online as you do offline.

Branding is all about perceptions, and the Internet is a big factor in molding perceptions today. After all, everyone is checking each other out on the Internet, and people are going to do it whether you want them to or not. Checking out people, products, and companies on the Internet is how we operate today. According to Jobvite, a vast majority of executive recruiters will use social networks to recruit candidates. And hiring managers at Fortune 500 companies are checking you out on the web and social networking sites as well, particularly on LinkedIn, the number-one business site.

Business managers search online for their employees. Recruiters research prospects online. Colleagues Google each other.

People don't have to know you personally to "like," "friend," "subscribe," or "follow" you online. A colleague can post a picture of you drinking at a party and tag your name to it. Then it's up to you to untag yourself before it hurts your brand.

 **A weak digital footprint is like a weak reputation.**

Privacy and anonymity are things of the past. Social media giants such as Facebook, LinkedIn, Google+, and Twitter, along with the massive proliferation of blogs and consumer websites, connect each of us to one another twenty-four hours a day, seven days a week. What people discover about you online can enhance your personal brand, or it can destroy your career if something completely inconsistent with your company's values appears. (And make no mistake, companies are mining the personal data you put online for one-to-one marketing and other purposes.)

If you don't show up on search engines like Google and Bing at all, that's telling about your brand, too. It's the equivalent of saying you don't exist!

## "Word of Mouth on Steroids"

As much as the Internet has changed the way we interact today, the latest digital revolution is taking place with new media, particularly social media. It's all part of what I call *cyberbranding*.

**Cyberbranding takes place in the dynamic digital world with content created and shared by anyone and accessible to everyone.**

*New media* refers to all the interactive forms of communication that use the Internet, such as blogs, websites, social networks, RSS feeds, and the like. One of the hottest areas of new media is *social media*, including Facebook, Twitter, LinkedIn, YouTube, and Pinterest, which are platforms for a peer-to-peer interactive dialogue and which foster the creation and exchange of user-generated content.

Social media magnifies and disperses word of mouth like never before. And it's something that you need to catch hold of because word of mouth has always been the best (and cheapest) tool for branding. After all, your brand isn't just what you say it is: it's what others say about you. And the more high-quality connections and recommendations you have on social media sites, the stronger your brand will be.

## Power to the People

Cyberworld is a democracy. It gives power to the people. Everyone can participate, not just the well connected or well informed. It offers on-demand access to content and information to one and all, anytime. Cyberbranding is the fast, low-cost way to brand yourself—and to connect with your colleagues in a genuine way. People want honesty and authenticity, not hype and gloss, and the online world is the place to present yourself.

Indeed, each of us can enter the world of new media and develop our own following by launching a website or publishing a blog or creating a profile page on Facebook or Google+. We can post videos on YouTube or pictures on Pinterest. Each of us can reach many people every time we post. Unlike traditional media, new media tend to be inexpensive to own and operate. Even kids can do it, and they do!

While we have more control in many ways, it's not absolute. Our readers or followers can respond and agree or disagree. They can take our message and pass it along, or change it and pass it along.

We don't have the same powerful arbiters that we do in traditional media, but we have arbiters just the same. The digiworld arbiters are less visible. They're the decision makers and programmers who make the software and set up the protocols for search engines, aggregators, and indexers. They may be less visible than the heads of CBS, ABC, or NBC, but they determine what counts and what doesn't in more ways than we may realize. You have to figure out how to score with them so you are visible on the Internet by mastering SEO, which allows you to be picked up by the aggregators and indexers. To master cyberbranding, you also need to develop engaging content and have a powerful visual identity.

## Make That 4.74 Degrees

We've all heard of six degrees of separation: the idea that six connections separate any two people. The concept was based on research done in the 1960s by American social psychologist Stanley Milgram and made famous by Joan Guare's 1990 play *Six Degrees of Separation* (and later by the game Six Degrees of Kevin Bacon).

Well, six degrees is outdated, thanks to social media.

According to a 2011 study by Facebook and the University of Milan, the average number of steps it takes to connect two people on Facebook is 4.74. The study looked at 721 million active Facebook users, and 4.74 was the average number of hops it took to connect people, including far-flung Facebook users in the Siberian tundra.

No doubt you know a "friend" on Facebook who knows someone who knows someone who knows that person. Cyberworld is connecting us quicker than ever.

## Think Cyber

The minute you print a brochure, it is out of date. Production is expensive. Distribution is expensive.

A well-done website, blog, and social media page are powerful ways to create a dynamic brand identity and a community of loyal fans. You can have your own website or blog to express your interests or market your business. You can use the company website or intranet to build visibility for your initiatives, or write guest posts on other sites. Social media sites like LinkedIn and Facebook make it easy for you to hang your virtual shingle out there, too.

(TM) **A website, blog, or social media page is worth a thousand brochures.**

Cyberworld offers the ultimate branding. It's a way to build a powerful visual and verbal identity quickly and affordably, reaching everyone you want to target and creating a brand community. Cyberworld allows you to display your own brand personality and always be up-to-date and relevant. It lets you be accessible to your customers or audience.

You always need to approach the design of your cyberbranding properties as powerful packaging and advertising for you, your business, or your ideas. Observe these eight principles for developing a great website or blog:

1. *Go for fast pages:* We're all in a rush, and many will be looking you up on the run using a mobile device. So you want your web pages to be fast in every way. For your website, make it easy for people to scan the page quickly and know what the site is about, both the big picture and tantalizing detail bits with links. You also want to be fast in terms of download and mobile speed by keeping images small and page length reasonable.

2. *Develop fresh, clear content:* There's so much noise out there, now more than ever, you need to grab the reader immediately. To be different, teach a new thing or provide a new interaction or beg to differ with the prevailing view. To be clear, don't be hard to read. Use fewer words and break up the copy into short paragraphs; use headlines and subheads like advertisers do in print ads.

3. *Intrigue with a distinct brand look:* You have seconds to make a first impression, so make sure your site has a great look. *Don't use a template design.* You'll look like everybody else—like a generic not a brand. Keep your website simple and uncluttered, and don't be afraid of white space. Use it generously around paragraphs and images. Select a dominant brand color or distinctive palette. Your visual identity should complement your verbal message and be consistent with your persona. To get inspiration for your web design, cruise around the Internet for sites that appeal to you, but customize so that yours is uniquely you.

4. *Convey a brand personality:* Use color, design, imagery, graphics, and verbal messages to create a brand personality that conveys your

voice and vision. Bring your personal DNA into the equation by writing in a personal style that engages visitors and builds a strong web community.

5. *Avoid clever navigation:* Navigation, navigation, navigation. Sometimes navigation is hidden in the most unlikely places. While it may be clever on the part of the web designer, if people can't navigate your site easily, they will move on. And navigation needs to work well on laptop screens as well as mobile devices.

6. *Be mobile friendly:* People are busy, and chances are they will try to check you out from their mobile phones, so install a mobile plug-in to transform your website and blog into a mobile-friendly version. This will cut down rich media and the number and size of images, so your site doesn't slow down the mobile experience.

7. *Solicit interaction and linking:* Empower your visitors with the ability to get more information via links throughout your site. Ask for visitor feedback. Include calls to action, inviting visitors to sign up for your e-zine or newsletter or make a purchase or get information. Link only with sites that complement what you do. If you align yourself with junk sites, you will pull down your own brand. Likewise, keep your links current, or you're signaling that you don't care, and visitors won't either.

8. *Measure:* Move over Don Draper, the computer geeks are in charge! In the old days of advertising, creative was king. Now with social media and new media, data junkies have the power. If you're not growing your audience, reevaluate and change your website or blog, or kill it. With Google Analytics and other measurement tools, it's easy to track where the traction is on your website and social media programs.

## The Secret of Bloggers and Tweeters

Blogging and tweeting stars—from top executives such as Tony Hsieh of Zappos to mommy bloggers like Heather Armstrong to celebrities like Shaquille O'Neal and Ashton Kutcher to thought leaders like Dan Pink—have something in common. They know that the more personal and real the content, the bigger the online following they will amass.

They realize that cyberbranding provides a way to connect with people directly and often. They tell stories and share their points of view. They include you so that you feel a part of their world, and you feel that you know them personally.

Rather than trying to sell something, they often simply write about where they are traveling, who they are meeting, and what they are thinking about. Like any great story, the plot of their tweets and blog posts keeps evolving, offering twists, cliffhangers, and emotion. When you choose to "follow" them, you are becoming a part of their story—and that makes you feel connected to them.

 **Make your posts and tweets less about your achievements and status and more about the journey— what you're thinking, doing, and observing.**

The more real you are, the more you will draw people in. Be the storyteller for your career, or for your business if you're an entrepreneur. Share what you're doing and who you're meeting. Reveal what your customers and clients are thinking, what their interests are, and what you're thinking about as a professional in today's world.

## The Power of Friendship

Social media lets you do something extraordinary: tap into the power of friendship. And it lets you do it in many ways. Social media like Facebook, Twitter, and LinkedIn make it easy for you to expand your network of acquaintances. They enable you to speak to many every time you speak.

Best of all, social media lets you easily tap into the selling power of a personal introduction from someone who knows you to someone he knows. Social media sites like LinkedIn also help you leverage the power of a professional endorsement or recommendation.

 **Marketers have always realized that the best way to sell something is to get other people to sell it for you.**

The selling power of friendship is what denizens of cyberworld use every minute on Facebook and other sites just by clicking the "Like" or "Retweet" buttons next to a particular bit of content. You tap into the power of friendships when you ask people to recommend you on LinkedIn or other social sites. Third-party endorsements are powerful for brands. After all, when you say it, it's bragging. When someone else says it, it's an expert opinion.

The Internet is a great place to make new friends with like-minded people. Follow the blogs and Twitter feeds of people whose writing and points of view you admire. To get to know them better, make comments from time to time on posts that you like. Or retweet a tweet with a comment. Before long, if you are simpatico, you will be part of each other's networks.

## Be Real or Get Out

We all seek experiences that enlarge our lives in some way, that touch our emotions and help us grow. The digital world can make you a part of that process. People don't need to know you well to become interested in your ideas and point of view, as long as you create a dynamic presence on the Internet and positive buzz in online forums.

 **We pass along what moves us emotionally—either positively or negatively.**

It turns out that we don't want to share facts and practical information as much as we do stories and emotions. This is true whether we're passing along an article, a video, or an ad.

Why? Research shows that we want to share strong emotions because we want to connect and feel solidarity with a group. We pass along things that surprise or move us because they excite us. Emotional content brings about what social scientists call a state of "high arousal."

When we read or see an article or ad that excites us, our nervous system mirrors these feelings. Our heart starts beating faster, our sweat glands open, and we're ready to do something. We respond in this way whether the stimulus is a horror movie or a love story. And when we're in a state of arousal, we're much more likely to pass along and share the news article, post, or video that aroused these emotions. And the Internet makes it easy to do that.

**BRAINSTORMER: Pass Me Along**

What kind of "emotional" content could you develop for your blog, your tweets, or your Facebook status updates for people to pass along?

## Be Easy to Pass Along

If imitation is the sincerest form of flattery, appropriation isn't far behind. Make it easy for people to pass along your content or your company information, whether it's an interesting story, a blog post, or your thought for the day.

The power of the Internet is leverage, which is why you want to connect with friends and colleagues and promote pass-along. Twitter's "Retweet" and Facebook's "Like" are two of the most powerful buttons on the web, so make it easy for people to follow you by linking them to your website, blog, and other digital properties so that people can easily spread the buzz about you.

And keep your ear to the ground for new ways to optimize your online presence. New things are happening every day—new sites, new tools, new apps—all designed to make your cyberbranding effortless and effective.

## Own Your Name

You want to make it easy for people to find you in cyberworld. Begin by owning your name's real estate on the Internet. Buy your domain name even if you don't have a website or blog set up yet. When you're ready to launch a blog or special site, you will have the rights to your name. Register your name on popular social media sites like LinkedIn, Facebook, and Twitter and branch out to other more targeted sites.

 **Claim your digital real estate: register YourName.com, set up your Facebook page under your name, etc.**

What do you do if another person owns your domain name or has staked out your name on a dominant social media site like LinkedIn? Consider using your middle initial, a middle name, a double-barreled last name, or another identifier.

## Go Big or Go Home

My philosophy is to begin with the five social media giants: LinkedIn, Facebook, Twitter, Google+, and YouTube and then branch out into other broad social media sites like Pinterest and more targeted niche sites that reflect your interests.

The reason is simple. In branding, the hottest spots are where the most people can be found, whether that's watching the game on Super Bowl Sunday, at the bazaar, or on Facebook. So make sure that you cover the big arenas first where there's lots of brand-building to be done then brand out to narrow media outlets where the crowd is small but very targeted.

Remember, branding is generally a balance between broad media and targeted media. You want to do both in establishing an effective brand building campaign.

## Leverage Cyberworld

There are some basic rules that will help you make the most of cyberbranding. To establish your brand's keywords, put yourself in the shoes of people who might search for you and your job skills. Research the most commonly searched keywords in your industry and job function. Make sure that those keywords are used in your online profiles and other online content in text format so that you can be picked up by search engines.

In cyberbranding, you always want to think of linking and leverage. In addition to the "Like," "Retweet," and other sharing tools, have links everywhere; include them on your website, blog, and social media pages so that viewers can easily learn more and so that all your platforms cross-promote. Repurpose your content so that it works in other formats and other media. For example, if you give a talk at an industry conference or local event, promote it using Facebook and Twitter, and post a short highlights video on YouTube after the event.

You can't do it all. That's why I say, automate your cyberbranding. There are social media management sites like TweetDeck and HootSuite that allow you to manage all of your social media in one place and repurpose messages to go out simultaneously. You can schedule blog posts or tweets in advance so that you can do a week's worth (or a month's worth) at once. You can always come back and post something topical.

Just because you can doesn't mean you should be ubiquitous on Facebook or other social sites. When you overshare personal details and post silly stuff multiple times a day, you can come across as having Social Media Attention Disorder (SMAD). If you tend toward this type of addiction, reserve it for a private feed to your close friends only.

After you establish yourself on the big social media sites, explore more targeted sites. One of the beauties of social media is the ability to find a community of people who are interested in the same things you are, people who are trying to solve the same problems that you are, people who are like you. There are social media for every type of interest, background, heritage, geography, job function, gender, age, you name it. At these specialized social media sites, more than at the giants, you are likely to forge bonds in a focused community setting.

## Brand Your Profile

For many social media sites, you'll be able to post an online profile. This is an opportunity to tell your personal or career story in a compelling, focused narrative that imparts your brand identity, the distinct, relevant value you bring to a professional situation.

People want to know your story, but you've got to make it interesting. You don't have to relate everything you've ever done, but nor should you dispense with the profile in a few terse sentences.

 **Tell your personal story flawlessly in a captivating narrative.**

The best profiles tell a story, a career story or a personal story, that ties all the pieces of your journey together into a coherent whole that's brief, compelling, and unusual. Think in terms of a meta-narrative, the central theme you want to relate and the overarching story you want to tell. Make sure that there is a plotline that ties your entire career story together with the theme.

Profiles with a captivating narrative flow are sticky; they're easy to remember. Weave in key accomplishments, credentials, and turning points in your career. Ditch aspects of your journey that take people off course for your brand, unless you can make them part of your story (car wreck leads to rare business opportunity). Avoid insider jargon, so that who you are and the value you offer is understandable to a broad audience.

Your profile needs to be flawless, particularly on the big social media sites, like LinkedIn, where recruiters prowl for candidates, reporters search for experts, and businesses search for suppliers. Make sure that your profile is well written and tells an integrated self-brand story with no grammatical errors. About 40 percent of résumés are riddled with misspellings and grammatical errors, studies show, and I suspect that the error rate on online profiles is about the same. (Note to self: Have two other people proof my profile before I post it.) The best profiles convey a sense of the person's personality and style as well as her accomplishments and credentials.

Many social media sites have sections where you can list your favorite music, interests, and links to YouTube videos, your blog, or your website. It's up to you to decide how much of your personal life, tastes, and idiosyncrasies you want to share. On many social media sites, you can keep a separate private setting for friends only.

 **BRAINSTORMER: What's Your Story?**

Explore drafting your online profile so that it has a focused, compelling narrative.

## Ace the Online Picture

If you've ever marketed yourself on Match.com or eHarmony.com, you know how important having a flattering picture is to your dating success. It is equally important for building your brand online.

Your picture will be examined more than you realize. Get a good-quality picture that lets your personality and brilliance shine. It's important to dress the part for your career and industry, so ditch the glam unless you are in the fashion industry and forgo the casual jeans and T-shirt unless you work at a tech start-up or are a garage mechanic.

 **A page with a profile picture is seven times more likely to be viewed than a page without one.**

For your main photo, select a headshot of you alone, not a picture with your dog, significant other, or a scenic view in the background. Don't think this means that you need to opt for a dull "corporate" shot. Although professionals in many industries should aim for a corporate look, you don't have to be expressionless. The best pictures have a natural feel and project warmth and openness. As secondary photos, you can add snapshots of you on the job, at a conference, or at a sporting event to create a broader brand portrait.

 **BRAINSTORMER: Picture Perfect**

Does your picture reflect your brand well? If you're not sure, ask a colleague to rate it for you.

## How LinkedIn Are You?

LinkedIn is the world's largest professional network, with over 100 million members and counting, so it has to play a leading role in your online branding tool kit.

LinkedIn is built on a series of powerful networking ideas. Its foundation is the power of connection and the value of an introduction from a trusted contact over a cold call.

Another important idea behind LinkedIn is that you have a network that is much bigger and more valuable than you realize. (An early tagline at LinkedIn was "Your network is bigger than you think.") The numbers are pretty astounding if you do the math. For example, if you have 45 connections and each of these first-degree connections has 45 unique friends of his own and each of those friends has 45 unique friends, then you have 91,125 people (45 × 45 × 45) you can reach through a LinkedIn introduction. What if you're linked with a superconnector who has more than 500 or 1,000 connections? The numbers can quickly snowball.

To make the concept of a personal introduction a socially powerful idea, the organizing principle of LinkedIn is *degrees of separation*. So you'll have first-degree (direct) contacts, second-degree contacts, and so forth.

To harness the networking power of LinkedIn, you'll need to master making requests to link and asking for help. You'll also need to become talented at requesting and making introductions. Otherwise, you've just got a list of names with contact information like you'd find in a phone book.

 **LinkedIn is about connection and degrees of separation. Use it to link up with colleagues and seek out the great networkers in your field.**

When you want to meet someone in your extended network on LinkedIn, you should ask for an introduction. Just as with traditional networking, you need to ask directly for something specific and to focus the request not on why you want to be introduced, but how you can add value to the contact you want to be introduced to. So it's not, "I want to meet your friend Marty because I think it would be cool to work at ABC Corp," but "I am interested in meeting Marty because his company is expanding in China and I've just launched a successful project there."

To make yourself attractive as a professional contact, think of LinkedIn as your narrative bio, résumé, cover letter, letters of recommendation, and business head shot all aggregated in one place where it will be looked at repeatedly. So it makes sense to give everything you place there a lot of attention. Look at the profiles of other professionals to get ideas for composing yours. Before you reach out to someone, use LinkedIn as a resource to find areas of connection and mutual interest, so that the engagement will be more successful.

 **Ladies, according to LinkedIn, in 2011 only 37 percent of its users were women, and men were more active in building networking contacts.**

Third-party endorsements are powerful for brands, and they are powerful for people, too. LinkedIn gives you a platform to display endorsements. Reach out to business colleagues and associates and offer to write a recommendation on LinkedIn for them. In return, ask them if they would recommend you. Recruiters often look for the "thumbs up" graphic that means you've been recommended, as well as at the number next to it that indicates how often you've been recommended.

It's smart to participate in LinkedIn groups or start your own group. Choose groups that are relevant to your industry, job function, and interests. Groups are a valuable way to keep up with the buzz in your industry and areas of interest as well as meet new people. You can post questions, sign up for weekly digests, and start discussions. You can form your own group (mine, on personal branding, is called SelfBrand).

My philosophy is to be easy to contact, so, if you agree, include your personal e-mail address in your Summary Profile or put it in the contact field and label it public. People can't add you to their network unless they have your e-mail address or send a LinkedIn InMail. A huge part of LinkedIn's appeal is its networking and messaging system, so it pays to be open and available.

### BRAINSTORMER: Three LinkedIn Actions

*Introduce:* Introduce two people through LinkedIn who could benefit professionally from knowing each other.

*Give:* Send a small "gift," such as an article, to someone you want to get to know.

*Request:* Make a request for an introduction, giving a specific reason you could benefit the other person.

## Human Branding on Facebook

While LinkedIn is great for your career identity and building a business network, Facebook—with more than 1 billion users and growing—gives you a broader social network. Many people use Facebook to humanize their personal brands and to provide more information about themselves as people through status updates and their profile page. It's also a way to stay in touch easily with a wide range of friends, colleagues, and acquaintances.

Think of Facebook as an extension of your desk or office, where people can get a sense of the person beyond the job through the pictures on your desk or framed on your office walls. Share photos and videos on Facebook that amplify your brand and interests in a positive way, the ones that you would actually place on your desktop at work.

The status update is one of Facebook's guiding principles. Use it to post current updates on what you, your friends, and family are doing and thinking.

 **Facebook is about sharing a broader range of your personal activities.**

**Use it for communicating a holistic brand story with a wider social audience.**

To make it easier to tell the evolving story of your life, Facebook launched a searchable, curated personal history called Timeline in 2012. Timeline enhances the value of your profile by giving pictures more prominence, including a large "cover" image, and by including the ability to highlight turning points such as accomplishments, relationships, job changes, and the like. Timeline gives you a host of options to tell a complete personal brand story from music to shopping, from travel to food, from news to giving. An algorithm dramatizes the important content on Facebook like a personal brag book would.

A key benefit of Timeline is what Facebook calls "frictionless sharing." Now there are new apps that seamlessly deliver your activities on outside sites into your Timeline profile.

Facebook has a lot of other tools for cyberbranding. You can add the Facebook "Like" button to your website or blog so that when people click it, a link to your website and a message that the person liked it appears on their news feed on Facebook. It's a way to get free advertising for you and your content.

You can also activate the "Subscribe" button so that others can connect with you without having to be friends on Facebook. Likewise, you can follow and subscribe to the news feeds of people you aren't friends with. With the "Subscribe" button, you can also customize the news feeds you receive from your friends, as well as how your news feeds are distributed (whether they are public or for friends only). And Facebook, as a leader in social networking, will continue to offer new tools to enhance the site's value.

## You've Got Talent

The number-one search engine is Google, but guess what's number two? YouTube.

So if you think YouTube is all juvenile pranks and amateur talent videos, think again. It can be an important arena for personal branding. Along with all the narcissism and idiocy on YouTube, you'll find a treasure trove of game-changing ideas as well as inspiring people from around the world. You can see the very best thought leaders speak at TED conferences—without an invitation. You can listen to an entrepreneur talk about her new invention. You can watch a how-to video to gain a new skill. It's all on YouTube.

Depending on what you do, videos can be a smart personal branding tool but you'll need video content to take advantage of it. To use YouTube effectively, it's smart to keep your videos short, about one to two minutes in length. If you're posting a major talk or media interview, trim it to eight minutes or less. As with text-based social media, aid searching by putting relevant tags and keywords in the descriptions for all your videos as well as in the tag section.

 **YouTube is about sharing videos with a wide audience. Keep your videos short and entertaining so your audience will want more.**

The key to successful videos is to avoid making a sales pitch or being overtly self-promotional. Aim to make your videos entertaining or enlightening. At the very least, they should inform and educate. Research shows that videos that are passed on to others provoke *high arousal*, meaning that people get emotionally involved with the content. You can check out the most-viewed and most-subscribed videos to get a good idea of what works.

## Tweeting and Twittering

How can you resist a communication tool that limits you to a handful of words? After all, how hard could composing a message in 140 characters (including spaces) be?

Twitter is so quick and easy to use that it took off like a rocket. On Twitter, everyone is a broadcaster who's promoting something—a link, a personal update, or a point of view. As brief as a tweet may be, tweeting takes practice and a little wit to master, which is why celebrities and senior executives often hire Twitter coaches. Think of Twitter as part microblog and part social network that can work as a micro PR feed.

The secret to attracting followers is to provide interesting commentary and quips. Use it to broadcast helpful riffs about what you are doing and thinking right now. Tweet about inside information in your industry. Tweet about your point of view on what's happening in your world or business. Tweet useful tips that your followers might find interesting. You can suggest interesting articles and books to read and provide a link.

The key is to provide interesting news, ideas, and a point of view that are fresh and reflect who you are and your brilliance as an observer or interpreter of your world. Do that and followers will come. If you're following 4,789 people and only nine are following you, that's a sure signal that people view you as a spammer not a tweeter. And that won't reflect well on Brand You.

As quick and simple as it is to use, Twitter is not without its pitfalls. Someone created a fake Twitter account for popular NBA star Shaquille O'Neal and tweeted negative messages. As a result, O'Neal hired a coach to help him tweet. Now Twitter is a dominant marketing tool for his personal brand. His coach introduced "Hide and Tweets" and "Random Acts of Shaqness" to humanize O'Neal's brand. He tweets about his doings in a fun way that's enabled him to build his own network of fans.

(TM) **Twitter is instant messaging for the masses. Use it as a mini PR feed that has the power of brevity and immediacy.**

When he retired, O'Neal didn't go the normal route of announcing it in front of TV cameras. He made the announcement in a video posted on Twitter, rewarding his fans with inside information that hadn't yet been released.

It's not a sin to repeat tweets or other digital messages. The entrepreneur Guy Kawasaki repeats each of his tweets four times and gets an average of

600 click-throughs each time, effectively expanding the views of each tweet from 600 to 2,400.

## The Tweeting Activist Artist

The Chinese artist and architect Ai Weiwei may be best known in the West for his design of the Bird's Nest Stadium for the Beijing Olympics in 2008, but in China his fans are so passionate that they're literally throwing money at him.

Ai was jailed for two months in 2011 for suspected income tax evasion, what many believe was a vendetta by the government for Ai's documentary publicizing the names of the children killed by collapsing schools and the reactions of ordinary people after the earthquake in Sichuan province.

To pay off his fine of $2.3 million, Ai turned to the Internet and reached out to his supporters for contributions, which he promised to repay in full. Fans sent money in the mail, through banks, and over the Internet. Others simply folded 100 yuan notes (about $16) into paper airplanes and sent them over the gate around his home in Beijing. In one week, he received almost $1 million.

Because he's an artist with strong branding instincts, Ai doesn't just send his fans a dull paper receipt. He conceived of a decoratively designed receipt that's like a beautiful piece of art for his fans to treasure.

Ai Weiwei was already famous in China before his arrest. His father, Ai Qing, is a famous modern poet in China who was "rehabilitated" during the Cultural Revolution. Ai Weiwei was one of the first celebrities sought out by Sina Weibo (a Chinese microblogging service similar to Twitter) to have a celebrity microblog in 2005, but his account was shut down by Chinese censors. Ai turned to Twitter as his primary communication vehicle, and after Twitter was banned in China, his Chinese fans have to "climb the wall" to pick up his tweets in Hong Kong.

Twitter gives Ai Weiwei a way to express himself personally and politically. According to Ai, "In the Chinese language, 140 characters is a novella." In Chinese, each character can represent a complete word or idea rather than just one letter of the alphabet, as in Western languages. Ai doesn't confine his political activities to Twitter and the Internet. In 2009, he used the Internet to recruit 1,001 Chinese people who had never been to

Europe to wander around a small town in Germany as an art performance called "Fairytale."

## The Kid Stays in the Picture

Even in the early days of the Internet, Gary Vaynerchuk saw that it could be a great vehicle for selling wine in his father's liquor store. He launched Winelibrary.com in 1998, and in 2005 Vaynerchuk discovered social media, particularly video, after seeing a *Saturday Night Live* clip. The SNL clip went viral online and it got Vaynerchuk thinking about how he might use online video to build a personal brand that would help grow the family wine business even more.

 **Digital media is made for personal branding. It gives you a big microphone to broadcast to many every time you speak.**

Vaynerchuk called his video blog WineLibraryTV.com, but later changed it to Daily Grape. The show's set was simple: a table, a chair, and a "big-ass glass." The fifteen- to twenty-minute show was filmed unscripted and uncut to keep costs low and reality high. Vaynerchuk didn't even have a mike. He sampled different bottles of wine and shared some historical facts and then talked about whatever came into his head as he smelled, swished, and tasted the wine. He came across as a regular guy with his plaid shirt and makeshift set. Vaynerchuk's Russian last name is long by naming standards, so his trademark introduction was to say his name slowly, clearly pronouncing each syllable: Vay–ner–chuk.

Vaynerchuk is spontaneous, fun, and has an interesting wine palate. With over 80,000 viewers a day at its peak, the video blog was a big sales generator for the family's wine business and Vaynerchuk's brand. He inked a multi-book deal on entrepreneurship with a major publisher. Now that his brand is highly visible, Vaynerchuk has moved on from the video broadcasts on wine to focus on his book franchise and high-priced consulting. But his vlog is what built his brand giving him visibility, celebrity, and an ardent fans base.

# Virtual Virtuoso

While the Internet has given us the ability to become mini media moguls, it has also transformed that popular mainstay of corporate life, the business meeting. With today's dispersed workforce and teams, another way people are connecting is through virtual meetings. Compared with face-to-face meetings around a conference table, the virtual meeting can seem like a sensory wasteland, whether you are leading the meeting or are an attendee. Unless it's a video conference, you have no idea whether the other members are listening to what you are saying, answering e-mail, or walking the dog. It takes special planning to keep your team involved from start to finish.

Here are some tips:

▶ *Keep the meetings brief and fast paced:* The shorter the better, but make the meetings no longer than ninety minutes. There is no margin for error so you need to spend more time planning the agenda and work flow.

▶ *Send the group a short prework assignment:* Let the team know that you expect them to be prepared to hit the ground running. So send them something that you plan to tee up at the beginning of the meeting for their comments. For example, you can send them the current quarter's sales numbers and ask the group to give their view on the top three challenges you face this year.

▶ *Change up the activities every five to seven minutes:* It's easy to lose the attention of meeting attendees unless you switch activities and give them things to do. So incorporate interactivity into the meetings. For example, you could show some slides then switch to brainstorming, so people can respond with suggestions. Try to avoid boring them with wordy PowerPoint slides. Rather, show slides with a visual and a few key points and elaborate verbally so that you engage the group.

▶ *Humanize meetings by posting pictures:* It may seem unnecessary, but posting the pictures of the attendees around a virtual table can help the team bond. The pictures can be posted at the beginning of the meeting and team members can even make a hard copy so they can visualize the team.

## Don't Skip Skype

It takes some thought and planning to perform at your best if you're doing a Skype interview or video conference meeting where your image is broadcast on a screen.

Somehow, Skype and other video conferencing systems are less flattering to Brand You than the in-person experience. So you need to put on your producer's hat, particularly if you're at home. Make sure that you have plentiful lighting. Turn on all the lights in the room and place lights in front of you to brighten your face. Make sure there are also lights behind you so that you are backlit, avoiding a flattened look. Have extra lights around so you can experiment to get the right effect.

Pose against a backdrop that is simple and static. Avoid sitting in front of a window if there is movement outside or near a cluttered desk that can take attention away from you and your message.

Check your image on the computer. You want your face to be centered on the screen with a straight site line between your eyes and the camera. Your makeup should look natural, but achieving that effect will probably require a little more attention to your makeup than usual. For men and women, make sure you have powder on hand so you can get rid of any shine on your face.

## Holistic Branding

As a brander, you will want to step back from time to time to look at your brand holistically. What are all the places where people touch your brand, both online and offline? What is the experience like, and is it consistent? What do people learn?

Do you know?

As a busy professional, it's easy to get so caught up working that you don't step back and look at how your brand is coming across holistically— both online and in person. To do that, you need to examine your brand from a 360-degree perspective. You need to step into the shoes of all of your different "customers," like marketing professionals do.

When you do that, you'll see there are a lot of contact points, what marketers call *touchpoints*, both in person and online.

**TOUCHPOINTS: All the contact points—both real and virtual—where people come into contact with Brand You.**

**BRAINSTORMER: Holistic Brand**

What are the main touchpoints, or contact points, between your brand and your "customers"?

How could you enhance each for more effective brand building?

*Offline Touchpoints:* List the main offline touchpoints where people come into contact with you, such as in person, over the telephone, in your office, etc. How can you make each touchpoint more consistent and powerful for your brand message?

1. _____
2. _____
3. _____
4. _____
5. _____
6. _____

*Online Touchpoints:* List the main online touchpoints, such as your website, blog, and Twitter, Facebook, and LinkedIn profiles and feeds, etc. How you could make each more consistent and powerful for your brand message?

1. _____
2. _____
3. _____
4. _____
5. _____
6. _____

There are potentially thousands of cyber touchpoints: social media like Facebook, Twitter, LinkedIn, as well as your blog, website, and thousands of other places where you can appear or your picture can be tagged. These virtual touchpoints are very fluid and mutable because other people can interact and make their own comments pro and con about your brand. You don't have total control over the content.

Still other touchpoints are more subtle: the way you come across on your voice-mail message, your e-mail signature, the way that you answer the phone. Marketers try to make all brand touchpoints as personal, meaningful, and experiential as possible. That way, you create a powerful emotional connection with others, even a feeling of community.

Thinking in terms of touchpoints is powerful for people, too. Real and virtual contacts or touchpoints affect the impression your brand makes in the minds of your "customers": your boss, business colleagues, clients, friends, and prospective bosses and associates. You want every one of your touchpoints to convey the right brand impression, to be as consistent (and consistently *positive*) as possible.

## Cyber Cuts

What do you do if a bad story about you appears in the media? What if the story comes up prominently on page one when you Google yourself? The good reputation you've worked so hard to create can go up in smoke in a flash.

You'll find that it's hard to erase a story from the Internet.

As a personal brander, you want to play a strong role in creating your story—the one you want told, not the story that someone else is assigning to you. Set up tools to monitor your cyberbranding. Use Google Alerts for your name and relevant keywords so you can check what is being said about you and your interests as you build your brand online. There are a number of reputation management tools you can use to track your personal brand and keywords, including Trackur, BrandsEye, and MyReputation.

One tactic for exerting control is to post frequent content on the Internet. Search engines give more weight to real-time updates, so if you are active on social media and new media, posting and connecting frequently, your media updates will impact organic search results, pushing the negative story down in page rankings.

You can ask people to write positive recommendations and endorsements on social media sites as well. That way, the bad story will look oddly out of place.

## Measure Your Brand Power

The Internet makes it easy to measure your brand's online influence. Measurement has always been a key component of branding. Television and radio provide marketers with measurement numbers of viewership, and if the numbers are low, broadcasters throw in *make-goods*, free spots so that a marketer gets the numbers they paid for.

Now you, too, are a media broadcaster, and you can measure the sort of viewership your media network is generating. Take a page from the Madison Avenue playbook and take a beginning *benchmark* measurement before you step up your branding efforts. Then, take additional measurements at periodic intervals to see the effects of your online branding.

The simplest way to measure your online presence is to set up Google Alerts for your name; Google will alert you by e-mail every time your name shows up on the web. You can use the Online ID Calculator to measure the strength of your online reputation, which looks at the volume of mentions and the relevance. There is also Klout, which you can link to your Facebook, Twitter, and LinkedIn accounts to measure your social influence. Klout measures thirty-five different variables in three basic areas: True Reach (the size of the engaged audience), Amplification (a measure of the engagement of the content), and Network (the influence level of the engaged audience). Klout synthesizes this into a numerical score ranging from 1 to 100.

There are tools specific to each social media platform, and no doubt more are being developed each day, for the personal brander as well as for entrepreneurs and business owners who want to track the effectiveness of social media marketing. On Twitter, for example, you can set up TweetBeep, Twitalyzer, or Crowdbooster. If you have a website or blog, you can insert a plug-in for Google Analytics to measure how many people are coming, the content of greatest interest, and other useful measures.

If people find that you have a weak brand online, they will assume you aren't as good as someone with a strong online reputation. If you have a weak score, figure out what you can do to increase your brand strength online, such as improving the quality and number of your profiles on social networking sites or setting up a blog and posting regularly and linking to other sites. Post short articles on e-zines that cover your areas of interest. Set up a Twitter account and tweet several times a week. Even posting book reviews on Amazon and other sites will help your online strength to trend up.

**BRAINSTORMER: Reputation Management**

What can you do in the next twenty-four hours to increase your brand strength online? What can you do in the next week? In the next month? What online tools will you use to measure your progress?

What is most effective today isn't traditional, in-person branding and marketing, as powerful as they are. What works best is a holistic approach that uses all the tools at your disposal to build a strong personal brand, both in person and online. Explore the new cyberbranding opportunities on social media to complement your in-person branding. What works today is connecting and building a community with your business colleagues, prospects, and like-minded people through traditional and virtual touchpoints.

**IN A NUTSHELL:** The eleventh secret of self-brands: Leverage the new social media world. It's low cost and democratic, unlike the old media world. And it gives you plenty of tools to make your personal brand more valuable.

# CHAPTER 12

# Think in Terms of Emotional Engagement with Your Key Target Markets

*Look fresh and merrily.*

William Shakespeare
*Julius Caesar* (II, 1)

**P**owerful brands touch people. Brands today are not about the product but about the relationship between the brand and the target market. That's why today's brand managers put a lot of emphasis on *emotional branding, brand personality, market segments,* and *total brand experience.*

We form the strongest bonds with brands we like, identify with, and feel emotionally connected with in our lives. Powerful brands make us feel more in control, more self-assured.

Ad agencies even help their creative departments develop advertising by writing descriptive brand briefs that bring the brand virtually alive.

The brand brief also defines and describes the target market for the brand. The target market not only is described in demographic characteristics such as age, income, and geography but is brought to life through softer characteristics such as lifestyle, attitudes, and way of thinking. The creative people really need to get under the skin of the target market in order to develop effective advertising for the brand.

The goal is to build a strong emotional bond between the brand and the target market through all branding activities: packaging, design, advertising, and other marketing programs.

## Think in Terms of Markets

Business success is built around relationships, too. Your success depends on what other people—your target markets—think of you. It doesn't matter who is "objectively" more qualified or talented. What matters is what the people making the decision feel about you and your abilities versus the other people you are competing with.

Think about all the people who are important to your brand—your boss, your clients, and your colleagues—in terms of target markets and follow these six rules of thumb.

### Rule 1: Prioritize Your Target Markets

Most people make the mistake of defining the market too broadly. So they don't give the most important consumers of their self-brands any more attention and service than they give to their less important consumers.

In branding, markets are defined and prioritized. No one has the resources or time to go after everyone. No brand can appeal to everybody. Neither can you. It's smart to pay more attention to the people who have the greatest impact on your brand's success. You want to create loyal customers by focusing on your most important customers.

Think in terms of primary and secondary markets:

▶ *Primary target market:* These are the key people who are the most important to your self-brand and who will deliver the best results for your brand. It could be your core group of clients and prospects. If you work in a corporation and don't have external clients, your boss and key senior executives may be your primary target market.

▶ *Secondary target market:* These people also have some impact on your brand and could become more important in the future.

## Rule 2: Create Loyal Customers

There's a saying in branding that you know a product has become a brand when your customers are your salespeople. That's why branders put so much focus on building a community among their customers. And they strengthen community ties through loyalty marketing programs or friendship branding with special events and rewards programs for customers. Communities make brands thrive. And happy communities grow into bigger communities since the word of mouth is so positive.

To build a community of "loyal customers" for Brand You, you must understand what makes the people you are targeting tick. Marketers often do segmentation studies and give the segments names like "Actives," "Show-Offs," "Family Values," "Worriers," and the like. These psychographic descriptors help marketers design sales and advertising messages.

You might want to look at your target markets that way, too. What are they looking for? What values are important to them? Given this understanding, what is the best way to appeal to this group of clients or that senior manager?

If you were a competitor, how could you top your performance with your primary target market? What would your clients love you to do that you are not doing now? Start doing it.

What are the sore spots? What are you doing that they don't like? Stop doing it.

What changes can you make to increase your target market's level of satisfaction?

The more precisely you define the target market and its needs and desires, the easier it is to package yourself and develop the best solutions, messages, and approaches to satisfy those needs and desires.

## Rule 3: Develop a Clear Value Proposition

In analyzing market segments, you're looking for an opportunity. With which group would you be most successful? What is the right self-brand strategy for this target market? What is your value proposition—what do you have to offer them that competitors don't?

If the target market is defined too broadly, your value proposition won't resonate with anyone because it will be too broad and vague. It will be impossible to build a strong brand identity, too. Your image will be too general to attract interest and loyalty.

In attacking a narrow target market, you need to make sure the segment has enough size and growth potential. You want to own a valuable target market niche.

Say you are a financial consultant targeting women. Which women are your best prospects? Women differ in age, income, education, lifestyle, marital status, geographic origin, and psychology.

Even women with high net worth may be too broad a target market. Maybe it's high-net-worth female executives and entrepreneurs. Or it could be women who are divorced or are planning to divorce. Or maybe it's widows. Or it could be women who have inherited money.

Each of these target markets has distinct needs and interests that would not be satisfied with an approach that targets the broader market of women in general.

## Rule 4: Build an Emotional Bond

Today, brand managers put such a strong emphasis on emotional branding because people form the strongest relationships with brands they like and care about.

It's often the emotional ties that bind. Rationally, we may be able to make a case for why the capabilities of one company are better than another's or why one person's experience is superior to that of another. Yet our gut may tell us something different. We choose the one that makes us feel more comfortable emotionally.

Your goal as a self-brand is also to build satisfied and loyal customers, people who have good things to say about you because they have strong feelings about you, too.

One simple thing to keep in mind will go a long way toward building a strong bond with your target markets: listen more and talk less.

Listening seems so simple, yet few have mastered the art. Listening helps in building strong relationships and engaging your target audience.

When you listen rather than talk, you flatter your audience. You'll create a great impression (and learn a lot at the same time). When you listen, you are telling people that you think they are smart and worth listening to. You are saying that you care about their concerns, that you feel something for them. Listening also says that you are the type of person who wants to learn and improve.

It's so simple and so powerful. By simply listening, you often engage your target markets more profoundly than by saying something profound.

## Rule 5: Think Outside-In

A cardinal rule of branding is to think first of what reaction you want from your target audience (outside), then figure out what you have to do to get that reaction (inside).

So don't begin with what you want (inside-out). Begin with what you want your target audience to do, then plan your action. For example, if you are a salesperson, the reaction you want, of course, is a sale. But if you go right into a sales message with a new client, you probably won't get the reaction you want. Most people don't want to be sold, but they do want to buy. A better tactic is to get to know what the client's needs are and avoid "selling."

Think in terms of *framing* your message. People are different and what would work with one sales prospect (or any target group) might be completely wrong for another. Frame your message and how you act so that you connect with people's wants and desires. You want to connect with their "bias," what's important and relevant to them.

## Rule 6: Attract through "Soft Power"

The term "soft power" was coined by Joseph S. Nye in a book about how to attract people to your ideas in the arena of world politics. We're all familiar with exerting power through the carrot (paying someone) and the stick (threatening someone). Soft power is the third way. It uses things like your values, style, and point of view to attract others to you.

As I've said, branding shows you a lot about how to develop a style and point of view and other soft power ideas. One thing to think about that will increase your ability to attract others to you is executive presence. An important component of executive presence is bearing—the way you inhabit space. How do you enter a room? Do you stand tall and walk purposefully? Do you make an entrance? Or do you slouch and look distracted? Something as simple and controllable as bearing, your posture and stance and the way you move, is a powerful self-branding device that signals a lot to your target audience.

The other important component of executive presence is comportment—your way of conducting yourself when interacting with others. It's knowing how to greet and make conversation with new people at an industry event. It's knowing how to lead a meeting or handle an irate client. It's knowing how to behave in expected and unexpected situations, regardless of how many eyes are on you.

Now, let's look at the people in your target markets.

## Guess Who's Number One?

If you work in a company, your boss is probably your number one target market.

Why?

Your boss has the most control over your self-brand (unless you have an internal network that's better than your boss, or very loyal external clients, or are related to someone important).

Look at Zoe's story. Warm and engaging, Zoe had an impressive background in brand management at well-known packaged goods companies. Unfortunately, she had spent her career building brands for others and had not done much to build her brand. Here she was, in her early forties, unable to get to the next level although she had been with the same company for eight years. She worked hard and had a loyal team, yet some colleagues with similar experience and levels of responsibility had been promoted to vice president, two levels above her.

What was she doing wrong? Her problem was a familiar one: "The boss doesn't appreciate me." How did Zoe respond to her problem? She avoided her boss!

Do you think that was a good tactic for achieving her goal of being promoted to VP? (She was ignoring her primary target market.)

## Think Truth or Consequences

Emotionally, I could understand why Zoe wanted to sit far away from her boss at meetings and avoid one-on-ones. But her behavior was career sabotage. It was completely counterproductive to her goal of becoming a corporate VP.

Zoe had established a distant, formal relationship with her boss. Things were so bad by the time we started working together that she was communicating with him primarily through e-mail and memos and as infrequently as possible.

In her performance evaluations, Zoe's boss gave her high marks in many areas but consistently low marks in leadership and communications skills. Her boss told her that she needed to play a stronger role in initiating projects, selling them to management, and increasing her visibility in the firm.

Of course, Zoe felt that she had done all these things, often more than colleagues who had been promoted. After all, she had forty-seven people reporting to her. But, her boss didn't perceive her as being a leader or having a high enough profile to be a VP.

## Perception Is Everything

The business world, like most places, operates on *perceptions*.

It really didn't matter that Zoe supervised a larger group than her colleagues had. She was viewed as a weak brand and not a vice president brand. And, in most companies, if your boss doesn't nominate you for VP, you will not have those two letters appearing after your name no matter how good you are.

So, if this happens to you, the choice is clear: you must either change your boss's perceptions of you or find a new boss somewhere else.

Zoe was stuck in an outdated junior image.

Our task was to develop a self-brand action plan that would change people's perceptions so that Zoe would be seen as the leader she is. She needed to improve her communication and presentation skills and dramatically increase her visibility inside and outside the firm.

## Take Action for a New Reaction

Above all, Zoe needed to stop avoiding her boss. She had to emotionally engage him in what she could do.

To begin that process, she had to build rapport with her boss by meeting with him, making eye contact, and interacting in a more relaxed manner.

Rather than approach him as the "boss" or the "enemy," Zoe had to approach him as a trusted confidant (even as a friend). She needed to replace her negative self talk with a positive mantra ("My boss is my ally").

Zoe had to approach him as if he were the way she wanted him to be. Often, if we treat people in a certain way, they start behaving to match. If that didn't work, her plan B was to launch a job search.

## Slay the Dragon

Zoe had to gain more confidence as a business presenter. She was great in front of her own team, but hated to present to her colleagues and senior executives. She hid behind a blizzard of PowerPoint bullets and spoke too fast to hide her nervousness.

Zoe told me that when she had to present to an important audience, her mind would go blank. The detailed slides were her safety net.

It turns out that Zoe had an inner critic, a voice inside her head that screamed, "You're not good enough" or "You'll forget something important and do a terrible job." It immobilized her and inhibited her performance.

The good news is that these feelings are common. I've had to fight an inner critic throughout my life, and many of my clients have had to as well. Here are some techniques to slay the inner critic:

- ▶ *Use positive self talk:* Talk back to your inner critic. Say, "That's not true. I *am* good enough!" One client even told me that she imagines her inner critic as a pesky crow on her shoulder who she shoos away.
- ▶ *Visualize a confident, successful you:* Many pro golfers are taught to visualize hitting the perfect shot as they approach the tee, even imagining exactly where the ball is going to land. Visualization can be powerful in business, too. It's like the avatar you might choose in an online game. I often visualize a poised, charismatic alter ego before I give a talk, and sometimes it even works!

▶ *Tune in to your body and your breathing:* Yoga emphasizes deep belly breathing and connecting with your physical body as a way of calming yourself and being present in the moment. You'll find the same techniques immensely helpful in business situations, too. Breathe deeply through your diaphragm, not shallowly through your upper chest. Even becoming aware of your body, of your feet firmly planted on the ground, can be a wonderful way to relax.

▶ *Have a pre-talk ritual:* Actors have a ritual that they go through before a stage performance. They do physical warm-up exercises, vocal exercises, visualizations, or they listen to a tape—whatever works to get them relaxed and ready to perform. Find your own ritual to get you in the zone. I have one that I've developed to deal with my pretalk jitters.

## Improve What You Can

Zoe also worked on slowing down her rapid-fire speech. She spoke so fast that I often had to replay her voice-mail messages to decipher them!

One of the first things she did was join Toastmasters. After she gained some experience with that group, she offered to give a talk at a local university in order to develop more confidence in her presentation skills.

Little by little, Zoe started getting a different response from her boss and others at her company as she became a better communicator. She also increased her visibility within the company by volunteering to lead an important strategic initiative.

When Zoe's boss selected her to represent him at an important company-wide meeting in Europe, we knew she had turned the corner. (And Zoe did get her happy ending. She made VP, and the company even added a new group to her department.)

## View Company Execs as a Market

Colleagues and senior executives at your company are important target markets

Henry, a financial services exec, is a master at developing formidable internal networks. The speed with which he put a network in place at his new firm was nothing short of "I came, I saw, I conquered."

Here's how he did it. When he started his new job, he saw an opportunity to put together innovative client events and programs directed at key client segments.

Rather than just put together programs that broke new ground with the client market, Henry also chose topics that were appealing to his consumer target and earmarked themes that appealed to key internal executives (his target market).

For example, the company's chief financial officer was involved in charitable groups that dealt with children and education. Henry put together a client event on America's education crisis, something of concern to the parent market segment his financial company was targeting. He invited a nationally recognized speaker on the topic and asked the CFO to introduce the speaker. Henry also put together a women's event with a well-known media figure and asked the firm's female executive vice president to make the introductions.

All the client events were successful with their target markets, and they were also a big coup for Henry. In short order, he had strong bonds with executives at all levels and in all parts of the company.

Looking at colleagues as a target market is important for anyone. You may not be able to apply Henry's maneuvers, but there are many opportunities at most companies to volunteer for projects that will put you in touch with a wider group of colleagues. Volunteer. Build relationships. It's much easier to be promoted with the support of other company executives.

## Offer Something Competitors Don't

Whatever your target market, you'll want to have a self-brand strategy that provides a compelling value proposition, a reason to choose you over your competitors.

One client, Kat, had a long career in video production and wanted to start her own business. The problem was that the video production category was crowded.

So we focused on a narrow segment of the market where she had special expertise: training videos and CD-ROMs for cosmetics companies. But there were some entrenched competitors here as well. When we started drawing up her strategy and value proposition for her target audience, we came up with a better idea.

Kat had some special attributes that set her apart and formed the core of our strategy. She was a woman (and could provide a woman's touch) in the video production business, which was dominated by men. She had a long history of producing high-end videos for top cosmetics brands. She knew how to get the lighting, makeup, and staging for top production values.

Kat also had a hidden asset. Before becoming a video producer, she had been a television morning show host in affiliate markets. Bingo! We had our strategy: strong on both sides of the camera.

Defining her business proposition this way dramatically improved the power of Kat's concept compared to those of her competitors. The value to clients was high-end know-how, whether they were preparing a video for their business or a media push that required someone to do a great job looking good in the public eye. It was a different idea, and one that resonated with her target audience.

Kat was able to tie together her assets: her strong client contacts, experience with some of the world's top cosmetics brands, experience as a television host, and a woman's touch to offer clients a clear value proposition.

> **BRAINSTORMER: Your Value Proposition**
>
> Unlike others in my industry, I _____ because
> _____

## Go with Your Gut

Like empathy, intuition is a powerful tool in business for making decisions, analyzing problems, and building relationships. An ad executive at a major global ad agency, Tara was known for her ability to psyche out her clients. Tara had the uncanny ability to unlock the *hidden agenda*—what clients really want but don't articulate—that can make the difference between success and failure in business.

Tara was great at reading body language in meetings. Once, an important prospect said very little as the meeting proceeded with its agenda. Tara sensed that something was amiss, and she wondered, "Gee, I think we missed something. Should I bring it up?" At the end of the meeting she said, "Before you make your decision, I would like to meet with you and show you one of our other proposals. In hindsight, I think it might fit your needs better."

It's amazing, but that exchange led to a close business relationship between Tara and the client. Afterward, Tara's colleagues at the company told her, "You have just added more value than we could have in building a relationship with this client." The important thing is to have the courage to act on your intuition when you feel something strongly.

## Don't Neglect the "L Factor"

Whether we like it or not, business is a popularity contest as much as high school ever was, just without the spit balls.

Likeability is the one thing all target markets must perceive in a brand, whether it is a product or a person. That's why marketers develop a *brand personality* for a product or a company. Marketers also measure brand likeability. A new ad campaign, association with a celebrity, or alliance with another brand dramatically influences a brand's likeability.

Unlike with a product, you don't need to manufacture a brand personality. But always remember that personality is an important differentiator for a brand. You'll find the road to success much easier if you are perceived as likeable. Especially in markets like today's where there is a lot of choice, having a likeable personality can spell the difference between success and failure. Here are five general principles you can use to influence likeability:

1. *The Attractiveness Principle:* We have already discussed the importance of looks and packaging in self-branding. Attractiveness influences that all-important first impression. It has a halo effect and leads to a lot of positive assumptions.
2. *The Similarity Principle:* Finding common ground or relevance is a good networking tool, and it also influences likeability. We like people who are similar to us in some way, whether it is in personality, lifestyle, political beliefs, or an old school tie.
3. *The Empathy Principle:* The best way to get someone to like you is to like them. Put the focus on others. Empathize with them, and they will like you.
4. *The Familiarity Principle:* We like people with whom we are familiar and have contact, whether it's through personal contact, via the

media, or by reputation. That's why visibility is important for people and brands.

5. *The Authenticity Principle:* Authenticity may be the cardinal rule of branding. You have to be yourself, not try to be someone else or fulfill other people's expectations and values.

Tom Hanks ranks high on most people's likeability meter. What makes him so likeable? Hanks is nice-looking, so he fulfills the Attractiveness Principle. But he's not too attractive, so he also taps into the Similarity Principle. Both his public and movie personae suggest that he is someone we could relate to, who treats others well, satisfying the Empathy Principle.

Hanks also fulfills the Familiarity Principle. Movies have made him famous and familiar. Many celebrities share their stories, experiences, and values through the media. Fans feel that they know the celebrity and often become emotionally involved in that person's life.

Above all, Hanks seems to be a regular guy. He seems open and unaffected, which fulfills the Authenticity Principle. He appears to be comfortable in his own skin. He seems like someone you could get to know and someone you would want to be. In a word, Hanks is likeable.

---

 **IN A NUTSHELL:** The twelfth secret of self-brands: Think in terms of markets. Determine what the market wants and what you can do to appeal to the market in a way no one else can.

# CHAPTER 13

# Become a Little Bit Famous

*Have more than thou showest.*
*Speak less than thou knowest.*

William Shakespeare
*King Lear* (I, 1)

**M**ost of us have low wattage on the visibility spectrum. We are unknown outside of a small network of friends and professional contacts. We are not boldface names.

But visibility and its companion, fame, are things you should think about. We're talking here of fame on *some* level—famous in your industry, famous in your company, famous in your division, famous in your hospital, famous in your school, famous in your neighborhood. And we're talking here of being famous for *something*—an idea, a belief system, a point of view, a major achievement, an area of excellence.

You can build visibility for yourself in a subtle or heavy-handed, tasteful or obnoxious, outdated or up-to-date manner, but if you don't participate, you will be left behind.

It is impossible to become a brand without visibility. Marketers want visibility for their brands because visibility builds *mindshare*.

Mindshare brings big rewards. You can get a higher price for your services. People will seek you out. You will attract people to your ideas.

**MINDSHARE: Awareness of your brand versus those of competitors in the target market. High mindshare for your brand means sales leadership and pricing power.**

More opportunities will be offered to you. And it will be easy to gain more visibility.

Of course, it is easy to scoff at the fame game as phony.

But the concept of visibility is part and parcel of our culture. It's not just the media machine that thrives on it.

Visibility is behind every product, every company, every nonprofit institution, every movement, and every person who achieves great things. Yes, visibility helps make the world go 'round.

## Become Top of Mind

Despite things we've been told, like "talent wins out," the reality is more that "visibility wins out."

Talent and ability are important, but visibility alone may explain the difference between a professional who is in demand and earns a large salary and another professional who is just getting by. The truth is that people who have a reputation outside the company's walls have more value.

One key measure of mindshare is *top of mind (TOM) awareness*. Market researchers ask questions such as, "When you think of category X, which brand comes to mind first?" Being top of mind, or the first brand mentioned by the target market, is a powerful advantage. It translates into sales leadership and gives you pricing power over your competitors.

It's the same with people. If you're visible and top of mind in your industry, people will make a lot of favorable assumptions about you. Fame tilts the playing field dramatically in your favor.

People assume that TOM performers are the top performers in their fields. If you are perceived as top of mind, you will be paid more, and more opportunities will come your way. You'll have what we in branding call *mindshare momentum*. Being the dominant, better-known brand in a category gives you strategic control.

 **Being top of mind = strategic control**

## Study the Branding Model

Brand managers build visibility and mindshare for their brands with a variety of tools: advertising, PR, events, product placement, Internet promotions social media programs, and hordes of other creative activities that bring the brand and its target market together.

Brand managers think in terms of (and measure) the *reach and frequency* of a brand message: how many people in the target audience saw a particular message or promotion and how many times they saw it. As a self-brand, you should think in terms of having a clear message and repeating that message so that people remember it too.

Advertisers track *net effective reach*, the optimum number of times the target market needs to be exposed to a message. They even track *wearout*, which is what happens when key market segments have seen a particular ad campaign enough times that it has become worn out and overexposed.

## Rub Shoulders With a Celebrity

The celebrity endorsement is a well-known standby in the advertising business.

Studies by ad agencies tell us why the celebrity touch is so powerful. It's not because consumers really think that the product will necessarily be better but because they notice and pay attention to more of the sales message and are more likely to buy a product when a celebrity is behind it. Look at how Paul Newman sold spaghetti sauce. The "copy the stars" syndrome is also at work here. We have a need to model ourselves on heroes and superstars. We give them mythic stature and want to emulate their style.

The touch of a highly visible celebrity can jump-start demand for a product, company, or event. Adidas partnered with designer Stella McCartney to add sizzle to its shoe line. Certainly her designs were a breath of fresh air for a brand that had become lackluster, but the celebrity wattage of her name helped a lot, too. Now, it's hard to find Adidas shoes in stock.

Even being associated with a celebrity in some way will give you an enormous boost in visibility. When Kevin Federline married Britney Spears and Guy Ritchie married Madonna, it placed them front and center in the news and raised their position in the celebrity spectrum (at least for the time they were married). Pairing up increased the star power of Catherine Zeta-Jones and Michael Douglas—not to mention the uberwattage of Angelina Jolie and Brad Pitt.

You can get a halo effect just by displaying a picture of yourself together with a "celebrity" in your office or home. Notice the interest in photo ops with the mayor, or the company chief executive, or a celebrity at a corporate outing.

Event planners seek out highly visible people to draw big crowds to corporate and civic events. Endorsement from a well-known person can move an unknown product or company into the big leagues. Former president Bill Clinton's endorsement of *The South Beach Diet* on a talk show boosted sales of the book almost overnight.

In summary, visibility gives you the following benefits:

- ▶ Credibility
- ▶ Awareness
- ▶ Differentiation
- ▶ Higher pay
- ▶ More visibility
- ▶ Awards of distinction
- ▶ Career opportunities

## Take the Hollywood Road

High visibility is often the strategy of choice for celebrities, television personalities, and sports stars when the worth of their personal brands depends on megavisibility. Sometimes visibility is the only strategy for a celebrity, for example, Paris Hilton and the Kardashians.

Celebrity-making involves positioning, image development, packaging, story line, marketing messages, and PR, all aimed toward building and extending a person's shelf life, just as in brand development. With celebrities, it's easy to tell who the stars are and who is at the red-hot center. You can look up each person's Q Score, Marketing Evaluations's ranking of celebrities in terms of their fame and popularity quotient, at *http://www.qscores.com*.

A high Q Score translates into getting tens of millions of dollars for the star role in a hot new movie. Advertisers want you for product endorsements. Publishers are eager to snag your new book. And fame opens up a list of opportunities that is long and growing longer as line extensions break new ground.

### (TM) THE HOLLYWOOD MODEL
### Talent + Packaging + PR = Star

Celebrities (and their agents) are constantly on the lookout for opportunities to gain visibility that would benefit their brands. You too should always keep your eyes open for ways to increase your visibility that are compatible with your self-brand and your profession.

## Opt for Business Visibility

It used to be that businesspeople shunned visibility, but that was before the days of the celebrity CEO. Selection of a brand CEO can drive up a company's stock.

Likewise, the troubles of a celebrity chief can drive down a company's stock, as happened when ex-chiefs Dennis Kozlowski and Bernie Ebbers did the perp walk. Now, in the new world of Sarbanes-Oxley, chief executives are also tuned into the risks of being in the spotlight.

### (TM) Modesty Is a Virtue but Visibility Pays

Many hardworking executives are visibility challenged. They undervalue the importance of volunteering to lead projects, taking credit for accomplishments, and getting to know a range of senior executives.

Of course, nothing beats a track record of accomplishment for brand-building visibility. Preet Bharara is the U.S. Attorney for the Southern District of New York. Targeting what he calls Wall Street's culture of greed, he's had high profile arrests and convictions of Wall Street executives to seal in his brand as a fearless and successful prosecutor.

Don't be afraid to toss your hat in the ring and ask for assignments, and volunteer to lead or be a part of projects and new initiatives. When Bria was a beginning employee, she was itching for a promotion. "I didn't have all that much to do at the time, and with little to do, I get bored and restless so I asked around to get more work. One Friday, a helpful executive dropped a pile of reports on my desk and said, 'Why don't you write a summary of these?'"

Bria had a lost weekend and she had a full report on Monday. She did it again and she did it again. And before long, Bria was promoted into a bigger job. A little extra work can pay off a lot—it helped Bria brand herself as an emerging leader who was willing to do whatever it takes to help the team win. So don't be afraid to ask.

When you're an important contributor or leader of a project or initiative, don't relinquish ownership either—you can always share ownership. Remember the lesson of John Adams, who ceded the task of drafting the Declaration of Independence to Thomas Jefferson because he thought Jefferson was the better writer. It was a mistake that Adams regretted for the rest of his life: "Jefferson ran away with all the stage effect," he lamented, "and all the glory."

Visibility means you're more likely to show up on Google when someone plugs in your name. Look at my client Richard, who held a series of senior management positions in retailing. When a PR release would go out about a new company initiative, Richard would tell the PR department to get a quote from one of his key lieutenants, instead of giving a quote himself. His recognition of subordinates made him a popular boss, but you can take this too far.

Richard is in transition now, and he is virtually nonexistent on Google searches. That's a problem. There's no paper or virtual trail to punctuate his impressive job history, so his role is diminished in the eyes of headhunters and prospective companies. Richard is competing with other senior managers with similar job histories who do have an impressive list of news clippings and links when their names are searched, and that makes them more desirable.

**BRAINSTORMER: Gauging Your G Score**

Gauge your visibility measure by Googling your name or using one of the social media brand measurement tools. How does Brand You measure up?

How can you work on building your G Score?

## The Rise of Celebrity

Now, along with the celebrity CEO, there is the celebrity chef, celebrity entrepreneur, celebrity doctor, celebrity lawyer, and celebrity hairdresser, you name it. People running businesses of all sorts realize that visibility helps their businesses flourish.

Political commentator Peggy Noonan commented on an unsettling trend in U.S. politics in the Republican primary race in 2011–2012. Some candidates appeared to be running not because they wanted to actually be president but as a "branding exercise" to help them sell books or get a cable TV contract.

In the new world of celebrity fascination, the good news is that you can always rebrand after a scandal—short of murder perhaps. Look at Martha Stewart. The damage was extreme because the company is essentially Stewart's self-brand. However, the company's stock regained positive momentum after Stewart and her company took charge of her self-brand again. After all, there is no sexier story than picking yourself up from a big fall and rebuilding your life for an against-all-odds second act.

## Create Buzz

Today, businesspeople have lots of avenues for visibility.

At the high end of the visibility spectrum, you can enhance your visibility through interviews on network and cable television or in consumer and business publications. You can give speeches at industry or outside events. You might choose to provide expert testimony. You could seek board seats at other companies or become involved with charities and philanthropic causes.

Like entertainment and sports celebrities, businesspeople are pursuing line extensions outside their areas of expertise as a way of expanding their brand footprint and perceived value. Buying a sports team, running for political office, and writing a book are all actions that pack a high visibility quotient.

Some businesspeople are even trespassing on celebrity turf by launching television shows, fueled by the success of Donald Trump and his reality show *The Apprentice*. After you've made piles of money, there's an attraction to becoming a "king of the hill, top of the heap" brand on television—the kind of fame and recognition we associate with television personalities. Publicity-driven CEOs such as Trump, Martha Stewart, and Richard Branson have turned PR into an art form. All are in a class by themselves, so adept are they at creating visibility and manipulating PR. Rappers are some of the best media and business crossover stars, adept at exploiting multiple media streams (think Sean "Diddy" Combs).

These days, no one is immune to the draw of visibility. In the past, academics were not known outside a small circle unless they published a best-selling book. Now, academics appear regularly on talk shows, speak around the country, and are quoted in the news along with being profiled in alumni magazines.

## Begin With Low-Visibility Tactics

Most people aren't able to talk about their companies or their jobs to the outside media unless they are senior executives and have been authorized to do so. You probably can't use high-visibility tactics unless you are involved in an activity outside your job, such as chairing a fund-raising drive for a nonprofit or supporting a cause of personal interest to you.

But you can use a lot of low-visibility tactics to achieve more visibility within your company and your industry.

Start by taking a more active role, such as volunteering for cross-functional projects at work. Ask to participate in or lead corporate initiatives to which you can make a contribution. Besides learning something new, you will come into contact with executives outside your area in the company. Even something low-key, like setting up a monthly brown-bag lunch and inviting senior executives and outside vendors to speak, will help get you noticed outside your department.

Brush up your presentation skills so that you are an effective communicator both internally at meetings and externally with industry and other groups. As you become better at speaking and communicating, more opportunities will come your way.

Look for ways to make your talks special or set up a dramatic introduction for someone else. Think about how you enter a meeting. Don't ever rush in. Enter slowly, and if you are in a company where you can pull it off, grandly. I'll never forget my high school experience of watching Margaret

Mead enter the auditorium from the back of the room and walk down the aisle with an enormous walking stick. What a grand entrance!

When you talk about your ideas and proposals, use the branding techniques discussed earlier, such as naming your ideas to make them big ideas and coining words and expressions. Write an article for the company newsletter, or suggest a story about your department's new initiative. Don't make the story about you. Make it about the project, the idea, or the accomplishment. Glory will flow back to you, and you won't appear to be self-promoting.

The box below contains a list of high-visibility and low-visibility tactics used by businesspeople. It not only is a good review of what we've just discussed but may spur additional ideas of your own.

### High-Visibility Tactics vs. Low-Visibility Tactics

| | |
|---|---|
| Expert on television | Project leader |
| Media interviews | High-level presentations |
| Book | Company projects |
| National media articles | Company newsletter |
| Charitable boards | Charitable activities |
| Corporate boards | Letters to the editor |
| Keynote speeches | Trade articles |
| Industry panels | Industry association activities |
| Website or blog | Proprietary reports |
| High-society events | White papers |
| Celebrity pal | Company website |

# Check for Room in the Channel

In seeking visibility, one thing you need to consider is whether there is "room in the channel," as they say in the business.

PR isn't a limitless thing. There is only so much room or coverage that can be absorbed by any one topic (with some notable exceptions, such as a juicy scandal).

As a rule, only a certain number of people can dominate each arena (unless you carve out a new arena, and as a talented brander, you just might be able to do that). Only a certain number of new faces can be highlighted each year. Yet, there is an insatiable desire for new faces, new voices, and new content. This creates the tension in the visibility sphere.

Look at a major American event that is filled with high-visibility celebrities, such as the Academy Awards. The media focuses on the winners in the big categories, but after that, visibility reaches just those celebrities who wore a fabulous (or awful) dress or say something especially provocative (or incoherent) on stage. The channel simply doesn't have enough room to give visibility to every important person at the event.

Likewise, it's harder to find room in the channel in a geographic market like New York City, which is already crowded with top talent in every field. It will be much more difficult to break out unless you come up with something very special.

## Dominate a Space

Look for an arena that is not already too crowded with others who staked out their spots before you. The first places to look are your job and your field. Then look at outside areas—cultural or political organizations or a cause that you are passionate about. Best of all, create a new cause or business idea to champion.

Every field produces celebrities: people who act as standard bearers. These people are the leaders who are active at industry events and are quoted on industry issues or on their specialty areas. Or they fill the role of expert, pundit, or contrarian. Every institution has a need for people to fill various archetypal roles. Some even become icons.

Think about where there might be room in the channel for you. Is it time for a changing of the guard? Are there issues in your field that are not well represented or even discussed? How can you get to know some of the influential people in the various arenas that interest you? Which ones would benefit most from your contribution?

## Your Breakout Story

Think strategically about your *breakout story*, the first story that launches you in the media. It is your most important story, since it will position you in the minds of others and have lasting consequences.

Another thing to think about is whether your field is mediagenic. Some industries are inherently more high interest than others. It's much easier to generate visibility if you are in a high-profile business area such as technology, media and entertainment, pharmaceuticals, and others that are of constant interest to the public. People in finance still get a lot of media attention but after the financial meltdown, most have had to fight negative branding whether personally deserved or not.

If you work for a coal company, you will likely have more trouble getting visibility for yourself and your company than if you are in a high tech startup. You will have to generate visibility outside of your industry or have business insights with universal appeal.

Harvey Mackay ran an envelope company, a business that does not usually generate much interest. Mackay won megavisibility through his first business book, *Swim with the Sharks*. The PR on the book and his business insights (and humor) catapulted Mackay into the big time as a business leader and philosopher on winning in business. And he followed up his first success with other best-selling business books.

## Toot Your Own Horn (Gracefully)

If you hope to succeed at visibility, you need to control how you are perceived. Whether it's becoming better known in a small pond (your company) or a big pond (your industry) or the ocean (nationally), it's smart to package your message. You need to package it with a good name and sound bite so that it will break through, but you must also package it so that you don't appear to be promoting yourself.

Here are the most important guidelines for promoting yourself effectively while avoiding the appearance of self-promotion:

- ▶ *Use a narrative or story format:* Presenting your accomplishments or ideas through dialogue and building suspense gets people involved in the story because it doesn't seem to be about you but about what happened.
- ▶ *Quote other people:* As they say, the best advertising is word of mouth. When another person sings your praises, it's the opinion of a third party, not your own judgment. ("I was really surprised when client Joe called to say . . .")

▶ *Put the spotlight elsewhere:* Don't focus on yourself. Put the spotlight on your new initiative or the company. Always make it about something larger than yourself.

▶ *Bring the audience into the story:* When you bring your audience into the story, it won't just be about you. ("I wish you could have been there when . . .")

## Leave a Role for Lady Luck

While I believe that you create your own luck, that doesn't mean people don't add a dollop of luck to their stories. They attribute their success to luck because the story goes over much better that way than telling people the truth. Namely, that you have been working 24/7 on building your career.

 **Luck is the big white lie in most success stories.**

Luck is a key element in most stories of achievement. Luck makes people look like they did not plan their success or use PR or managers to promote themselves. Many people think it is somehow wrong to go after success.

The reality in almost every case is the opposite. Almost no one achieves great things or becomes a well-known self-brand without wanting it and working very hard to achieve it. Strategy and planning have more to do with achieving success than luck does.

People who achieve great things work smart in order to achieve their goals, often with the help of coaches, branding experts, and PR specialists. But most people would rather not hear about all that planning and hard work.

So if you say, "Gee, I just got lucky. They needed an architect to design the new arts center, and I guess I was in the right place at the right time," or, "I didn't mean for this to happen," people will respond in a positive way.

## Master the Media

Today, more than 70 percent of news comes from PR sources. The media have a tremendous need for content, and, as a person who is interested in promoting your self-brand, you'll need to know how to give them good content that will benefit you and your organization.

Never make a media interview about you. Make the interview about what you did or your point of view, not about you personally. By making the project, the new product, or the new initiative the focus of the interview, you will not be the center of attention, but attention will come to you.

 **Remember, your job is to stay on message. The reporter's job is to get you to say something off message.**

Prepare a media talking points memo in advance of big meetings and certainly before a media interview. Include the most likely questions and role-play your answers beforehand. Think of stories, anecdotes, and sound bites ahead of time. Is there a way to present elements of your story as news?

It is also smart to be prepared with at least one point of view that's different from the prevailing view if you want maximum media coverage.

If a question is off track, bring the reporter back to the message you want to give. Reporters are looking for a good story. A good story is when you say something controversial. It's your job to stay in control of the message, no matter what question you are asked. So master the pivot, move sideways and answer the question with the message you want to give.

## Guard Your Reputation

People at the top of their game often develop a false sense of invulnerability.

In fact, they are more vulnerable.

You should realize that you will be living in a fishbowl when you become a boldface name.

People will scrutinize your words and actions more closely than they did when you were not so well known. Some will be looking for mistakes or questionable activities. Jealous competitors may try to take potshots at you.

And as much as the media likes to build people up, it also likes to take people down. The story of Ms. Big's fall from grace sells. As does the juicy scandal that Mr. Big got caught up in. When something like this happens, it gives people the feeling of schadenfreude, or delight in the misfortunes of others.

And you have a lot to lose. The name you spent a lifetime building can be tarnished or even torn down very quickly. Studies show that it takes a lot of promotion of good acts to build a reputation, yet just a little promotion of one bad act to tarnish it.

That's why it's wise to adopt the mind-set that there are no secrets and that people will find out everything. If you're presented with the chance to be involved in something that would truly destroy your reputation if it were known, let that opportunity pass you by. More than losing possessions, losing your reputation will severely damage your self-brand identity.

If you are about to get caught in a PR nightmare, try to take control of the story. The old PR saying goes, "Tell them everything and tell them first."

**(TM) Reputations take a long time to build, but a short time to destroy.**

If the news gets out in front of you, there are still things you can do. Look at how Jack Welch handled the bad publicity about his rich retirement package from GE. Rather than let the "greedy" label stick, he gave back some of the excessive retirement perks. A year later, he came out with a book, *Winning*, to get his brand back in the mindspace he wants to own. Welch is giving the profits from the book to charity, a fact he spells out at the bottom of the book's dedication page. This is a generous thing to do, but also a smart thing if he wants to change misperceptions about being greedy. These smart moves got Welch's brand back intact and he's active today as a global business statesman.

Of course, sometimes bad news stories can have a silver lining. Hillary Clinton's image improved after the Monica Lewinsky scandal. People saw her in a more sympathetic light. Likewise, Martha Stewart's travails and prison stint helped humanize her. And Paris Hilton's appeal only increased after her sex tape made its way into the consumer media.

Managing your reputation is a skill you must master if you intend to build your self-brand, whether you're well known in a national or international arena or a little bit famous in your company or community.

Build your reputation and visibility with finesse. You want to be known for something, but not for being a self-promoter.

The key to doing self-promotion well is to do it without looking like you are doing it. And that indeed is an art worth learning.

**IN A NUTSHELL:** The thirteenth secret of self-brands: Make yourself a little bit famous. Find an arena you can dominate and build a self-brand identity.

# CHAPTER 14

# Develop an Action Plan That Gets You All the Way from A to Z

*Action is eloquence.*

William Shakespeare
*Coriolanus* (III, 2)

Defining a great self-brand strategy is one thing. Making your strategy a reality is another.

You may have a great strategy and a focused visual and verbal identity, but you'll never get anywhere until you pay off your brand promise with an action plan. Without a tactical plan, your success is left to chance.

Executing a self-brand strategy requires persistence and action. Brand managers use a marketing plan to tie it all together, and you should, too.

## Plot a Career Strategy

Margot was a finance major and started out in the treasury area of a major global company. One day after she had been there for six years, her boss called her into his office. Something about her boss's serious tone got her worried that she might be axed.

But she was wrong. "You have talent, Margot. You could go somewhere in this company. You have the potential to be a senior leader, even CFO someday," he said. "But to do that, you can't stay in treasury. You have to move around to other business areas so that you can learn about all the company's businesses and meet people across the firm."

Margot hadn't thought of moving around. She liked her boss and her colleagues. It's counterintuitive, but the best time to move is when you're happy. That's when you have the most support internally.

Margot hadn't looked at her career strategically, at building a finance career with varied business experiences and increasing the value of her human capital. And her path wasn't always easy. She made a number of lateral and promotional moves. In one move, she was put in charge of a troubled, complex business unit, and all her new colleagues used a lot of jargon in meetings that she didn't understand. Margot would nod and take careful notes and go to her direct reports to help translate what they were talking about. Gradually, she mastered the jargon and turned the unit around.

Over the next ten years, Margot worked in various divisions of the company, learning the different businesses and building relationships with a wide range of colleagues. She branded herself as a popular well-rounded leader. Her moves gave her the track record and relationships to become CFO of the company.

When you're thinking of your career and where you're going, ask yourself, as Debby, a coaching colleague, advises, "Is it better?" Is the new situation better than where I am now in some way? It could be better in terms of money, position, learning new businesses, or whatever else is important to you.

## Commit to Action

The hardest part of a big endeavor is getting started. You must, of course, start.

Most people become so daunted by the task of developing a personal branding plan that they procrastinate. The key is to get started with a personal brand audit to determine the best positioning for Brand You. Make sure that you "package" your brand with a visual and verbal identity that communicates your brand message. Then start with a short plan (aim for five pages). Lay on one tactic after another that will help you reach your goal.

Things will add up. Often, just implementing one action item leads to another item. (Even if it's the wrong one, you will be learning. And learning leads to the next step.) Writing the action plan is important because it forces you to tie your strategy to tactics and to set specific goals and target dates.

**BRAINSTORMER: Making a Plan**

If you have already done the brainstormers in the other chapters, you're halfway there. Pull together the goals from the brainstormer in chapter 1, the SWOT and competitive analyses you did in chapter 2, and the strategy statement from chapter 4 and combine them in one document, your self-brand action plan. Then, list specific things you can do to achieve your goals and implement your self-brand strategy.

A self-brand action plan includes the following:

- ▶ *Goals:* Lay out the path you plan to take by setting two or three concrete goals for yourself.
- ▶ *SWOT analysis:* Review your strengths and weaknesses and the opportunities and threats you see in the marketplace. Include an analysis of your key competitors.
- ▶ *Target markets:* List your primary and secondary target markets.
- ▶ *Self-brand strategy:* Define your self-brand strategy, the brand positioning that sets you apart from competitors and offers a benefit to your target market. Make it short and punchy, like a mantra. (Reread chapter 4 and the ten self-brand strategies outlined there if you need to refresh your memory.) Follow your strategy statement with three to five proof points (reasons to believe your strategic positioning).
- ▶ *Time frame:* Set a time frame to check your progress against.

▶ *Tactics:* Outline a series of specific marketing and professional activities that will help you reach your goals. Include the amount of time scheduled for each tactic and the likely results.

▶ *Measurement:* Measure the success of your action plan by noting your progress toward achieving your concrete goals.

Use the brainstormer to get started on your action plan.


## Stay Relevant

A self-brand marketing plan is not carved in stone.

Situations change. You change. Sometimes there's a mixture of self-imposed change and market-induced change.

Change always creates new challenges and opportunities. It requires new strategies and tactics. So, look at your action plan periodically to make sure that your strategy and tactics are right for the current marketplace. Fortunately, people are more adaptable and can change tactics or even strategies more easily than most companies and products can.

Look at my own career. I started out as a Japanese art historian working at the Seattle Art Museum. I pursued a Ph.D., but left before finishing my dissertation. Then I trekked to New York City to seek my fortune. I worked at two ad agencies on a range of products and companies. Then I was a corporate branding executive on Wall Street before I became an entrepreneur.

I'd like to tell you that I became an entrepreneur as a result of a lot of careful planning and a blinding flash of insight—a big idea that I knew couldn't fail. But . . . it didn't happen that way. The truth is, I was forced into entrepreneurship when I lost my high-powered corporate branding job right after 9/11.

Saying goodbye to a Wall Street job—the security, the prestige, the good paycheck—was scary but exciting at the same time. (Never mind that it felt like my *only* realistic option.)

The demand for what I was doing—marketing financial services companies and products—was drying up, and that situation was unlikely to turn around anytime soon.

I had periodically harbored thoughts that I'd do something entrepreneurial at some point (particularly after a bad day at the office). Now, I had to do it.

I may have been a reluctant entrepreneur at first, but after the initial shock of job loss wore off, I was determined to find an idea and develop a business plan quickly. I had to start selling something soon if I was going to survive. And the business idea I came up with was launching a branding and professional development company, which I named SelfBrand.

## Move the Plot

If you take over a new job, the first 100 days are the most important. Notice how the media follows the first 100 days in office of a new president. Your behavior and actions when you start a new job will be scrutinized and will have a strong impact on how you are perceived over the long haul.

Remember the importance of first impressions. Come out of the gate running, with an action plan. Create a vision and a plot for your team to follow and rally around. And keep the plot moving along in the direction you want.

Your self-brand is constantly changing whether you do anything or not. If you don't keep a successful narrative going, the story line could get away from you, and you will be regarded as yesterday's sensation.

Take Luke. Because of his hard work and the successful team projects that he led, he rose quickly at an industrial company. He was known as an innovative leader who could execute because he knew how to make things happen in the manufacturing plants.

After being at the company for a number of years, Luke grew a little bit complacent and wasn't working as hard as he had in the past. All that careful branding as the innovative leader who could execute through final product was beginning to fade from the corporate memory.

Then Luke got a new boss who came from the outside and didn't know about his past deeds. And Luke didn't have any recent accomplishments that might have kept his leadership alive in his new manager's memory.

Six months later, Luke was given a tough job review. All of a sudden, his star, which had been on the rise for so long, was flickering out.

Was the new boss's assessment fair? Probably not.

Did the new boss have his own agenda? Probably.

But the greatest learning experiences often come from bad bosses.The less-than-stellar review certainly woke Luke up to the fact that he wasn't bulletproof.

## Discard Doubts

Self-confidence usually takes a beating in a situation like Luke's. His certainly did.

He started second-guessing himself and doubting his abilities. He circled the wagons and shut himself in his office. And that led to more depression and inaction.

Self-confidence or the perception of self-confidence is a big career booster. And the lack of it is a career buster. To be a successful self-brand, you have to protect your self-confidence. Otherwise, when you feel you are under attack, even if you were once as supremely self-confident as Luke, you will come across like a wimp. For a while, Luke was almost a basket case.

He needed to start believing in himself again and put the experience in perspective. The new boss's bad review was just one person's opinion in a long career of achievement.

Luke needed to protect himself from the impact of his boss's negative perception by focusing on what he knew to be true about himself and by taking action.

## Fight Back

Many people get bogged down in what the boss did or didn't do.

It is impossible to control what other people do and think. But you can always control your reaction and what you are going to do.

Luke initiated an action plan with a two-pronged offensive. One group of tactics addressed his boss's concerns about his performance. The other group of tactics supported a major job search.

After the negative review, Luke wrote his boss a long, positive memo about his performance evaluation. In it, he detailed bullet point by bullet point the actions he was taking to address each performance item. He also met with human resources to create a record of his contention that, even though he felt the performance evaluation was unduly harsh, he was committed to turning things around.

 **You can't always control a negative situation. But you can control how you respond to it.**

Luke took these steps even though he suspected that the new boss had given him the unfavorable evaluation because he wanted to bring his own person in to fill Luke's position.

## Do a Self-Audit

Sure, Luke had made some mistakes. Maybe he hadn't stayed current and on top of new trends. For one thing, many of his company's competitors were outsourcing or locating new plants in Asia. Luke and others at his company were behind on this trend, so now competitors had a pricing advantage. But since Luke was in trouble (and the corporate politicians could sense it), he got more than his share of the blame.

Perhaps Luke had become too reactive, building his workday activities around the many e-mail and text messages he got each day. He realized that he wasn't bringing enough strategic vision and big picture ideas to the business. He hadn't been as innovative in coming up with new product ideas and technology or in initiating better processes as in the past.

But he didn't really recognize the person described in his new boss's harsh evaluation. Nor was the boss very helpful when Luke approached him for direction on an important company issue.

Why did Luke take these steps with his boss and HR?

A job search takes time, and he needed to buy time in which to find something else. There was also the possibility (however unlikely) of turning things around with his new boss or locating another position in the firm. In any case, as long as Luke was working at the company, he had to try to build a positive relationship with his boss, a key target market.

## Create a New Brand Position

Of course, Luke felt set up. But once he accepted the unfairness of the situation, he was able to take charge. We did the SWOT analysis and developed a strategy and an action plan. Luke started setting his own agenda, rather than leaving it to his boss.

Luke's action plan got him to refocus on what had made him great in the first place. He had built his brand on his hands-on, innovative yet nurturing style of leadership. His roots were in operations, and he knew how to build teams within the organization to innovate and get things done. He had been a master of managing from the bottom up and sideways across the organization.

The key thing Luke needed to do was change perceptions—of his boss, other key executives, even the rank and file in the field. He knew his boss was raising the issue with senior management of whether Luke was the right leader for today's highly competitive global marketplace. He needed to create a different impression. He needed to show that he was able to lead in innovation and manufacturing with pricing power over his competitors.

Initially, Luke concentrated on actions that would lead to positive outcomes. His relationship with field operations had always been a source of business inspiration and had given him a performance edge. Luke started visiting the manufacturing plants and field offices more frequently.

He also worked on some small projects that allowed him to score several early victories. He pressed forward on a new product that did much better than expected in the marketplace. And he put together his own team to explore outsourcing and manufacturing outside the United States.

## Mission Impossible

Luke also volunteered to lead the company's big initiative to increase competitiveness by taking a more global approach to manufacturing and other functions where it made sense. No one else wanted to take it on (at least in the lead role). It was a difficult project with a lot of moving parts. In a way, Luke had nothing more to lose but a lot to gain.

The project increased his visibility among many executives with whom he normally didn't come into contact, including the president. He updated his boss frequently on the project's progress, so that the boss would have no reason for complaint. The global initiative also gave Luke hands-on knowledge of and experience with China, India, and other low-cost manufacturing and outsourcing centers his company was exploring. Luke found that his strong interpersonal and team-building skills served him well on the new global playing field. He made important contacts and was building relationships that would be valuable to his company in the future. (Of course, Luke realized that the new initiative made him infinitely more attractive as a job prospect, if it came to that.)

By focusing on his strengths (his creativity, relationship with operations employees, and his ability to lead cross-functional team projects), Luke also drew attention to the weaknesses of his new boss, who was numbers driven, a poor people person, and not that innovative (at least in Luke's opinion).

🔵 **When you have a competitor or a detractor with a weakness, emphasize your strength in the same area.**

It came about naturally in Luke's case, but it's a smart strategy to use with any competitor: look at your competition's weaknesses, and position a weakness against a key strength of yours. Emphasize where you are strong and they are weak. Luke's strength with people and with organizing global teams emphasized his boss's lack of people skills.

## Carry a Brag Book

The more Luke took charge of his life, the less victimized he felt and the more success he had in his job hunt and at his company.

As a way of marketing himself effectively, Luke put together a brag book so that he had all his successful initiatives at his fingertips. It was a nice presentation folder that contained the following self-brand marketing pieces:

► Letters of recognition
► Key initiatives, organized in a case study format (challenge, action, results), like a new business pitch
► Awards for achievement
► Luke's letters in recognition of others
► Testimonials and references

Luke polished up his elevator speech and put together a résumé that sold his accomplishments as a dynamic leader and innovator in his industry, highlighting his leadership of the firm's globalization initiative. He put together a one-page achievement addendum to the résumé that marketed three key projects in a crisp case study format (challenge, action, results). He put a little marketing polish on each with a short quote from a former boss, colleague, or client about how well Luke handled the project. The one-pager was a good document to use as a leave-behind or send with a follow-up letter.

In interviews, Luke had a strong self-presentation and a leave-behind (the one-pager or the brag book). He developed interesting narratives on each of his key projects, linking together his accomplishments and portraying himself as a "man of the people" and an "innovative manufacturing leader." He did his homework on each company so that the meeting would be a conversation, not a one-way question-and-answer session.

## Create Signature Successes

Luke didn't waste much energy on unproductive activities like complaining about his new boss. He focused on his strengths and on activities that would lead to positive outcomes—*signature successes* that would put him on the radar screens of senior executives and on a better track with his new boss, or that would help him locate a desirable job at another company.

Here are some of the tactics in his action plan and measurement goals:

Volunteer for a major company initiative to demonstrate leadership, to build stronger ties throughout the company, and to become an expert in Asian manufacturing and outsourcing. *Measurement:* Achieve project goals set by company president.

Send a memo about the performance review to the boss and to HR, outlining specific actions for addressing critical areas. *Measurement:* Send a monthly memo to the boss and to HR and meet quarterly with both to evaluate progress.

Get in better touch with operations by planning two to three trips a month and scheduling regular times to talk to operations management. *Measurement:* Trips scheduled and calls made each month.

Revise résumé and develop a compelling cover letter, achievement addendum, and brag book for job search. Customize the résumé and letter for each interview. *Measurement:* Set a target date for document completion.

Develop a short list of companies to explore and a networking list of contacts. *Measurement:* Ten discussions or meetings per month, with a company, a recruiter, or a networking contact.

Luke's action plan kept him busy and focused on his goals. The outcome in his case was interesting and totally unexpected. About seven months after Luke completed his internal makeover and began his external job hunt, his boss got a new boss. And within six months, the boss who had been trying to push Luke out was sent packing.

## Keep Your Narrative Current

But Luke probably won't be resting on his past accomplishments anytime soon. More than ever before, Luke realizes that being happy and powerful in your life requires action. You have to get out there and do it. You have to keep your narrative moving along so it is relevant and vital.

Whether you are an executive, a professional, or an entrepreneur, a self-brand action plan also helps you create a sense of value added—the X factor—that sets your self-brand and your business apart from the rest.

After all, the whole point of branding and the action plan is to help you prepare to win. You need to have both the sizzle and the steak to win in today's marketplace.

## Lead With Your Strong Suit

Always play to your strengths and your authenticity. It's easy to forget this maxim as we're offered different opportunities in life.

Take Julius. Julius was an entrepreneur who built a small but successful niche in financial services. After a few years, one of his clients offered to buy his business and put Julius in charge of the division at the company.

Julius was smart, creative, and visionary. He was decisive and made things happen. He was charismatic and a super salesman. And he was likeable.

Sounds like all the right traits to succeed in a large global company, right?

Wrong!

Sure, his intelligence, salesmanship, and creativity were valued at the company, but many of the strengths that made Julius a great entrepreneur were weaknesses in a large corporate environment.

At heart, Julius was a maverick. He was used to making decisions himself, so he got frustrated with the bureaucracy. Sometimes he didn't go through channels. He rubbed managers the wrong way when he didn't solicit their help or win their buy-in. Sometimes he became angry and emotional in dealing with colleagues when he felt they weren't being cooperative.

Before long, Julius was no longer running the division—his baby, the business he had created from scratch. The company brought someone in over him. Julius was now number two.

## Remember What Made You Great

When I first met Julius, he was angry. He felt like a victim, even a failure. He was so upset that he wasn't going to work.

Interestingly, the company wanted Julius to come back either in the number two role or in another position. The company valued his intelligence and sales skills and even signed off on a coach.

Julius may have felt like a failure because he was no longer running his business, but the word "failure" hardly applied. As an entrepreneur, he had created and sold a business for great profit at a young age. Not many people achieve that in a lifetime.

The key question Julius needed to answer was "Do you want to be an entrepreneur brand or a corporate executive brand?" He also needed to find out what he had to learn from this experience. What behaviors should he change or improve on so that they wouldn't haunt him the next time around?

## Do a 360-Degree Turn

Just as brand managers do market research with key target markets, we did a self-brand audit, confidential interviews with ten people, including senior executives, colleagues, direct reports, and family members. (People often tell me that they may have a bit of a difficult reputation at work, but they are completely different at home. Yet, when I talk to their spouses, they tell more or less the same story I hear at the office!)

Our goal in the audit was to gauge perceptions of Julius: who he was, what his strengths and weaknesses were, and what was different and even remarkable about him.

Branding is a game of perceptions. This is true whether the brand is for a company, a product, or a person. What you want to say and do are less important than what the market experiences of you. What are you doing that the target market loves? What are you doing that is tarnishing your brand and turning off your customers?

Target markets often have insights about you and how you bring meaning to the world that you can't see because you're too close to the brand. That's why marketers constantly keep in touch with their target markets through focus groups, one-on-one interviews, and larger surveys.

## Focus on Strengths and Authenticity

When we did the market research on Julius, we found the following key themes:

> Julius made a great first impression (likeable, smart, strong self-presentation) but tarnished the image by being overly emotional for a corporate environment.
>
> Julius was smart and creative and had an entrepreneurial flair, but follow-through in a corporate environment could be a problem.
>
> Julius was a super salesperson who developed strong client relationships, but he needed to translate those people skills to his interactions with colleagues at work. (In other words, he would fare better if he tried to woo colleagues as if they were clients.)

Like all of us, Julius had formidable strengths and weaknesses. Of course, he could transform himself so that he would perform well in a corporate environment, but should he?

In so many ways, Julius was a natural entrepreneur. He had the smarts, creativity, and drive to develop and incubate business ideas. He was interested in gaining financial rewards for himself and his investors. (His concern about his earn-out at the company was another area that rankled the more traditional corporate execs at the firm.)

By focusing on his authenticity and his strengths, Julius was able to focus on the path that was right for him. So what if he couldn't succeed running a division in a large corporation? The best positioning strategy for Julius was to build on his strengths as a maverick and an entrepreneur.

Rather than accept the corporate post the company was offering him, Julius presented a proposal to the division president about creating the new position of intrapreneur. As an intrapreneur, Julius would be responsible for coming up with ideas for start-ups that would expand business with the company's existing customer base.

Julius also explored ideas for business start-ups outside the company and put together a business plan for the one with the most promise.

Now, Julius had a self-brand strategy and an action plan that played exactly to his strengths. With these, he was able to see good options for his future.

## You Can Always Rebrand

Few people have had as dramatic a rebranding as Hillary Clinton. When Clinton was first lady, she got low popularity scores in polls, yet today, as secretary of state, she is not only popular in the United States—often more popular than her boss, President Obama—she is widely regarded to be doing a great job as a globe-trotting diplomat.

How did Clinton successfully rebrand herself from distrusted, unpopular president's wife to admired global diplomat? How did she go from being viewed as inauthentic, divisive, and self-serving to authentic, team-oriented, and altruistic?

Clinton did several things that had a big impact. For one, when she ran for the U.S. Senate from New York, she didn't play the diva role or come across like she felt entitled to the job. She was humble, and began her political journey on a "listening tour," traveling widely around New York State to meet ordinary people as well as state political and business leaders. She sought to understand their perspectives, questions, and concerns. Everywhere she went, people were impressed with her knowledge of the state and its issues.

When Clinton won her seat in the U.S. Senate, she kept a very low profile initially, even though she was a "celebrity" senator. Gradually, people began to see Clinton differently. Her colorful pant suits seemed appropriate for her leadership style. She was a hard worker. She was knowledgeable. She was effective. She may have lost the Democratic nomination for president but as U.S. secretary of state, Clinton went on to establish herself as a strong, capable, and authentic leader on the world stage. She regularly tops polls of the most-admired people.

## Branding Lessons Abound

There are personal branding lessons all around you, every day. Observe successful people in the media, in your company, and in your community, and you'll soon discover that branding lessons are everywhere.

Of course, corporate icons, Hollywood celebrities, and star athletes (who often have brand advisers to help them) are particularly fertile examples to look at for branding and rebranding lessons as well as for cautionary tales about the overexposure, arrogance, and excesses that can destroy a brand. Look at the way Angelina Jolie transformed her brand from her early days, when she wore her husband's blood in a vial around her neck, to today, with her focus on being a mother of six children and a global humanitarian. It's not easy to create a strong self-brand that lasts through the decades or even beyond your death as brand icons do. Here are some factors behind personal brand icons who have kept their brand in demand:

- ▶ *Begin early, and continuously evolve your brand:* We've all heard about an "overnight success," but it's a myth. Usually there are years of work in the trenches followed by equally hard work to stay relevant. Look how Clint Eastwood has interlaced his acting career with periods as a mayor and then a successful film director. Hillary Clinton has deftly navigated her brand from lawyer to first lady to senator and secretary of state. Who knows what her next act will be.
- ▶ *Create a distinctly personal visual identity:* Close your eyes and think of Michael Jackson. Notice the visual trademarks of his "packaging": the sequined glove, the military-style jackets, the mirrored aviator glasses, the black shoes and stark white socks, the masks. Or think of Sarah Palin and her distinctive updo hairstyle and rimless glasses.
- ▶ *Attach a verbal identity that positions Brand You:* Brands think in terms of owning a word, a phrase, or a tagline that captures the brand positioning. Frank Sinatra was "The Chairman of the Board," Elvis Presley was "The King," and Bruce Springstein is "The Boss." In politics, President Ronald Reagan was "The Great Communicator," underscoring his remarkable ability to connect with people through his words and personal style.
- ▶ *Be visible:* Visibility is important for brands, and it's important for people too. President Bill Clinton keeps his personal brand and narrative alive and highly visible through the Clinton Global Initiative, his charitable foundation.

▶ *Seek powerful alliances:* You can't do it alone. If you look at most high profile personal brands, you'll notice that they cultivate professional and personal relationships with other power brands.

## Keep Your Own Scorecard

One thing I have found in working with all types of clients is that practically anything is possible. This is true whether your goal is a promotion or a new job, getting the corner office or getting into the right school, rejoining the workforce after a long absence, or rebranding the family business.

Think of your goals. Brainstorm. Take baby steps first. Create a chain of links. What is one little thing you can do to get yourself moving in the direction of achieving your goal? What else can you do? Start building links on a chain to get yourself from one point to the next.

Apply the branding mind-set and the branding process.

If what you're doing isn't working, try something else. Branders change tactics all the time. Even if a tactic is working great for you now, at some point it won't work as well or will wear out. Like a brand manager, you will have to change and refresh your experience and marketing programs. Marketers refresh the brand experience all the time. They might try a new advertising campaign, a new promotion, a special event, new packaging, a celebrity tie-in, or experiment with a new social media program to engage its audience.

The best way to come up with a good idea for your brand is to think of a lot of ideas. You may not be able to use them all, but some will be worthwhile. Focus on the best ideas that reflect your self-brand strategy and see where they lead you. Try a different tactic and see where it takes you.

When things are going well and you're on a roll, that is the time to push for more. That is the time for bold actions and new projects. Ask for the big raise or the promotion. Seek out more visibility and take your brand to the next level.

Above all, keep your own scorecard. You'll get a lot of feedback and advice when you enter the personal branding arena, but ultimately, all your moves are up to you. Nobody can assess and manage Brand You as well as you can. And, never forget, you're never really finished unless you drop out. Branding is the journey of a lifetime.

**IN A NUTSHELL:** The fourteenth secret of self-brands: You'll never get to where you want to go in life without setting concrete goals and realizing it's the journey that gets you there.

 **AFTERWORD**

*Nothing is either good or bad,*
*but thinking makes it so.*

William Shakespeare
*Hamlet* (II, 2)

**B**usiness success, like branding, is a game of perceptions.
If people think you are at the top of your game, you are. If people think you are a bit player, you will be one until you change their thinking.

When you are competing for something—whether to head up the company, the new business pitch, or the PTA—it doesn't matter who is "objectively" better for the job. What matters are the impressions in the minds of other people. Those perceptions about you control your destiny.

Self-branding is a way of thinking and doing to help you take back control of your destiny and create positive perceptions for Brand You. It isn't just about self-promotion (though that will be a result). Self-branding shows you how to maximize your assets in a way that will benefit both you and the company. You'll be able to perform better and be more effective by thinking strategically in terms of markets and needs. You'll harness soft power through "packaging" a compelling visual identity and verbal identity. You'll learn how to differentiate yourself so that you are relevant and memorable.

The world of brands is not static. Neither is yours. Branding is a way of thinking and responding to changing market conditions. When things are going well, that is the time to step up your branding programs and go for big gains in the marketplace (introducing new initiatives, seeking a big promotion, starting a new venture, and so on).

*There is a tide in the affairs of men*
*which taken at the flood, leads on to fortune.*

William Shakespeare
*Julius Caesar* (IV, 3)

Markets can shift, too. They can even disappear completely, leaving you as relevant as the buggy whip. But branding gives you a method for repositioning, rebranding, and relaunching yourself and your business arena. You don't want to end up adrift in the tough business marketplace lamenting, "How could this have happened?" or "How can I be riffed? I've worked here for twenty years!"

You want to be able to smell change coming and focus your energies on analyzing the new marketplace and finding new ideas and options. You need to be opportunistic and develop tactics to get back in the game for a successful second act. And, whether it's a big pond or a small pond you're swimming in, you need to have a good understanding of your competition so that you can keep what you offer relevant as the market twists and turns, or as your company gets downsized or merged.

While I have presented a lot of guidelines for self-branding, there are no hard and fast "branding rules." You can break a branding principle and still be phenomenally successful. The branding highway is filled with brands that broke a guideline (or two or three) and were a hit anyway. It happens all the time. (Remember, branding is more an art than a science.)

*Fair is foul. Foul is fair.*

William Shakespeare
*Macbeth* (I, 1)

Just as there are no concrete branding rules, there are no hard and fast business or life rules. Something that worked for someone else may work for you, but it may not. Something that was a career buster for one person may be the critical event leading to a wonderful opportunity for you.

You'll have to use your own brain and instincts, your aptitudes, and your special uniqueness and abilities—that's what makes branding so fun and interesting. But there are some guidelines to keep in mind as you take your personal brand out in the world:

Sunny beats gloomy
Sparkle beats drabness
Authenticity beats pretending
Consistency beats muddle
Difference beats conformity
Strategy beats luck
Tactics beat inaction
Engagement beats aloofness
Visibility beats low profile
Perception beats reality

Just as no two people are the same—even if they are twins—no two people have the same brand assets. As a self-brander, your job is to manage the asset that is you through the good times and the bad.

The good news is that you are in control of your brand—you are in charge of crafting your brand and taking it out in the world. You are the brand manager and the creative director. You are the screenwriter and the editor. You get to select the core brand concept, your message, and the direction (including changes in direction) you want to take your brand. (And the bad news is everything above too.)

Almost nothing is objectively "good" or "bad." It's our perception of whether it's good or bad that makes it good or bad.

Each of us is unique, with a brain, looks, strengths, and experiences that are powerful assets. Anyone you know, or have known, and anything you have ever done or thought about can be an asset.

If you think something is an asset, it is. If you see it as a stepping-stone to your self-branding goal, it is. If you see it as a dead end, it is. We all have hundreds of assets and opportunities. But they are worthless unless we recognize them as positive things and take action accordingly.

In business, as in life, success is much more likely if you feel positive about yourself and your experiences, and if you stay in the moment rather than hold onto past glories or the way things used to be.

But even more important to your success is cultivating positive perceptions in the minds of others about who you are and what you've done and what you can do. You need to attract people to your ideas and abilities. You need to have that "something more" so that people want you and no one else. Self-branding gives you strategies and guidelines for harnessing those outside perceptions and market dynamics so that you can make the most of your most important asset, You.

# ➡ ACKNOWLEDGMENTS

This book started with an idea, an idea that wouldn't die in spite of the thick file of rejection letters from literary agents and publishers. Finally, my networking paid off and a lunch with a high school friend, Nancy Capizzi DeMeo led to a publisher. This new edition came about at a lunch I had with my publisher, Nick Brealey, when he was visiting New York City in 2011. We talked about how the book still had legs in terms of sales. Given the revolution taking place in social media, I lamented to Nick that there were now so many new opportunities to build a personal brand that didn't exist when the book was originally released. So, we cooked up the idea for a new edition.

I couldn't have done this book without people. After all, self-branding is about people.

I owe a large debt to my clients, who let me get involved in their stories, ideas, and makeovers, and who let me work with them to find the magic that was in them and the world around them all along. (And they'll be happy to know, I have used pseudonyms throughout the book to protect their privacy.)

In writing the book, I owe a special thanks to Gary Andrew Gulkis, who has the poet's appreciation of language and improved the writing in so many ways. Gary was always ready to take a call and brainstorm anything that was on my mind, large or small, and for that I am deeply grateful. Long a student of Shakespeare, Gary was the one who suggested using the Bard for all the quotes in the book. Thanks, Gary, for everything!

A number of colleagues were especially helpful in brainstorming ideas for this book. Elizabeth Hitchcock was a great cheerleader and offered smart suggestions and support. Tom Blanco was a sounding board and offered the insightful perspective of an executive recruiter. Tim Davis, who has the comedian's instinct for words and timing, not only has helped me improve my talks, he was always a good sounding board for ideas I was exploring. Margot Rutledge helped with the sales at SelfBrand and is a wonderful motivator. Nancy Settle-Murphy provided insights on how to make the most of virtual meetings. And Wen Zhao Ben and Barbara Krafte offered marketing wisdom in various ways. I want to thank Polina Viro, a computer programmer with a designer's sensibility and a mathematician's analytical skills, who helped rebrand the SelfBrand website and did numerous other programming and social media assignments. Polina, you are a gem! I also want to thank Ren Li who assisted in the development of the SelfBrand Personal Strategy Test and other marketing projects whose intelligence and artistic eye were greatly appreciated. There are other friends and business colleagues who offered their support in various ways. Thank you all.

I must name Al Ries in this accounting. Al gave me my start in the world of advertising and branding. And it took some faith, since I had spent the previous four years doing graduate work in Japanese art history. No other ad agency would let me in the door with those credentials. But Al must have seen something in me. (Of course, it helped that an employee quit two days after my interview, so my timing was lucky.) In any case, Al, along with Jack Trout, taught me the ropes about brand strategy and advertising. Al's way of thinking and writing has always been an inspiration, so I am thrilled that he said yes when I asked him to write the foreword to my book. Thanks, Al. Any book on personal branding owes a debt to Tom Peters who wrote the first article on personal branding and launched the Brand You genre. Tom was also generous enough to read the original manuscript and endorse this book. Thanks, Tom.

I also want to thank the team at Nicholas Brealey Publishing, particularly Chuck Dresner, Jennifer Delaney, andVanessa Descalzi in Boston, and Nicholas Brealey, Tom Viney, and Andrew Menniss in the London office. Thanks also to Susan Lauzau who did the copyediting and Ashley Gilliam who did the proofreading.

I am grateful for family members who were willing to indulge me in this project as I searched for a writing voice and a publisher. Thanks to my sisters Kevin Bishop, Jean Anderson, and Joan Ford, who heard me talk about this project on the phone more times than they would like to remember.

Finally, there are my husband Mike and our son, Ramsey, who put up with takeout food more than I'd like to admit during my writing jaunts. I couldn't have done it without you guys. Thanks.

# → ABOUT THE AUTHOR

From Madison Avenue to Wall Street to the halls of academe, Catherine Kaputa perfected her ability to market products, places, and companies. Catherine first learned brand strategy from marketing gurus Al Ries and Jack Trout at Trout & Ries Advertising. Early in her career she led the award-winning "I ♥ NY" campaign at Wells, Rich, Greene.

For over ten years Catherine was SVP, Director of Advertising and Community Affairs at Citi Smith Barney and at Shearson Lehman Brothers, where she was in charge of global branding and advertising for corporate, wealth management, and investment banking. During that time, Catherine also developed and taught a graduate-level course on branding and advertising at New York University's Stern School of Business.

Catherine came to appreciate that branding's potential was to help people not just products. Branding can help individuals define and own their career identity and create their own performance success. That's why Catherine launched SelfBrand LLC, a New York City–based personal branding company and wrote the award-winning book *You Are a BRAND! How Smart People Brand Themselves for Business Success*, winner of the Ben Franklin Award for Best Career Book and a bronze IPPY award, and rated a Top 10 Employee Training Book in China (Chinese language edition). To date, the book has been translated into ten languages. This new edition has about one-third new content.

Catherine's second book, on women achieving leadership success, is *The Female Brand, Using the Female Mindset to Succeed in Business* (2009).

Her third book is *Breakthrough Branding: How Smart Entrepreneurs and Intrapreneurs Transform a Small Idea into a Big Brand* (2012).

Catherine is active as a speaker, workshop leader, and coach. She specializes in offering dynamic and fun presentations to a wide range of organizations as part of motivational and group meetings, personal development, sales training, diversity and women's initiatives, and branding programs for entrepreneurs and intrapreneurs who want to transform a small business into a big brand. She works in various formats: as a keynote speaker, workshop leader, or panel moderator.

Catherine has been featured on CNN, NBC, and MSNBC, as well as in *Fortune, The New York Times, The Wall Street Journal, USA Today, The Financial Times, The London Observer,* and other media.

Catherine's speaking clients include PepsiCo, Microsoft, Intel, Citi, UBS, KeyBank, Commerz Bank, Unilever, Time Warner, Con Ed, Cardinal Health, Marsh, AT&T, and others.

To learn more, visit Catherine's website, *www.selfbrand.com*, and her blog, *www.artofbranding.com*. You can follow her on Twitter @catherinekaputa, Facebook, YouTube and other social media. To talk to Catherine about speaking at your event, e-mail her at *catherinekaputa@gmail.com* or contact *selfbrandpr@gmail.com*.

# RESOURCES

Arruda, William, and Kirsten Dixson. *Career Distinction: Stand Out by Building Your Brand*. Hoboken, N.J.: Wiley, 2007.

Beckwith, Harry. *What Clients Love: A Field Guide to Growing Your Business*. New York: Warner Business Books, 2003.

Beckwith, Harry, and Christine Clifford Beckwith. *You, Inc.* New York: Business Plus, 2007.

Beers, Charlotte. *I'd Rather Be in Charge*. New York: Vanguard Press, 2012.

Bridges, William. *Creating You & Co.: Learn to Think Like the CEO of Your Own Career*. Reading, MA: Addison-Wesley, 1997.

Cialdini, Robert B. *Influence, Science, and Practice*. Boston: Allyn and Bacon, 2001.

Corcoran, Barbara, with Bruce Littlefield. *If You Don't Have Big Breasts, Put Ribbons in Your Pigtails*. New York: Portfolio, 2003.

D'Alessandro, David F., Michele Owens, and Michael Owens. *Career Warfare: 10 Rules for Building a Successful Personal Brand and Fighting to Keep It*. New York: McGraw-Hill, 2003.

Ferrazzi, Keith, and Tahl Raz. *Never Eat Lunch Alone: And Other Secrets to Success One Relationship at a Time*. New York: Currency, 2005.

Ferriss, Timothy. *The 4-Hour Workweek*. New York: Crown, 2007.

Frankel, Alex. *Word Craft: The Art of Turning Little Words into Big Business*. New York: Crown, 2004.

Gerstner, Louis V., Jr. *Who Says Elephant's Can't Dance?* New York: HarperBusiness, 2003.

Gladwell, Malcolm. *The Tipping Point: How Little Things Can Make a Big Difference*. Boston: Little, Brown, 2000.

Gladwell, Malcolm. *Blink: The Power of Thinking Without Thinking*. Boston: Little, Brown, 2005.

Godin, Seth. *Unleashing the Idea Virus*. New York: Free Press, 2000.

Godin, Seth. *Purple Cow: Transform Your Business by Being Remarkable*. New York: Portfolio, 2003.

Heath, Chip, and Dan Heath. *Made to Stick*. New York: Random House, 2007.

Kawasaki, Guy. *The Art of the Start: The Time-Tested, Battle-Hardened Guide for Anyone Starting Anything*. New York: Portfolio, 2004.

Kiyosaki, Robert T., and Sharon L. Lechter. *Rich Dad, Poor Dad*. New York: Warner Books, 2000.

Klaus, Peggy. *Brag! The Art of Tooting Your Own Horn Without Blowing It*. New York: Warner Business Books, 2003.

Lehrer, Jonah. *Imagine: How Creativity Works*. Boston: Houghton Mifflin, 2012.

Levinson, Jay Conrad. *Guerilla Marketing: Secrets for Making Big Profits for Your Small Business*. Boston: Houghton Mifflin, 1998.

Levitt, Steven D. and Stephen J. Dubner. *Freakonomics: A Rogue Economist Explores the Hidden Side of Everything*. New York: William Morrow, 2005.

Mackay, Harvey. *Dig Your Well Before You're Thirsty: The Only Networking Book You'll Ever Need*. New York: Currency, 1999.

MacKenzie, Gordon. *Orbiting the Giant Hairball: A Fool's Guide to Surviving with Grace*. New York: Viking, 1996.

Morgan, Nick. *Give Your Speech, Change the World*. Boston: Harvard Business Review Press, 2005.

Montoya, Peter. *The Brand Called You: The Ultimate Brand-Building and Business Development Handbook to Transform Anyone into an Indispensable Personal Brand*. Santa Ana, CA: Peter Montoya, 2003.

Peters, Tom. *The Brand You 50*. New York: Knopf, 1999.

Rein, Irving, Philip Kotler, and Martin Stoller. *High Visibility: The Making and Marketing of Professionals into Celebrities*. Chicago: NTC Business Books, 1997.

Ries, Al, and Laura Ries. *The 22 Immutable Laws of Branding: How to Build a Product or Service into a World-Class Brand*. New York: HarperBusiness, 2002.

Ries, Al, and Laura Ries. *The Origin of Brands: Discover the Natural Laws of Product Innovation and Business Survival*. New York: HarperBusiness, 2004.

Ries, Al, and Jack Trout. *Positioning: The Battle for Your Mind*. New York: McGraw-Hill, 1981.

Rivkin, Steve, and Fraser Sutherland. *The Making of a Name: The Inside Story of the Brands We Buy*. Oxford: Oxford University Press, 2005.

Roffer, Robin Fisher. *Make a Name for Yourself: 8 Steps Every Woman Needs to Create a Personal Brand*. New York: Broadway, 2000.

Sanders, Tim. *The Likeability Factor: How to Boost Your L-Factor and Achieve Your Life's Dreams*. New York: Crown, 2005.

Steinberg, Neil. *Hatless Jack: The President, the Fedora, and the History of American Style*. New York: Plume, 2004.

Trout, Jack, with Steve Rifkin. *The Power of Simplicity: A Management Guide to Cutting Through the Nonsense and Doing Things Right*. New York: McGraw-Hill, 1999.

Trout, Jack, with Steve Rifkin. *Differentiate or Die: Survival in Our Era of Killer Competition*. New York: Wiley, 2002.

Trout, Jack. *Jack Trout on Strategy*. New York: McGraw-Hill, 2004.

Welch, Jack, with Suzy Welch. *Winning*. New York: HarperBusiness, 2005.

White, Ronald C., Jr. *The Eloquent President: A Portrait of Lincoln Through His Words*. New York: Random House, 2005.

Whyte, David. *Crossing the Unknown Sea: Work as a Pilgrimage of Identity*. New York: Riverhead, 2002.

# INDEX